NEW PERSPECTIVES ON LANGUAGE AND EDUCATION: 64

Perspectives on Language as Action

Festschrift in honour of Merrill Swain

Edited by
Mari Haneda and Hossein Nassaji

W0007554

MULTILINGUAL MATTERS
Bristol • Blue Ridge Summit

DOI https://doi.org/10.21832/HANEDA2937
Library of Congress Cataloging in Publication Data
A catalog record for this book is available from the Library of Congress.
Names: Haneda, Mari., editor. | Nassaji, Hossein, editor. | Swain, Merrill, honouree.
Title: Perspectives on Language as Action: Festschrift in honour of Merrill Swain/Edited by Mari Haneda and Hossein Nassaji.
Description: Bristol ; New York, NY : Multilingual Matters, 2019. | Series: New Perspectives on Language and Education: 64 | Includes bibliographical references and index.
Identifiers: LCCN 2018046143 (print) | LCCN 2018054814 (ebook) | ISBN 9781788922944 (pdf) | ISBN 9781788922951 (epub) | ISBN 9781788922968 (Kindle) | ISBN 9781788922937 (hbk : alk. paper) | ISBN 9781788922920 (pbk: alk. paper)
Subjects: LCSH: Language and languages—Study and teaching—Foreign speakers. | Second language acquisition. | Immersion method (Language teaching)
Classification: LCC P51 (ebook) | LCC P51 .P434 2019 (print) | DDC 418.0071—dc23
LC record available at https://lccn.loc.gov/2018046143

British Library Cataloguing in Publication Data
A catalogue entry for this book is available from the British Library.

ISBN-13: 978-1-78892-293-7 (hbk)
ISBN-13: 978-1-78892-292-0 (pbk)

Multilingual Matters
UK: St Nicholas House, 31-34 High Street, Bristol BS1 2AW, UK.
USA: NBN, Blue Ridge Summit, PA, USA.

Website: www.multilingual-matters.com
Twitter: Multi_Ling_Mat
Facebook: https://www.facebook.com/multilingualmatters
Blog: www.channelviewpublications.wordpress.com

The policy of Multilingual Matters/Channel View Publications is to use papers that are natural, renewable and recyclable products, made from wood grown in sustainable forests. In the manufacturing process of our books, and to further support our policy, preference is given to printers that have FSC and PEFC Chain of Custody certification. The FSC and/or PEFC logos will appear on those books where full certification has been granted to the printer concerned.

Typeset by Deanta Global Publishing Services Limited.
Printed and bound in the UK by CPI Books Group Ltd.
Printed and bound in the US by Thomson-Shore, Inc.

Contents

Part 3: Sociocultural Perspectives on Second Language Teaching and Learning

Part 4: Issues and Developments in Language as Social Action

Contributors

Editors

Mari Haneda is an associate professor of world languages education and applied linguistics in the Department of Curriculum and Instruction at the Pennsylvania State University. She obtained her master's and doctoral degrees from the Ontario Institute for Studies in Education/ University of Toronto. Drawing on qualitative research, her research has centered on the education of multilingual students, L2 literacy development, ESL teachers' work, teacher learning and classroom interaction. Her work has appeared in journals such as *Applied Linguistics*, *TESOL Quarterly*, *Linguistics and Education* and *International Journal of Bilingual Education and Bilingualism*.

Hossein Nassaji is professor of applied linguistics in the Department of Linguistics at the University of Victoria, Canada. His recent books are *Corrective Feedback in Second Language Teaching and Learning* (2017, Routledge, with Eva Kartchava); *Interactional Feedback Dimension in Instructed Second Language Learning* (2015, Bloomsbury Publishing); and *Teaching Grammar in Second Language Classrooms* (2010, Routledge, with Sandra Fotos). He is currently the co-editor of *Language Teaching Research* published by SAGE Publications.

Chapter Authors

Siv Björklund is professor of language immersion at the Faculty of Education and Welfare Studies, Åbo Akademi University. She belongs to the pioneer research team of Swedish immersion classes in Finland at the end of the 1980s, and has since been actively involved in immersion research and education in Finland and internationally. Her research encompasses Swedish language, content and language integrated learning and bi- and multilingual education. Recent research projects focus on the relation between languages and identity in immersion programs as well as the development of emancipatory writing among students with Swedish as a first or second language.

Patricia (Patsy) Duff is professor of language and literacy education at the University of British Columbia. Her main scholarly interests and publications are related to language socialization across bilingual and multilingual settings; qualitative research methods in applied linguistics (especially case study and ethnography and complementary approaches to classroom research); issues in the teaching, learning and use of English, Mandarin and other international and/or heritage languages in transnational contexts; the integration of second language learners in schools, universities and society; multilingualism and work; and sociocultural, sociolinguistic and sociopolitical aspects of language(s) in education.

Tara Williams Fortune is director of the Immersion Research and Professional Development Project at the Center for Advanced Research on Language Acquisition, University of Minnesota. Tara devotes most of her professional time to the continuing education of immersion educators throughout the US and abroad. Publications include two co-edited research volumes on immersion education, a research-to-practice handbook on struggling immersion learners and articles in journals such as *Foreign Language Annals, Modern Language Journal, Annual Review of Applied Linguistics* and *Journal of Content-Based and Immersion Education (JICB)*. In 2016, she received the US Paul Pimsleur Award for Research in Foreign Language Education.

Próspero N. García is an associate professor at Rutgers University-Camden. His research expertise lies in the fields of Spanish second language (L2) acquisition and pedagogy, Vygotsky's sociocultural theory of mind, L2 evaluation and assessment, technology-enhanced language learning, teacher training and development, and bilingual education. His most recent publications study the role of conscious conceptual manipulation in the internalization of grammatical categories in heritage and L2 classrooms. His work has also explored the role of agency and emotion in the development and internalization of scientific concepts, and the implementation of dynamic assessment as a tool to foster L2 development.

Joan Kelly Hall is professor of applied linguistics and director of the Center for Research on English Language Learning and Teaching (CRELLT) at the Pennsylvania State University. Her research centers on documenting the specialized interactional practices and actions of teaching and learning found in instructional settings. Her work appears in journals such as *Applied Linguistics, Journal of Pragmatics, The Modern Language Journal* and *Research on Language and Social Interaction*. Her most recent book is *Essentials of SLA for L2 Teachers: A Transdisciplinary Framework* (2019, Routledge).

Tae-Young Kim (PhD OISE/University of Toronto) is professor in the Department of English Education at Chung-Ang University, Seoul,

Korea. His research interests center around L2 learning and teaching (de)motivation, and the contribution of sociocultural theory and activity theory to L2 motivation. He co-edited *Second Language Teacher Motivation, Autonomy and Development in the Far East* (2019, Springer). He has authored or co-authored over 110 papers and book chapters, and his recent work has been published in international journals such as *System*, *Language and Intercultural Communication*, *Educational Gerontology*, *Educational Studies* and *The Asia-Pacific Education Researcher*.

Celeste Kinginger is a professor of applied linguistics at The Pennsylvania State University, where she teaches courses in second language acquisition and education as well as advanced seminars, most recently, Narrative Approaches to Multilingual Identity and Second Language Pragmatics. She is affiliated with the Center for Language Acquisition in the university's College of Liberal Arts. Her research has examined telecollaborative, intercultural language learning, second language pragmatics, cross-cultural life writing and study abroad. Her current work includes a nationwide survey and qualitative investigation of language study abroad alumni, funded by the US Department of Education.

James P. Lantolf is the George and Jane Greer professor in language acquisition and applied linguistics at The Pennsylvania State University. He is director of the Center for Language Acquisition, was co-editor of *Applied Linguistics* and founding editor of the journal *Language and Sociocultural Theory*. He is a past-president of the American Association for Applied Linguistics and a recipient of its Distinguished Scholarship and Service Award. He is also Changjiang professor in applied linguistics in the School of Foreign Studies at Xi'an JiaoTong University, China.

Sharon Lapkin is professor emerita at the Ontario Institute for Studies in Education of the University of Toronto. Her research has centered on French second language education in studies ranging from large-scale program evaluations to qualitative studies of language learning in progress. She served for close to 10 years as co-editor of the *Canadian Modern Language Review* and is currently a director of Canadian Parents for French, a not-for-profit promoting opportunities for Canadian youth to learn and use French.

Roy Lyster is professor emeritus of second language education at McGill University in Montreal. He has a PhD in applied linguistics as well as a BEd and an MEd from the University of Toronto, and an MA from the Université de Paris VII. His research examines content-based second language instruction and the effects of instructional interventions to counterbalance form-focused and content-based approaches. He is author of a module called *Content-Based Language Teaching* (2018, Routledge), and two books: *Learning and Teaching*

Languages Through Content (2007, Benjamins) and *Vers une approche intégrée en immersion* (2016, Les Éditions CEC).

Brandon Sherman is an educational research manager at Indiana University – Purdue University Indianapolis, working on the US Department of Education-funded professional development project, Partnering for Radical School Improvement. His areas of interest include instructional coaching, instructional technology, post-humanism, dialogic interaction, TESOL and qualitative research methodology.

Linda Steinman, originally from Montreal, has lived and taught in Toronto since the early 1970s. A faculty member at York University's Department of Languages, Literatures and Linguistics since 2005, she currently teaches undergraduate credit ESL courses and graduate courses in narrative inquiry, Vygotskian sociocultural theory and case studies in applied linguistics. Linda co-authored a textbook with Merrill Swain and Penny Kinnear: *Sociocultural Theory in Second Language Education: An Introduction through Narratives* (2015, Multilingual Matters) now in its second edition.

Elaine Tarone is distinguished teaching professor emerita, University of Minnesota-Twin Cities. She is widely published in the area of second language acquisition research, on topics such as interlanguage variation, diglossia in immersion classrooms (Tarone & Swain, 1995), the impact of literacy level on oral L2 processing, learner language analysis and ludic language play. She is co-author or co-editor of several books, including *Interlanguage: 40 years later* (2014, John Benjamins), *Exploring Learner Language* (2009, OUP), and *Literacy and Second Language Oracy* (2009, OUP). She served as director of the Center for Advanced Research on Language Acquisition (CARLA) at the University of Minnesota from 1993 to 2016, and continues to offer summer institutes at CARLA on learner language analysis for teachers.

Diane Tedick is a professor in second language education at the University of Minnesota. Her research interests include student language development in immersion and dual language classrooms, content-based language instruction and immersion teacher education and professional development. Her publications have appeared in journals such as *Applied Linguistics, Language, Culture and Curriculum, The Modern Language Journal* and *International Journal of Bilingual Education and Bilingualism.* She co-founded and edited the international research journal *Journal of Immersion and Content-Based Language Education,* published by John Benjamins. In 2013 and 2016, she received the US Paul Pimsleur Award for research in foreign language education.

Annela Teemant (PhD, Ohio State University, 1997) is professor of language education at Indiana University – Purdue University Indianapolis. Dr Teemant's scholarship focuses on using critical sociocultural theory and pedagogy to prepare general education teachers for multilingual learners. She has been awarded five US Department of Education grants focused on ESL teacher preparation.

G. Richard Tucker (PhD, McGill University) is Paul Mellon University professor of applied linguistics emeritus in the Department of Modern Languages. Prior to joining Carnegie Mellon, he served as president of the Center for Applied Linguistics in Washington, DC (1978–1991), and as professor of psychology and linguistics at McGill University (1969–1978). He has published more than 230 books, articles and reviews concerning diverse aspects of second language learning and teaching. In addition to his work in North America, he has spent a number of years living and working as a language education advisor for the International Division of the Ford Foundation in Southeast Asia and in the Middle East and North Africa.

Yuko Watanabe holds a PhD in language and literacies education from the Ontario Institute for Studies in Education of the University of Toronto. Her research interests include second language writing, peer interaction, languaging and sociocultural theory. She is currently teaching applied linguistics at Brock University and translation studies at the University of Toronto.

Rémi A. van Compernolle is an associate professor and Williams S. Dietrich II career development professor of second language acquisition and French and Francophone studies at Carnegie Mellon University. His research extends cultural-historical psychology to second language development, with a specific focus on L2 pragmatics and sociolinguistics, concept-based instruction, dynamic assessment and pedagogical interaction. In addition to numerous articles and book chapters, he has published two monographs, *Sociocultural Theory and L2 Instructional Pragmatics* (2014, Multilingual Matters) and *Interaction and Second Language Development: A Vygotskian Perspective* (2015, Benjamins).

Foreword

James P. Lantolf

If ever a scholar in applied linguistics deserved a Festschrift in celebration of a massively impactful academic career, it is my colleague and dear friend, Merrill Swain. Perhaps more than anyone else in our field, Merrill has shaped research in multiple domains of inquiry, including immersion education, second language acquisition (SLA), sociocultural theory (SCT) and language testing. What is more, her work has not only influenced multiple generations of applied linguistics scholars, but it has also found its way into classroom practice. A career of such magnitude demands to be memorialized in a volume of the type you are about to read. While I cannot here do justice to the full trajectory of such a stellar research record that Merrill has constructed over the past 40 years, I would like to highlight what I consider to be her most significant accomplishments. I can only hope that others, and Merrill herself, would concur.

Merrill earned her PhD degree in psychology from the University of California, Irvine, working with someone who would eventually become one of the leading figures in SCT, Michael Cole, but who at the time was working in experimental psychology. She joined the faculty of what was then the Modern Language Centre (MLC) founded by H.H. Stern at the Ontario Institute for Studies in Education in 1968 (following Merrill's retirement, the MLC changed its name to the Centre for Educational Research on Language and Literacies in 2010). Merrill identified very closely with the MLC and its graduate program in second language (L2) education.

From very early in her career, Merrill made her scholarly presence felt in the relatively young field of applied linguistics, in particular with regard to immersion education. While she authored and co-authored numerous publications on this topic, in my opinion one of the most revealing studies on the effects of immersion education on language development was Tarone and Swain (1995). The article brought into focus observational data on a Spanish immersion program in Minnesota as well as interviews with an English learner in a mainstream classroom in Australia and an L2 French immersion learner in Canada. The analysis revealed that immersion learners in these different settings experienced a similar problem: as they moved to more advanced levels in school they increasingly avoided interaction with their peers in the L2. The authors speculated that the reason for this is that a diglossic situation emerges in which the L2 is restricted to academic topics, while the first language (L1) remains the learners' respective vernacular language for everyday communicative interaction. This is because classrooms do not provide them with opportunities to use the L2 as a vernacular language. A bit later, Merrill and her colleague Sharon Lapkin co-authored an important article (Swain & Lapkin, 2013) that brought to bear on immersion education the theoretical constructs of SCT, in particular the relevance of learners' L1 as a tool for learning the new language. The authors also argued for the need for educators to pay attention to the dialectical interpenetration of cognition and affective among immersion learners. The topic of emotion and cognition is something Merrill returned to later in her career as she began to examine the relevance of Vygotsky's notion of *perezhivanie* (see Vygotsky, 1994) for L2 development (see Poehner & Swain, 2016).

Merrill, of course, did not limit her research gaze to immersion education and instead broadened its scope, quite naturally, I believe, to encompass SLA. In 1980, she co-authored, with Michael Canale, what was to become the first of numerous seminal publications in SLA – Communicative Competence (CC) – a work that expanded the concept of CC originally proposed by Del Hymes in 1972 to include strategic competence, an especially important feature of CC for L2 users (Canale & Swain, 1980; Hymes, 1972).

In 1985, Merrill proposed the *output hypothesis*, yet another important concept for SLA that challenged the then dominant perspective asserted by Krashen and others that languages were learned exclusively through *comprehensible input* (Swain, 1985). The hypothesis was updated and refined in at least two of Merrill's subsequent publications (Swain, 2000, 2005). By that time, however, she had already made her transition to SCT and was now beginning to view output from the perspective of *languaging*, but I get ahead of myself. I will return to this aspect of Merrill's research shortly. According to the output hypothesis, language production also plays an important function in acquisition to the extent that it provides learners with the opportunity to notice gaps in their grammar and what is indeed available in the input; it affords opportunities for learners to test their hypotheses regarding target language structures, and it allows them to reflect on the language and as a result potentially make adjustments to their interlanguage grammar.

In 1993, I had the distinct pleasure of encountering Merrill in person for the second time in my career. The first time was when I heard her give a lecture in 1978 when I was on the faculty of the University of Texas at San Antonio. At the time, I was involved in research on the history of Spanish and the Spanish dialectics of the San Antonio area. Since I was also teaching Spanish, I thought I would attend the lecture that Merrill gave on bilingualism and immersion education. It was, for me, one of the most interesting talks I had heard to that point in my still young career. However, it had a profound effect on my thinking as it provided the initial impetus that eventually pushed me away from historical linguistics and dialectology to the study of SLA. Our second meeting some 15 years later was on a more personal level. It occurred at the Georgetown University Roundtable, honoring the former Georgetown professor and my colleague at the University of Delaware, Bob Di Pietro, who had sadly passed away the previous year. Merrill asked Bill Frawley and me to meet her for a drink after the day's session. At the meeting, she expressed her interest in SCT, the area that Bill and I had been working in for the previous five years or so. Since Bill was less interested in SLA than I was, Merrill and I continued our interactions on the potential relevance of SCT for the study of L2 development. Following numerous e-mail exchanges regarding SCT and L2 and at least one visit to the MLC at OISE, it became clear that she had indeed shifted her theoretical orientation to SCT. Among her early influential studies on SCT-L2 was her co-authored article (Nassaji & Swain, 2001). In this study, the researchers assessed in quite a creative way one of the central claims of Aljaafreh and Lantolf (1994), which proposed that feedback as mediation was most effective when it was sensitive to learners' zone of proximal development (ZPD). In their study, Nassaji and Swain showed that feedback that was random was less effective than mediation negotiated between tutor and learner and that was therefore presumably within the learner's ZPD.

In 1997, while I was on the faculty at Cornell University, our graduate program in linguistics sponsored the Summer Linguistics Institute, which included a substantial curriculum in SLA, including a course on SCT-L2 that Merrill and I co-taught. Subsequently, when I moved to Penn State, we continued to co-teach an SCT-L2 course in three more summer institutes that took place in 2002, 2005 and 2009. In each case, my inclination was to teach the course in a lecture format; Merrill, however, in her commitment to the importance that Vygotsky assigned to dialogue, insisted that we had to incorporate significant opportunities for the students to interact among themselves on many of the topics addressed in the course. This approach clearly made for a far more interesting and engaging experience for everyone involved.

During the 2002 institute, Merrill pointed me to an article on dynamic assessment that she had recently come across. I was at that time unaware of the concept and of its importance for rethinking the dialectic between language teaching and language assessment. I shared the article with Matt Poehner, then a student in our doctoral program, who developed the topic into his dissertation and who has subsequently developed the concept into a significant and influential research program. We owe much to Merrill for opening up a new line of important SCT-L2 research.

Continuing with the testing topic, but outside the scope of dynamic assessment, Merrill alerted testers to the relevance of 'collaborative dialogue' for a more robust assessment of learner development (Swain, 2001). Traditionally in oral assessment practices, learners are assessed on the basis of their performance during interviews with trained test administrators, such as in the case of the American Council on the Teaching of Foreign Languages (ACTFL) Oral Proficiency Interview. However, based on Vygotsky's notion of mediation, Merrill proposed that the dialogue that emerges among learners working in small groups can reveal a great deal about their language development when its focus shifts from solving a task to solving language problems that arise during the task-completion activity. This was known at the time as 'collaborative dialogue', which eventually Merrill reconceptualized as *languaging*, the topic I turn to next.

Returning to the output hypothesis, Merrill's expanded interest in SCT led her to reconceptualize her earlier theorizing on the role of output in light of the principles of Vygotsky's theory. In particular, the notion that speaking plays a central role in mediating our thinking process. According to Merrill (Swain, 2006a: 96), output was too static a notion, which by the year 2000 she had begun to recast as a verb rather than a noun. However, she was still uncomfortable with 'verbalizing' because it seemed to limit the mediating function of language to speech, and she felt, along with Vygotsky, that writing also plays a central role in the thinking process (indeed, Vygotsky referred to writing as 'written speech'). She believed that *languaging* was a more appropriate means of capturing how language activity (spoken or written) can lead us to 'a new understanding, a new insight' (Swain, 2006a: 96) relating to a particular matter, and in this case, the matter is the process of learning a new language. Although languaging has a long history in domains such as psychotherapy, Marxist theory and even in applied linguistics (see Lado, 1979), Merrill's adaptation of it as a way of recasting the output hypothesis has left its mark on the field. Languaging, construed as a problem-solving activity for language learning, can occur in dialogic interaction with others or with the self and it can occur through the medium of the L1 or the L2. An important consequence of languaging, as Merrill cautioned (Swain, 2006b), relates to research using verbal protocols as data. Typically, in such research, participants are asked to externalize in speech or at times in writing, what they are thinking when they engage in some type of language activity such as reading or writing, taking a test, carrying out an information gap task, etc. In Swain (2006b), she documents instances in which languaging during tasks can indeed influence and change the very activity that the research is trying to access via verbalization.

In the spirit of Vygotsky's quest to make psychology relevant for improving people's lives not only through education but through other forms of practical activity, Merrill and her colleagues, in particular

Sharon Lapkin, extended the concept of languaging to praxis-based research with elderly individuals. A series of case studies (Barkaoui *et al.*, 2011; Lapkin *et al.*, 2010; Swain & Lapkin, 2011; Swain *et al.*, 2013) demonstrated the power of languaging to regenerate the apparently diminishing cognitive, affective and linguistic capacities of several residents of a care facility for the elderly in the Toronto area. Not only are these studies important for their immediate practical value, but they are also theoretically significant because they show that development is a process that can indeed continue throughout one's life, provided appropriate forms of mediation are made available.

I think it is important at this point to highlight Merrill's co-authored *Sociocultural Theory in Second Language Education,* now in its second edition (Swain *et al.*, 2015). In some respects, this work has been seen by many as the 'antidote' to Lantolf and Thorne's (2006) book that introduces the central concepts of SCT and surveys the L2 research informed by the theory. The unique feature of the former monograph is its sensitivity to a readership who indeed might well be interested in SCT-L2 but who may not have the background to grapple with the latter work. Again, I believe Merrill's text demonstrates her keen awareness of how to make a complex theory understandable, a talent that not all of us possess. The uniqueness of the approach is made clear in the work's subtitle – *An Introduction through Narratives* – which has the dual goal of explaining the concepts and of informing the novice that it is ok to struggle with the theory itself.

Merrill received well-deserved recognitions for her scholarly and service contributions to applied linguistics. Among these are her election as president of the American Association for Applied Linguistics in 1998. The same organization recognized her with its Distinguished Scholarship and Service Award in 2004. The Canadian Association of Second Language Teachers named her as their Robert Roy Distinguished Educator in 2003. In 2006, she was named *Language Learning* Distinguished Scholar at the Beijing University of Foreign Studies. Finally, the University of Vaasa, Finland, awarded Merrill an honorary doctorate in 2011 for her research on immersion education.

I cannot conclude this woefully inadequate commentary on Merrill's academic achievements without mentioning that she was a major figure among major figures in what was once perhaps the pre-eminent graduate program in applied linguistics and language education. Long before I was fully committed to applied linguistics, I heard colleagues discussing the high-quality research and the stellar graduate students emanating from the MLC at OISE. Merrill's retirement, along with virtually all of her contemporaries at the MLC in recent years, represents an immeasurable loss to our field. It will be all but impossible to fill this gap. Although in retirement Merrill has reoriented her life toward interests outside of academia, including working for the betterment of her

Toronto neighborhood, she has without question left an indelible mark on applied linguistics. To this day, however, I, and many others in our field, continue to call on Merrill for assistance, insight and criticism of our own work. Kudos and a resounding BRAVISIMA!

References

Aljaafreh, A. and Lantolf, J.P. (1994) Negative feedback as regulation and second language learning in the zone of proximal development. *The Modern Language Journal* 78, 465–483.

Barkaoui, K., Swain, M. and Lapkin, S. (2011) Examining the quality of measures of change in cognition and affect for older adults: Two case studies. *Journal of Aging Studies* 25, 62–72.

Canale, M. and Swain, M. (1980) Theoretical bases of communicative approaches to second language teaching and testing. *Applied Linguistics* 1, 1–47.

Hymes, D.H. (1972) On communicative competence. In J.B. Pride and J. Holmes (eds) *Sociolinguistics* (pp. 269–293). London: Penguin.

Lado, R. (1979) Thinking and 'languaging': A psycholinguistic model of performance and learning. *Sophia Linguistica* 12, 3–24.

Lantolf, J.P. and Thorne, S.L. (2006) *Sociocultural Theory and the Sociogenesis of Second Language Development*. Oxford: Oxford University Press.

Lapkin, S., Swain, M. and Psyllakis, P. (2010) The role of languaging in creating zones of proximal development (ZPDs): A long term care resident interacts with a researcher. *Canadian Journal on Aging* 10, 477–490.

Nassaji, H. and Swain, M. (2001) A Vygotskian perspective on corrective feedback in L2: The effect of random versus negotiated help on the learning of English articles. *Language Awareness* 9, 34–51.

Poehner, M. and Swain, M. (2016) L2 development as cognitive-emotive process. *Language and Sociocultural Theory* 3 (2), 219–241.

Swain, M. (1985) Communicative competence: Some roles of comprehensible input and comprehensible output in its development. In S.M. Gass and C.G. Madden (eds) *Input in Second Language Acquisition* (pp. 235–253). Rowley, MA: Newbury House.

Swain, M. (2000) The output hypothesis and beyond: Mediating acquisition through collaborative dialogue. In J.P. Lantolf (ed.) *Sociocultural Theory and Second Language Learning* (pp. 97–114). Oxford: Oxford University Press.

Swain, M. (2001) Examining dialogue: Another approach to content specification and to validating inferences drawn from text scores. *Language Testing* 18, 275–302.

Swain, M. (2005) The output hypothesis: Theory and research. In E. Hinkel (ed.) *Handbook of Research in Second Language Teaching and Learning* (pp. 471–484). Mahwah, NJ: Erlbaum.

Swain, M. (2006a) Languaging, agency and collaboration in advanced second language proficiency. In H. Byrnes (ed.) *Advanced Language Learning. The Contributions of Halliday and Vygotsky* (pp. 95–108). Washington, DC: Georgetown University Press.

Swain, M. (2006b) Verbal protocols: What does it mean for research to use speaking as a data collection tool? In M. Chalhoub-Deville, C. Chapelle and P. Duff (eds) *Inference and Generalizability in Applied Linguistics: Multiple Research Perspectives* (pp. 97–113). Amsterdam: John Benjamins.

Swain, M. and Lapkin, S. (2011) Languaging as agent and constituent of cognitive change in an older adult: An example. *Canadian Journal of Applied Linguistics* 14, 170–192.

Swain, M. and Lapkin, S. (2013) A Vygotskian sociocultural perspective on immersion education: The L1/L2 debate. *Journal of Immersion and Content-Based Language Education* 1, 101–129.

Swain, M., Lapkin, S. and Deters, P. (2013) Exploring the effect of languaging activities on cognitive functioning: The case of an older adult in a long-term care facility. *Activities, Adaptation and Aging* 37, 1–18.

Swain, M., Kinnear, P. and Steinman, L. (2015) *Sociocultural Theory in Second Language Education. An Introduction through Narratives* (2nd edn). Bristol: Multilingual Matters.

Tarone, E. and Swain, M. (1995) A sociolinguistic perspective on second language use in immersion classroom. *Modern Language Journal* 79, 166–178.

Vygotsky, L.S. (1994) The problem of the environment. In J. Valsiner and R. Van der Veer (eds) *The Vygotsky Reader* (pp. 347–348). Oxford: Blackwell.

Introduction

Mari Haneda and Hossein Nassaji

> All words have the 'taste' of a profession, a genre, a tendency, a party, a particu-
> lar work, a particular person, a generation, an age group, the day and hour. Each
> word tastes of the context and contexts in which it has lived its socially charged
> life; all words and forms are populated by intentions.
>
> Bakhtin, 1981: 293

When we, the co-editors, think of applied linguistics, the term evokes various images, memories and felt experiences, which take us back to our graduate studies in Canada in the late 1990s at the Ontario Institute for Studies in Education of the University of Toronto (OISE/UT). We were fortunate to learn directly from Merrill Swain through our coursework in the second language (L2) education program and to learn about her ongoing research through internal presentations. She made an indelible mark on us as individuals and as scholars in applied linguistics and L2 education. What we took away from our experiences with her was that we needed to grow continuously as scholars, which would require intellectual curiosity, persistent efforts, rigor and integrity in our academic pursuits and the courage to question our own theoretical and methodological assumptions.

Swain's Contributions

Merrill Swain is now professor emerita at OISE/UT, having taught and conducted research there for over four decades. Her research interests include bilingual education and second/foreign language learning, teaching and testing. Her present research focuses on the role of collaborative dialogue and 'languaging' in second/foreign language learning. During her career, she has been president of the American Association for Applied Linguistics (AAAL) and vice president of the International Association of Applied Linguistics (AILA); she was also the recipient of AAAL's 2004 Distinguished Scholarship and Service Award.

This co-edited volume has been compiled in honor of Merrill Swain's multiple scholarly contributions to the field of applied linguistics. Its aim is to celebrate her groundbreaking accomplishments and to pay tribute

1

to her as an academic, leader, mentor and role model. Her work has contributed substantially to the knowledge base of the field, and her ideas
have had a significant influence on a range of subfields of L2 research,
including immersion education, mainstream second language acquisition
(SLA) and sociocultural theory/SLA. Swain has been recognized as one of
the most prominent scholars in applied linguistics by renowned peers in
the field (de Bot, 2015: 40–41). Among the applied linguists selected by de
Bot as notable scholars in the field, many commented on Swain's work;
the following are indicative of the nature of her contributions:

'She is to be admired for her versatility and long-term commitment to
  applied linguistics scholarship'.
'She had the guts to change her mind about the foundational assumptions of her research AFTER she had already become a universally
  celebrated scholar in our field'.
'Critical but fair, she has influenced many researchers in our field by setting a high standard for both quantitative and qualitative research'.
'Very supportive for upcoming young researchers and graduate students'.
'Her work on communicative competence, the output-hypothesis and the
  relevance of languaging as a source of SLA'.

What is remarkable about Swain's work is that her scholarship spans
a number of complementary research areas, ranging from immersion
education to output, collaborative dialogue, languaging, and testing
and assessment. The approaches that she has taken in her research are
multifaceted and range from large-scale quantitative program evaluation
to investigations, both qualitative and quantitative, of a range of issues
that include students' achievement in French immersion, first language
development and its role in L2 learning.

Her French immersion research, albeit conducted mainly in Canada,
has been embraced and brought to bear on many content-based L2
instructional contexts around the world, for example in Australia,
Brunei, China, Fiji, Hong Kong, India, Japan, Korea, New Zealand,
Singapore, the US and many countries in South America and Europe
(OISE News, 2016). Indeed, evidence of the influence of her work is to be
seen throughout the chapters that make up this book.

Swain's work in other areas has also been pioneering and has had
wide-ranging implications for theory and practice. She was one of the
first to draw attention to the important role of L2 production and how it
facilitates language acquisition. Her comprehensible output hypothesis,
which she proposed in the 1980s, has motivated substantive research
in this area, and even after the three decades since its introduction this
construct is still being used as an impactful theoretical lens to understand
and describe the various roles verbal production plays in L2 development. Fundamental to the output hypothesis are such notions as pushed

and modified output as well as the idea that output is not simply a sign that learning has taken place but also a cognitive process that promotes language acquisition.

Two further influential theoretical constructs derived from Swain's work are languaging and collaborative dialogue. These constructs highlight the importance of the ways in which producing language – particularly 'in an attempt to understand and problem-solve [collectively] to make meaning' (Swain, 2005: 95) – assist language development. Using a Vygotskian perspective, Swain (2006: 89) has emphasized opportunities for 'languaging,' which she has defined as 'the process of making meaning and shaping knowledge and experience through language'. Swain (2006: 97) has suggested that languaging in both speech and writing mediates cognition by serving 'as a vehicle through which thinking is articulated and transformed into an artifactual form'. In keeping with her growing interest in sociocultural theory, Swain has also argued for collaborative dialogue as a way to examine the interaction between L2 learners when they attempt to co-construct knowledge.

A third area in which Swain's work has been influential is that of testing and assessment. Her contributions in this area began with her seminal paper, co-authored with Michael Canale, in 1980: 'Theoretical Bases of Communication Approaches to Second Language Teaching and Testing' (Canale & Swain, 1980). In the article, three components of language proficiency (grammatical, sociolinguistic, strategic) were identified and theorized, to which Canale (1983) subsequently added discourse competence. In 1983, Swain articulated four principles for the development of communicative tests. A decade later, when statistical exploration of results from communicative tests had yielded low internal reliabilities, Swain (1993a) suggested that these low levels of internal consistency were indicative of the complexity of L2 proficiency and argued, therefore, that traditional testing theory could not account for the variation inherent in communicative language behavior (see also Lapkin, 2013: 5481).

This Volume: Aims, Content and Organization

By assembling this volume, titled *Perspectives on Language as Action*, we wish to recognize Merrill Swain's contributions to the fields of SLA and L2 education. The topics addressed by the contributors are varied and reflect the breadth and depth of Swain's contributions, expertise and interests. The chapters have been written by her colleagues (some of whom were formerly her students), who have built on Swain's research or have extended it to different contexts. The book has been organized into four parts: (1) Immersion Education, (2) Languaging, (3) Sociocultural Perspectives on Second Language Teaching and Learning and (4) Issues and Developments in Language as Social Action. In the Foreword, Jim Lantolf discusses Swain's academic contributions and also describes the impact of her work on his own development as an applied linguist.

Part 1: Immersion Education, consists of three chapters that explore ways in which Swain's scholarship has informed and impacted immersion education and research. In Chapter 1, Roy Lyster discusses ways in which Swain's (1985, 1988, 1993b) seminal papers, which underscored the importance of pushing students to produce language, brought about a turning point in the conceptualization of immersion pedagogy. Lyster explores the impact of this pioneering work on immersion pedagogy and the broad field of content-based language teaching worldwide. He also illustrates how Swain's work has been instrumental in the development of his own program of research.

In Chapter 2, Tara Fortune and Diane Tedick critically consider *translanguaging* practices, for which a number of renowned L2 education scholars have increasingly provided overt support. Fortune and Tedick pose a thoughtful question as to whether translanguaging practices can be beneficial for all learners in all instructional settings. While respectfully acknowledging the merits of translanguaging in some contexts, they present evidence-based arguments that invite a re-examination of the ubiquitous support for translanguaging practices in bilingual and immersion programs. Calling for more research in this area, they ultimately argue for the importance of taking account of the contexts and purposes of different bilingual and immersion programs, as well as students' needs (e.g. language-majority versus language-minority students), in making recommendations as to what constitute optimal pedagogical practices.

Siv Björklund, in Chapter 3, describes the characteristics of Swedish immersion in Finland and discusses the developmental trajectory of its immersion programs. She explains that, while building largely on French immersion research and practices, to which Swain has made major contributions, Swedish immersion education involves multiple languages, given the multilingual context of Europe, in contrast to French immersion that uses just two languages. Björklund also examines recent research trends in Swedish immersion and the challenges that lie ahead in terms of research and practice.

In Part 2, three chapters focus on the role of languaging. In Chapter 4, Yuko Watanabe examines the role of languaging in the development of L2 writing. She explores how languaging helps university English learners interact with peers and with themselves. Using data from a study in an intact Freshman-level English course for English-major students in a Japanese university, the study found that languaging mediated L2 writing and that the quality of languaging changed according to the nature and kind of interaction among learners.

In Chapter 5, Tae-Young Kim reports a study that investigated the effect of languaging on Korean elementary and junior high school English as a foreign language (EFL) students' learning motivation. Students, who

were divided into three languaging groups and one control group, participated in the study. The first languaging group wrote a learning diary in
which they reflected on their experiences of learning English. The second
group wrote about their opinions after watching a video clip and the third
group participated in peer discussions after watching a video clip. Of all
the groups examined, Kim found that the students in the opinion-writing
group showed the most significant increase in their motivation. The author
concludes that opinion writing can be used as an effective languaging tool
in L2 classrooms to enhance EFL learning motivation.

In Chapter 6, Rémi van Compernolle and Celeste Kinginger discuss
some of the ways the notion of languaging has been extended to the
teaching of L2 pragmatics, with a focus on 'tu' versus 'vous' (T/V) in
French. Highlighting the difficulties of the T/V systems, they explain
how languaging can be applied to concept-based pragmatics instruction
in various educational settings.

Part 3 addresses the contributions of sociocultural perspectives in various educational contexts. In Chapter 7, Hossein Nassaji examines the role
of collaborative output. The chapter provides an overview of the theory
and research in this area by first discussing the theoretical underpinnings
of collaborative output and then examining empirical research that has
explored its effectiveness. It also discusses how such opportunities can be
created in L2 classrooms. The chapter concludes with the implications of
these studies for classroom pedagogy and also for future research.

In Chapter 8, Próspero García addresses the contribution of sociocultural theory to our understanding of the links among emotion, cognition
and language learning. Drawing on the notion of *perezhivanie* (the functional unity of cognition and emotion that forms the lived experiences of
human beings), García examines mediated interview data collected from
three in-service Spanish-language teachers in teaching aspectual contrasts
in Spanish. He concludes that by considering development as the unity
of emotion and cognition, one can observe how teachers' emotions were
fostered and were impacted by their cognition.

Sharon Lapkin, in Chapter 9, tells the story of how insights gained
from Swain's research on L2 learning in a French immersion setting
informed a subsequent multiple case study in a long-term care facility
in their research project funded by the Social Sciences and Humanities
Research Council (SSHRC). Lapkin suggests that the shift in focus from
pedagogical to a gerontological context is connected to Swain's 'developing the construct of languaging (Swain, 2006), to her life experiences and
to her immense creativity'.

In Chapter 10, Linda Steinman describes not only how Swain has
contributed to the field of L2 learning but also how she has served as an
effective mentor for her students, including herself. Discussing mentorship as a form of mediation, the author delineates the quality of mentorship that she experienced with Swain.

The final part, Part 4, explores other important issues related to language as social action, particularly from sociocultural, sociolinguistic and interactional perspectives. In Chapter 11, Elaine Tarone reviews emerging research that describes bilinguals who have acquired multiple voices in their L2, as displayed in two language domains: presentational (e.g. rehearsed 'mirroring' of other voices) and interactional (e.g. unrehearsed constructed dialogue in narration). Building on Swain's work using multiple perspectives to understand language development, Tarone shows how the emotion-infused target language voices, including complexity, accuracy, fluency, suprasegmentals and accompanying non-verbals, manifested themselves in these domains and what characteristics they had. The implications of the analysis are also discussed.

In Chapter 12, Patsy Duff describes current debates and perspectives with respect to the use of multiple languages in the classroom. Duff reviews the research that has addressed these debates and the various positions proposed as solutions. They range from grammar-translation, through communicative language teaching, to some current theoretical and pedagogical trends that promote the deliberate use of teachers' and learners' languages and their metalinguistic knowledge in classrooms (e.g. translanguaging, or as multilingual, heteroglossic pedagogy and social practice). Duff explains how and why various perspectives/positions on this topic have changed over time, and how a more nuanced approach might be taken. The chapter concludes with suggestions for future research with the aim of providing a more finely tuned perspective on the use of multiple languages in L2 pedagogy.

In Chapter 13, using a case study approach, Mari Haneda, Brandon Sherman and Annela Teemant illustrate how a kindergarten teacher, Lisa, who had to work in an increasingly restrictive instructional environment in a US inner-city school, experienced 'assisted performance' (Tharp & Gallimore, 1988) through critical sociocultural instructional coaching (Teemant et al., 2014) and how the instructional coach participated in the process of Lisa's learning. Drawing on video-recorded longitudinal coaching conversations, the chapter focuses on teacher growth in which Lisa was initially observed to have difficulty but succeeded in growing professionally as she enacted the kinds of practice that she had originally thought to be impossible with her young emergent bilingual children. Also examined is how the coach assisted the teacher in overcoming the challenges she faced.

In the final chapter, Chapter 14, Joan Kelly Hall begins by describing language teaching as a sophisticated profession that requires a range of linguistic and interactional resources. Drawing attention to the need for a framework that can explain the highly specialized competence required for language teaching, the author describes a practice-based approach, that of ethnomethodological conversation analysis (EMCA), and argues that this framework could provide a deep understanding of language teaching as a specialized and situated social practice. Recent research on EMCA is reviewed and its implications for L2 teaching are also discussed.

Part 4 is followed by the co-editors' concluding comments. The book closes with an Afterword written by Dick Tucker who has known Merrill Swain since she was a graduate student.

Audience

We hope that this volume will be of value to L2 researchers and students in teaching English to speakers of other languages (TESOL), second/foreign language education and applied linguistics, as well as to L2 teachers and teacher educators. Given that the theoretical perspective on language as action is becoming increasingly popular in the field of L2 education, the book will be of particular interest to graduate students, L2 researchers and teachers who are interested in learning more about the key ideas in this area and their implications for L2 teaching and learning. Part 1 will appeal to the audience whose interests include immersion education. Parts 2 and 3 will be of interest to those who are interested in exploring ideas derived from the sociocultural perspective in language education, and Part 4 to those who are interested in exploring other issues including those about the application of sociocultural, sociolinguistic, and interactional perspectives to L2 teaching and learning.

Acknowledgments

We would first like to extend our appreciation to the chapter authors for their contributions, and also for acting as peer reviewers for many of the chapters. We would also like to thank other external reviewers, including Kimberly Buescher, Sarah Creider, John Hellermann and Gordon Wells. Our special thanks also go to Jim Lantolf for helping us conceptualize this volume at its inception stage.

References

Bakhtin, M.M. (1981) *The Dialogic Imagination: Four Essays*. M. Holquist (ed.) and C. Emerson and M. Holquist (trans). Austin, TX/London: University of Texas Press.

Canale, M. (1983) From communicative competence to communicative language pedagogy. In J.C. Richards and R.W. Schmidt (eds) *Language and Communication* (pp. 2–14). London: Longman.

Canale, M. and Swain, M. (1980) Theoretical bases of communicative approaches to second language teaching and testing. *Applied Linguistics* 1, 1–47.

de Bot, K. (2015) *A History of Applied Linguistics: From 1980 to the Present*. Abingdon/New York: Routledge.

Lapkin, S. (2013) Swain, Merrill. In C.A. Chapelle (ed.) *The Encyclopedia of Applied Linguistics* (pp. 5479–5483). Hoboken, NJ: Wiley.

OISE News (2016) See https://www.oise.utoronto.ca/oise/News/Merrill_Swain.html (accessed 24 February 2018).

Swain, M. (1985) Communicative competence: Some roles of comprehensible input and comprehensible output in its development. In S. Gass and C. Madden (eds) *Input in Second Language Acquisition* (pp. 235–253). Rowley, MA: Newbury House.

Swain, M. (1988) Manipulating and complementing content teaching to maximize second language learning. *TESL Canada Journal* 6, 68–83.

Swain, M. (1993a) Second language testing and second language acquisition: Is there a conflict with traditional psychometrics? *Language Testing* 10, 193–207.

Swain, M. (1993b) The Output Hypothesis: Just speaking and writing aren't enough. *The Canadian Modern Language Review* 50, 158–165.

Swain, M. (2005) The output hypothesis: Theory and research. In E. Hinkel (ed.) *Handbook of Research in Second Language Teaching and Learning* (pp. 471–84). Mahwah, NJ: Erlbaum.

Swain, M. (2006) Languaging, agency and collaboration in advanced second language learning. In H. Byrnes (ed.) *Advanced Language Learning: The Contribution of Halliday and Vygotsky* (pp. 95–108). London: Continuum.

Teemant, A., Leland, C. and Berghoff, B. (2014) Development and validation of a measure of critical stance for instructional coaching. *Teaching and Teacher Education* 34, 136–147.

Tharp, R. and Gallimore, R. (1988) *Rousing Mind to Life: Teaching, Learning, and Schooling in Social Context*. New York: Cambridge University Press.

Part 1
Immersion Education

1 Pushing Immersion Forward

Roy Lyster

Merrill Swain: Distinguished Immersion Scholar

In 2016, the Center for Advanced Research on Language Acquisition (CARLA) at the University of Minnesota conferred its first ever Distinguished Scholar Award at its Sixth International Conference on Immersion and Dual Language Education. The inaugural recipient was none other than Merrill Swain, in recognition of her role as a leader in the field of immersion education, having made significant contributions in the areas of both research and service.

Merrill Swain's seminal papers on immersion in the 1980s emphasized the importance of student production. Her output hypothesis triggered a turning point in the conceptualizations of immersion pedagogy and has been a source of inspiration for many researchers including myself. The output hypothesis can be seen as an important stage in her thinking, acting as a bridge between her earlier large-scale, evaluative research on immersion education, and moving toward a Vygotskian sociocultural approach to second language acquisition (SLA), emphasizing the interpersonal and collaborative co-construction of knowledge in the language learning process.

Merrill Swain began her long and productive career in 1973 at the Ontario Institute for Studies in Education at the University of Toronto, where she is currently professor emerita. During her career, she co-authored or co-edited 12 books or special issues related to immersion education, 95 book chapters and 135 papers in refereed journals. In addition, she co-supervised a remarkable total of 64 PhD students. Given the extent of her prolific career that was always moving forward, this chapter will focus on only a small part of it, namely, her early work conducted specifically in French immersion classrooms in Canada. Whereas Swain's earlier notions of functionally restricted input and the need for pushed output derived directly from her observations of immersion classrooms, her later research covered many contexts other than French immersion classrooms, ranging from adult university-level learners of French second language (L2) (Swain *et al.*, 2009) to aging adults living in long-term care facilities (Motobayashi *et al.*, 2014; Swain, 2013). Readers interested in her entire career will need to continue reading this timely volume dedicated to her wide-ranging contributions, aptly edited by Hossein Nassaji and Mari Haneda.

As for this chapter, it is devoted entirely to Swain's early pioneering work in French immersion contexts and its impact on immersion education. I suspect that many new scholars will be more familiar with Swain's later work, but I want to stress the importance of knowing her earlier work and its direct impact on moving French immersion forward at a time when its instructional practices still needed to be more clearly defined and based on research evidence. I will conclude that this body of seminal research is not always taken into account in the ever-increasing implementation of various types of content-based L2 programs around the globe. The purpose of this chapter is thus to highlight Swain's pioneering work in French immersion while rekindling the collective memory about its importance in program design and implementation.

Advocate for Change

Initial conceptualizations of immersion education and other forms of content-based language teaching underestimated the extent to which the target language needs to be attended to. It was initially believed that the L2 would develop naturally through exposure to comprehensible input in the form of content teaching and that students would pick up the language given sufficient time and input. Yet, as early as 1974, Merrill Swain (1974: 125) expressed concern about the L2 development of French immersion students, stating that 'some of the errors do not disappear' even after many years in immersion. To explain this, she argued that, first, teachers tend to ignore spoken errors so as not to disrupt the flow of communication and, second, communication with peers tends to 'reinforce their own classroom dialect of French' (Swain, 1974: 126).

Then, in a subsequent and well-known paper, Canale and Swain (1980) also drew from immersion findings (e.g. Harley & Swain, 1978: 11) to support their assertion that 'even with young children, grammatical accuracy in the oral mode does not improve much after a certain stage, perhaps when the learners have reached a level of grammatical accuracy adequate to serve their communicative needs'. They put forth that 'there seem to be no strong theoretical reasons for emphasizing getting one's meaning across over grammatical accuracy at the early stages of second language learning' and proposed instead 'some combination of emphasis on grammatical accuracy and emphasis on meaningful communication from the very start' (Harley & Swain, 1978: 14).

Thus, from the beginning, Merrill Swain was aware of some of the limitations of immersion education and subsequently became an advocate for change and a key player in proposing solutions. And, solutions were indeed proposed in her seminal papers that followed (Swain, 1985, 1988).

Pushed Output

In the first seminal paper, Swain (1985) proposed that comprehensible input alone is insufficient for successful L2 learning. She argued that exposure to input via subject-matter instruction engages comprehension strategies that enable students to process language semantically but not necessarily syntactically. Learners can draw on pragmatic and situational cues, vocabulary, real-world knowledge and inference to comprehend language sufficiently, without processing structural elements in the language. Bypassing language structure in this way, however, is harder to do when producing the language. Swain thus argued in favor of ample opportunities for student output and the provision of feedback that would push students to express themselves more precisely and appropriately. Having to produce the target language allows students to become more aware of language structure – if they are pushed to convey their meaning in precise and comprehensible ways. This is called pushed output.

In the second paper, Swain (1988) illustrated how subject-matter teaching does not on its own provide adequate language teaching; language used to convey subject matter, she argued, needs to be highlighted in ways that make certain features more salient for L2 learners. She reported that content instruction did not invite much student production, was restricted in the range of language functions it generated, did not necessarily engage students in form-function analyses and provided students with feedback only very inconsistently.

Swain (1988) argued that typical content teaching tends to involve more teacher talk than student talk. She reported findings from an immersion observation study in which only about 14% of the turns produced by sixth-grade students were considered to be sustained (i.e. more than a clause in length). Swain concluded accordingly that typical content teaching does not provide opportunities for sustained student production. In light of (a) the input-based instructional approach associated with content teaching, (b) observations of minimal production by students and (c) their lower-than-expected levels of grammatical competence, Swain (1993: 159) proposed the output hypothesis: 'through producing language, either spoken or written, language acquisition/learning may occur'.

In 1993, Swain was an invited contributor to a special issue of *The Canadian Modern Language Review* to commemorate its 50th year. In her contribution, she expounded upon the output hypothesis by proposing four ways in which output may play a role in L2 learning (Swain, 1993). First, output provides learners with opportunities for meaningful practice of their linguistic resources and thus for developing automaticity in using these resources. Second, output pushes learners to move from semantic processing to syntactic processing and, as a result, to notice what they do not know or know only partially. When learners notice a gap between what they need to say and what they know how to say, they can respond in one of three ways: (a) ignore the gap; (b) identify the gap and pay attention to relevant input; or (c) search their own linguistic knowledge for information that might help close the gap by generating new knowledge or consolidating existing knowledge. Third, output has a metalinguistic function that enables learners to use language in order to reflect on language. Fourth, as learners stretch their interlanguage to meet communicative needs, they use output as a way of testing hypotheses about new language forms and structures, which in turn generates responses from interlocutors about the comprehensibility or well-formedness of their utterances.

Empowering language learners to engage actively in increasing the accuracy of their L2 production is thus at the core of the output hypothesis. When learners seek input to bridge gaps in their knowledge, they demonstrate agency over their learning as they discover aspects of the L2 of which they were previously unaware. Moreover, by incorporating hypothesis testing into the output hypothesis, Swain adds an element of conscious play and experimentation to the process of language learning.

I thought I was pushing my students in their output but I wasn't

Studying at the Ontario Institute for Studies in Education in the 1980s with Merrill Swain, Birgit Harley, David Stern, Sharon Lapkin and Jim Cummins was indeed an exciting time for me. I was a French immersion teacher from 1982 to 1988, during which time I completed my MEd and then began my doctorate in 1988, right on the heels of Swain's two seminal papers. Yet, perhaps as a typical doctoral student, I was skeptical about the idea that all that immersion students needed was to produce more output – or at least that's how I interpreted the output hypothesis at the time. In a professional journal, Swain and Lapkin (1986: 8) wrote that there 'seems to be very little real exchange of information which goes on in immersion classes' and that there is 'little working through of ideas interactively'. In a graduate paper I wrote, which became my first publication (Lyster, 1987), I reacted to their article as follows:

> I have always tried to maintain a highly interactive classroom in which students are free to communicate amongst themselves as long as they do so in French, and in which group discussions and the expression of opinions form a significant part of the learning process. This approach seems to help students to develop fluency, but not accuracy. (Lyster, 1987: 714)

I have subsequently had the opportunity to analyze my 'highly interactive classroom' and have come to better understand a key component of pushed output that was missing. Here is the story (from Lyster, 2016).

In 1988, my eighth-grade students and I participated in a video produced by the Ontario Institute for Studies in Education in Toronto. In addition to the final product (a professional video about 75 minutes long used for immersion teacher education), I was given a video tape with hours of unused footage. From this source, I was able to transcribe various exchanges between me and my students for the purpose of analyzing my questioning techniques in terms of their effectiveness. The following exchange was extracted from a discussion during our study of the novel *Max* by Monique Corriveau (1966). Focusing on the plight of the eponymous character in Chapter 2, I asked students to put themselves in his shoes and to imagine how he must have felt as he took refuge overnight in a small projection room in the Aquarium du Québec. In doing so, I thought I was creating opportunities for sustained student output.

T: Maintenant, faites semblant que vous êtes Max et que vous êtes entré en cachette dans l'aquarium. Vous allez dans cette salle de cinéma qui est toute vide parce qu'il y a personne, y a pas de réunions en ce moment et vous devez passer la nuit là et vous êtes tout seul sauf les poissons. À quoi est-ce que vous penseriez si vous étiez Max? À quoi est-ce que vous penseriez? Tim?

T: *Now, pretend that you are Max and you've sneaked into the Aquarium. You go into the theatre and it's empty because there's nobody, there are no meetings going on, and you have to spend the night all alone, except for the fish. What would you think about if you were Max? What would you think about? Tim?*

S: Euh, après la nuit, où est-ce que tu vas passer.

S: *Um, after the night, where you're going to pass.*

T: Oui, oui. Liz ?

T: *Yes, yes. Liz?*

S: Hum, dans le matin, comme si tu, hum, allais dehors et si, comme si quelqu'un va te voir.

S: *Um, inside the morning, like if you, um, went outside and if, like if someone is going to see you.*

T: Oui, peut-être. Quelles seraient peut-être les émotions de Max à ce moment-là? Oui?

T: *Yes, maybe. What would Max's emotions maybe be then? Yes?*

S: La peur.

S: *Fear.*

T: OK, peut-être la peur. Autre chose? Dan?

T: *OK, maybe fear. What else? Dan?*

S: Peut-être la tristesse.

S: *Maybe sadness.*

T: Peut-être, oui, parce qu'il est tout seul. Oui?

T: *Maybe, yes, because he's all alone. Yes?*

S: Con... euh, confusé, c'est, euh...

S: *Con... um, confuse.*

T: Qu'il est confus.

T: *He's confused.*

S: Oui, confus.

S: *Yes, confused.*

T: Oui, oui, c'est bien, oui.

T: *Yes, that's good. Yes?*

S: Fâché.

S: *Angry.*

T: Oui, très fâché.

T: *Yes, very angry.*

S: Mais ça ne fait rien si, euh, le public le voit, n'est-ce pas, parce que le policier n'a pas, euh, dit à le... comme le public ne sait pas que Max est probablement coupable.

S: *But it doesn't matter if the public sees him, right, because the police didn't say, like, the public doesn't know that Max is probably guilty.*

T: Oui, c'est bien, sauf que... qu'est-ce qu'on avait écrit dans le journal ? Est-ce qu'on avait publié son nom ? On n'a pas publié sa photo, mais est-ce qu'on a publié son nom ? Oui ou non ? Jason ?

T: *Yes, that's good, except that, what had been written in the newspaper? His picture hadn't been published, but was his name published? Yes or no, Jason?*

S: Oui.

S: *Yes.*

T: Oui, tout à fait. Dans l'article de Lebrun, il a dit qu'on soupçonne Max. Oui ?

T: *Yes, exactly. In Lebrun's article, he said that Max was a suspect. Yes?*

S: Il serait très soucieux.

S: *He would be very concerned.*

T: Oui, très soucieux, c'est un très bon mot. OK. Très inquiet.

T: *Yes, very concerned. That's a really good word. OK. Very worried.*

Presumably with the goal of encouraging more complex language, I was trying hard to get students to articulate the emotions that might be felt by someone hiding and being sought after. Although the initial questions had been planned with this in mind, I clearly had not planned any follow-up questions. I did not provide any corrective feedback and did not follow up with elaboration questions to push students beyond their useful but very short utterances: *la peur* (fear), *confus* (confused), *fâché* (angry). Instead, I was quick to affirm their responses with 'yes' or 'that's good'. Yet, as Wong and Waring (2009) have since noted, the use of approval markers such as these may inhibit learning opportunities insofar as they serve a 'finale' function that precludes further attempts by others to articulate their understanding or explore alternative answers. So, instead, I should have asked these students to explain why Max would be afraid, confused or angry. I also could have expected longer utterances with subject pronouns and verb phrases more consistent with those in the questions, that is, either first- or third-person subject pronouns and verbs in the conditional to identify probable yet uncertain feelings: *J'aurais peur* (I would be scared); *Il serait confus* (He would be confused); *Il serait fâché* (He would be angry). If it's worth the time, in the context of this novel study, to ask these questions about feelings, then it must be worth the time to expect more than fragmented answers of only one or two words.

In their seminal study of classroom discourse, Sinclair and Coulthard (1975) found that the most typical teaching exchange consists of three moves: an initiating (I) move by the teacher; a responding (R) move by the student; and an evaluation (E) move by the teacher. It is this IRE sequence that I was following in the above abstract.

The IRE sequence is seen as the quintessence of transmission models of teaching and typical of teacher-centered classrooms. It has been criticized for engaging students only minimally and for maintaining unequal power relationships between teachers and students. Nevertheless, the IRE sequence continues to permeate classroom discourse, probably because it helps teachers to monitor students' knowledge and understanding (Mercer, 1999). By assessing their students in an ongoing manner in the course of interaction, teachers are better equipped to plan and evaluate their teaching. Furthermore, IRE exchanges can develop into more equal dialogue if, in the third turn, the teacher avoids evaluation and instead requests justifications or counterarguments (Nassaji & Wells, 2000). In this regard, the evaluation move needs to be replaced by a follow-up move that aims to: (a) elaborate on the student's response or provide clarification; (b) request further elaboration, justification, explanation or exemplification; and (c) challenge students' views (Haneda, 2005). This kind of push helps students to deepen their understanding of ideas and concepts and provides opportunities for students to use language that is more complex than that found in the shorter answers observed by Swain and her colleagues. This would be pushed output.

Functionally Restricted Input

In addition to limited opportunities for student output, Swain (1988: 75) characterized immersion classroom input as 'functionally restricted' and illustrated this with two examples. The first was the finding that singular *vous* as a politeness marker was almost completely absent from classroom input, which helps to explain its absence from immersion students' sociolinguistic repertoire. The second was the finding that 75% of all verbs used by immersion teachers were restricted to the present tense or imperative forms, whereas only 15% were in the past tense, 6% were in the future tense and 3% were in the conditional mood, which helps to explain immersion students' limited use of conditional forms and their inaccurate use of past tense forms.

To illustrate functionally restricted input, Swain provided an example of a history lesson (translated from French to English) in which sixth-grade students are listening to their teacher initiate a discussion about life in late 18th-century Antilles:

> How do you think these plantations … are going … to change … life in the Antilles? […] These people are going to sell their sugar, rum, molasses, brown sugar. They are going to make money. With the money, they are going to buy clothes, furniture, horses, carriages … all they want and they are going to bring them back to the Antilles. (Swain, 1988: 71)

Even though this was a history lesson about events that took place almost 200 years earlier, the teacher used the immediate future tense to convey her message, which Swain (1988) qualified as 'superb from a content teaching point of view', but then continued:

> Its use has brought the distant past into the lives of the children, got them involved, and undoubtedly helped them to understand the social and economic principle that this historical unit was intended to demonstrate. However, as a language lesson these examples illustrate several problems—problems which may arise in any instructional setting based on authentic communication; problems which arise at the interface of language and content teaching. (Swain, 1988: 72)

Swain (1988: 76) provided many useful pedagogical suggestions that are worth revisiting. Two that stand out for me are that teachers need to (a) be aware of their language use so that they can engineer contexts that demand specific and otherwise infrequent uses of language and (b) explore content sufficiently so that language in its full range emerges.

At the Interface of Language and Content Teaching: Problems and Solutions

The problems that arise at the interface of language and content teaching, as noted by Swain (1988), have also been addressed elsewhere. For example, in their immersion classroom observation study, Swain and Carroll (1987: 191) noted an important paradox: 'Although one goal of immersion is to learn language through learning content, a general observation about the classes is that form and function are kept surprisingly distinct'. They found that it was relatively rare for teachers (a) to refer during content-based lessons to what had been presented in a grammar lesson and (b) to set up content-based activities specifically to focus on form related to meaning. Instead, they observed many lessons set aside to focus on grammar, during which time formal rules, paradigms and grammatical categories were presented. These decontextualized grammar lessons emphasized the learning and categorizing of forms rather than relating these forms to their communicative functions, and appeared to have minimal effect on students whose exposure to the target language was primarily message oriented and content based (Swain, 1996).

In light of these findings, Swain (1988) argued that content teaching needs to be manipulated and complemented in ways that maximize L2 learning, and suggested that, to do so, teachers need to draw students' attention to specific form/meaning mappings by creating contexts that allow students to notice and practice L2 features in their full functional range (see also Harley & Swain, 1984; Swain, 1996). In spite of the observation that 'practice gets a raw deal in the field of applied linguistics' (DeKeyser, 2007: 1), Swain and her colleagues have been advocating the importance of both reception and production practice activities for years. For example, Harley and Swain (1984) proposed a twofold need to promote greater accuracy in the French produced by immersion students:

(1) for the provision of more focused L2 input which provides the learners with ample opportunity to observe the formal and semantic contrasts involved in the relevant target subsystem (this does not necessarily involve explicit grammar teaching); and
(2) for the increased opportunity for students to be involved in in activities requiring the productive use of such forms in meaningful situations. (Harley & Swain, 1984: 310)

An example of such an instructional sequence was subsequently implemented in Harley's (1989) study of the effects of instruction on sixth-grade immersion students' use of the past tenses in French (i.e. *the passé composé* vs. *imparfait*). The instructional treatment began with the reading of a traditional legend about werewolves that had been enhanced in the sense that past tense forms occurred frequently and the functional distinctions between the two tenses were made salient by the narrative. Then, students were asked to identify the two different past tenses in the text and, based on the narrative, to infer the different functions of each tense. Then, for production practice later in the treatment, students created childhood albums in which they described various childhood memories, both orally and in writing, along with authentic photographs, depicting either specific and completed actions or ongoing and incomplete actions in the past. Each student's album concluded with five questions about his or her past that the student was then asked by a classmate during an oral interview that was audio recorded so that other students could listen to it later.

Collaborative Dialogue

Possibly because of the difficulty of implementing practice activities that push students to use specific forms for communicative purposes, Swain turned her focus to the students themselves to explore how their attention may be drawn to language during student–student interaction involving collaborative tasks. This line of research has shown that when learners work collaboratively to complete tasks with a linguistic focus, they engage in 'meta-talk' in which they 'use language to reflect on language use' (Swain, 1998: 68).

Kowal and Swain (1994) conducted a study with eighth-grade French immersion students working in pairs to complete a dictogloss (Wajnryb, 1990), a text reconstruction task designed to encourage students to reflect on their own output, and described by Kowal and Swain (1994) as follows:

> A short, dense text is read to the learners at normal speed; while it is being read, students jot down familiar words and phrases; the learners work together in small groups to reconstruct the text from their shared resources; and the various versions are then analyzed and compared in a whole class setting. (Kowal & Swain, 1994: 10)

Based on the interactions recorded while students worked in pairs to reconstruct their texts, Kowal and Swain illustrated how the task enabled students to 'notice the gap' between what they wanted to say and what they were able to say, which in turn led them to make language form the topic of their discussions as they worked collaboratively to fill the gap. Students formed hypotheses, which they tested out against the dictionary, the teacher and each other. Kowal and Swain concluded that this type of collaborative task (a) allowed for reflection and better understanding, which led to the creation of new knowledge and the consolidation of existing knowledge; and (b) encouraged learners to move from the semantic processing dominant in comprehension to the syntactic processing needed for production.

Similarly, Swain and Lapkin (1998, 2001, 2002) investigated the use of collaborative writing tasks and their potential for encouraging immersion students to use language as a means of reflecting metalinguistically on their use of the target language. They demonstrated that students used language in this way as they completed dictogloss and jigsaw tasks. Swain and Lapkin concluded that the writing component common to both tasks was an important factor in encouraging students to focus on form. In addition, through analysis of think-aloud protocols with immersion students about their writing, Swain and Lapkin (1995) found that the students' oral output, as they thought aloud, triggered noticing and led them to attend to grammatical form, which in turn, they suggested, provided propitious opportunities for language learning to take place.

The Impact of Swain's Seminal Research on Pedagogy

The impact of Swain's seminal work from the 1980s on immersion pedagogy can be seen in her collaborative work with her colleagues (e.g. Harley *et al.*, 1990), which laid the groundwork for a series of quasi-experimental studies conducted in French immersion classrooms ranging from second to eighth grade. The instructional treatments in these studies were initially characterized as 'functional-analytic teaching' following the work of Allen (1983) and Stern (1983, 1992), and later as form-focused instruction (FFI), which is designed to draw learners' attention to target features 'as they are experiencing a communicative need' (Loewen, 2011: 582), thereby differing considerably from decontextualized language instruction. These studies demonstrated the variable effects of FFI on a range of challenging target features in French: grammatical gender (Harley, 1998; Lyster, 2004), second-person pronouns (Lyster, 1994), conditional verb forms (Day & Shapson, 1991), functional distinctions between perfect and imperfect past tenses (Harley, 1989), verbs of motion (Wright, 1996) and derivational morphology (Lyster *et al.*, 2013). Taken together, the results of these studies showed that, in more than 75% of the 40 tests given either as immediate or delayed posttests to assess both knowledge and productive use of the target features, students participating in the FFI improved more than students left to their own devices to 'pick up' the target forms from the regular curriculum (Lyster, 2016).

It is this particular line of research and its pedagogical implications that have driven much of my own research and professional development work with teachers, both in terms of reactive FFI that includes corrective feedback, and proactive FFI that entails a sequence of noticing, awareness and practice activities (Lyster, 2007, 2016, 2017). My program of research on corrective feedback (e.g. Lyster & Ranta, 1997) was especially inspired by Swain's early work, as it sought to determine which feedback moves more than others lead to 'pushed output' (Swain, 1985, 1988). In the context of observational research and with the aim of examining corrective feedback in terms of its illocutionary force, we borrowed the term 'uptake' from speech act theory to refer to the range of possible utterances made by students in response to corrective feedback. The notion of uptake in classroom studies was employed to identify patterns in teacher–student interaction that included various learner responses following teacher feedback. We found that what we called the negotiation of form (later known as prompts) was more likely than recasts in immersion classrooms to push learners toward self-repair. Distinguishing the negotiation of form and the negotiation of meaning was also important for Swain (1985), who was one of the first to question the effectiveness of negotiation for meaning if its only purpose was mutual comprehensibility rather than pushing students to produce language that is not only comprehensible, but also accurate. Lyster and Ranta's (1997) identification of prompts as an important instructional strategy for pushing learners toward more accuracy was supported by de Bot's (1996) psycholinguistic interpretation of Swain's output hypothesis: He argued that L2 learners benefit more from being pushed to retrieve target language forms than from merely hearing the forms in the input, because retrieval and subsequent production stimulate the development of connections in memory. As Swain (1995: 131) argued, when learners are pushed in their output during interaction with others, specifically through feedback provided by teachers or peers, they are able to 'reprocess' their output in ways that reveal the 'leading edge' of their interlanguage.

It remains difficult to assess the direct impact of SLA research on actual classroom practices, but I would venture to say that in school-based immersion programs, following the publication of Swain's (1985, 1988) seminal work, there was a shift in emphasis from an input-driven curriculum to one where student production plays a more substantial role. For example, Day and Shapson (1996) and Salomone (1992) both reported having observed considerably more opportunities for immersion students to engage in sustained language production than the minimal amount reported by Swain and her colleagues. Similarly, in their study of immersion classrooms, Lyster et al. (2009: 374) observed 'extensive opportunities for student production along with peer and teacher feedback, as well as opportunities for student-initiated discourse'. In a similar vein, since Swain's (1988) observation that teachers provided feedback after only 19% of their students' grammatical errors, immersion teachers have been observed using corrective feedback more frequently, in response to as many as 56% of students' grammatical errors in French immersion (Lyster, 1998) and after more than 60% of students' overall errors in French immersion (Lyster & Ranta, 1997), Japanese immersion (Lyster & Mori, 2006) and English immersion (Lee, 2006).

That the impact of Swain's seminal work is apparent in school-based immersion programs may reflect their propensity for language across the curriculum whereby language develops mainly through its purposeful use, learning occurs through talking and writing, and language use contributes to cognitive development (Mercer, 1999). In this regard, because of its emphasis on 'using language to learn', Day and Shapson (1996) advocated language across the curriculum as the driving force behind effective school-based immersion programs.

In contrast, however, research conducted at the tertiary level suggests that some content-based programs have been implemented in ways that integrate neither a strong language focus nor extensive opportunities for student production. This may be the result of a simple time factor whereby university students have much less time in class (possibly three hours per week), unlike school-based immersion programs where students are engaged with the target language for at least half the day for five days per week. Or, it may be the case that Swain's (1988: 68) argument that 'not all content teaching is necessarily good language teaching' has not been taken into account.

An important concern expressed by Swain (1988) is that content teaching can take on a lecture format without providing sufficient opportunities for interaction and student production. To explore this, one of my MA students (Moriyoshi, 2010) conducted an observational study of two post-secondary, content-driven classes in Japan: a geography class and a sociology class taught in English. In addition to an analysis of 7.5 hours of video-recorded observations, 76 participating students were administered questionnaires and two native English-speaking teachers were interviewed and also completed a questionnaire. The results revealed that the instructors provided extensive comprehensible input to students, focusing exclusively on content and especially on content-obligatory vocabulary items, while students had limited opportunities to produce the language. Of the total words spoken, the instructors uttered 93% and students the remaining 7%. Notwithstanding, both teachers and students perceived the classes in a positive light, considering them to be effective for improving both listening skills and content knowledge.

In the context of college-level, content-based Italian courses focusing on Italian geography, Musumeci (1996: 314) found that teachers 'supplied key lexical items and provided rich interpretations of student responses, rather than engage in the kind of negotiation which would have required learners to modify their own output'. Also at the post-secondary level, Pica's (2002) study of content-based ESL in the US showed that, during discussions of film reviews, the focus was on comprehensibility and not on L2 development. The majority of students' erroneous utterances went unaddressed in any direct way: 'Although there was a good deal of negotiation for meaning, the focus of the discussion was on defining unfamiliar lexical items and clarifying factual information rather than on calling attention to grammatical items' (Pica et al., 2006: 307).

More recently, Rodgers (2015) reported similar findings in his study of post-secondary literary/cultural studies courses in French L2 and Spanish L2. He found few student contributions beyond the sentence level, and these contributions were in response to teacher-directed questions focusing on a particular word, phrase or concept. The instructors focused on the communication of content-related ideas rather than on language-related issues. At the end of the semester, speaking abilities showed little evidence of significant improvement, and when students were asked what they got out of the course, 80% mentioned greater content knowledge, while only 13% mentioned having improved their language skills.

Similar results were reported by Arias and Izquierdo (2015) in their study at a Mexican university of two courses taught in English: Culture of English-Speaking Countries and L2 Materials Development. They found that the instructors, although trained as foreign language teachers, favored content, only erratically attending to inaccurate language. Similarly, in the case of the growing number of post-secondary programs in Europe adopting English as the medium of instruction (EMI), Smit and Dafouz (2012: 3) noted that language learning remains 'of secondary importance'.

Conclusion

This chapter has highlighted some of the key findings yielded by Swain's pioneering research and some of its impact on immersion pedagogy. Specifically, Swain's (1985: 248) seminal papers underscoring the importance of pushing students 'toward the delivery of a message that is not only conveyed, but that is conveyed precisely, coherently, and appropriately' triggered a turning point in conceptualizations of immersion pedagogy. Accordingly, her work became a source of inspiration for me and many colleagues engaged in classroom-based research and professional development work with teachers.

Swain identified the benefits of comprehensible input in SLA while attributing a complementary role to student production. At the same time, she identified the limitations of classroom input – specifically the oral language to which classroom learners are exposed – and argued convincingly that it needs to be manipulated and complemented to maximize L2 learning. However, I end with a concern that some content-based programs are adopted without sufficient knowledge of her research and are thus implemented with the expectation that students will pick up the language through mere exposure to content teaching.

The effectiveness of content-based language teaching has been attributed to its capacity to enrich classroom discourse through substantive content, which provides a motivational basis for purposeful communication and a cognitive basis for language learning. For this to happen, students need to engage with the target language in its full functional range, as argued by Swain, and teachers need to engage with a range of instructional practices considered effective for integrating content and language. Specifically, teachers need to be adept at scaffolding content learning while ensuring continued target language development, and stakeholders responsible for program implementation need to appreciate this dual role of teachers as the *sine qua non* of program effectiveness. However, some content-driven L2 programs appear to be implemented with a fleeting reference to the success of Canadian immersion programs but without sufficient awareness of the limitations of these programs, as identified in Swain's early work, and without preemptively initiating, through professional learning opportunities for teachers, the solutions that she and her colleagues proposed. There is no doubt that her seminal research should be an indispensable resource for all program stakeholders.

References

Allen, P. (1983) A three-level curriculum model for second-language education. *The Canadian Modern Language Review* 40, 23–43.

Arias, A. and Izquierdo, J. (2015) Language attention in content-based instruction: The case of language instructors teaching content in a foreign language in Mexican Higher Education. *Journal of Immersion and Content-Based Education* 3 (2), 194–217.

Canale, M. and Swain, M. (1980) Theoretical bases of communicative approaches to second language teaching and testing. *Applied Linguistics* 1, 1–47.

Corriveau, M. (1966) *Max*. Toronto: Copp Clark Pitman.

Day, E. and Shapson, S. (1991) Integrating formal and functional approaches to language teaching in French immersion: An experimental study. *Language Learning* 41, 25–58.

Day, E. and Shapson, S. (1996) *Studies in Immersion Education*. Clevedon: Multilingual Matters.

de Bot, K. (1996) The psycholinguistics of the output hypothesis. *Language Learning* 46, 529–555.

DeKeyser, R. (ed.) (2007) *Practice in a Second Language: Perspectives from Applied Linguistics and Cognitive Psychology*. Cambridge: Cambridge University Press.

Haneda, M. (2005) Functions of triadic dialogue in the classroom: Examples for L2 research. *The Canadian Modern Language Review* 62, 313–333.

Harley, B. (1989) Functional grammar in French immersion: A classroom experiment. *Applied Linguistics* 10, 331–359.

Harley, B. (1998) The role of form-focused tasks in promoting child L2 acquisition. In C. Doughty and J. Williams (eds) *Focus on Form in Classroom Second Language Acquisition* (pp. 156–174). Cambridge: Cambridge University Press.

Harley, B. and Swain, M. (1978) An analysis of the verb system used by young learners of French. *Interlanguage Studies Bulletin* 3, 35–79.

Harley, B. and Swain, M. (1984) The interlanguage of immersion students and its implications for second language teaching. In A. Davies, C. Criper and A. Howatt (eds) *Interlanguage* (pp. 291–311). Edinburgh: Edinburgh University Press.

Harley, B., Allen, P., Cummins, J. and Swain, M. (eds) (1990) *The Development of Second Language Proficiency*. Cambridge: Cambridge University Press.

Kowal, M. and Swain, M. (1994) Using collaborative language production tasks to promote students' language awareness. *Language Awareness* 3, 73–93.

Lee, J. (2006) Corrective feedback and learner uptake in English immersion classrooms in Korea. Unpublished master's thesis, International Graduate School of English, Seoul.

Loewen, S. (2011) Focus on form. In E. Hinkel (ed.) *Handbook of Research in Second Language Teaching and Learning, Vol. 2* (pp. 576–592). New York: Routledge.

Lyster, R. (1987) Speaking immersion. *The Canadian Modern Language Review* 43, 701–717.

Lyster, R. (1994) The effect of functional-analytic teaching on aspects of French immersion students' sociolinguistic competence. *Applied Linguistics* 15, 263–287.

Lyster, R. (1998) Negotiation of form, recasts, and explicit correction in relation to error types and learner repair in immersion classrooms. *Language Learning* 48, 183–218.

Lyster, R. (2004) Differential effects of prompts and recasts in form-focused instruction. *Studies in Second Language Acquisition* 26, 399–432.

Lyster, R. (2007) *Learning and Teaching Languages through Content: A Counterbalanced Approach*. Amsterdam: John Benjamins.

Lyster, R. (2016) *Vers une approche intégrée en immersion*. Montreal: Les Éditions CEC.

Lyster, R. (2017) Content-based language teaching. In S. Loewen and M. Sato (eds) *The Routledge Handbook of Instructed Second Language Acquisition* (pp. 87–107). New York: Routledge.

Lyster, R. and Ranta, L. (1997) Corrective feedback and learner uptake: Negotiation of form in communicative classrooms. *Studies in Second Language Acquisition* 19, 37–66.

Lyster, R. and Mori, H. (2006) Interactional feedback and instructional counterbalance. *Studies in Second Language Acquisition* 28, 269–300.

Lyster, R., Collins, L. and Ballinger, S. (2009) Linking languages through a bilingual read-aloud project. *Language Awareness* 18, 366–383.

Lyster, R., Quiroga, J. and Ballinger, S. (2013) The effects of biliteracy instruction on morphological awareness. *Journal of Immersion and Content-Based Language Education* 1 (2), 169–197.

Mercer, N. (1999) Classroom language. In B. Spolsky (ed.) *Concise Encyclopedia of Educational Linguistics* (pp. 315–319). Oxford: Pergamon.

Moriyoshi, N. (2010) Content-based instruction in Japanese college classrooms: Focusing on language, content, or both? Unpublished master's thesis McGill University.

Motobayashi, K., Swain, M. and Lapkin, S. (2014) Autobiographic episodes as languaging: Affective and cognitive changes in an older adult. *Language and Sociocultural Theory* 1, 75–99.

Musumeci, D. (1996) Teacher-learner negotiation in content-based instruction: Communication at cross-purposes? *Applied Linguistics* 17, 286–325.

Nassaji, H. and Wells, G. (2000) What's the use of 'triadic dialogue'?: An investigation of teacher–student interaction. *Applied Linguistics* 21, 376–406.

Pica, T. (2002) Subject-matter content: How does it assist the interactional and linguistic needs of classroom language learners? *The Modern Language Journal* 86, 1–19.

Pica, T., Kang, H.S. and Sauro, S. (2006) Information gap tasks: Their multiple roles and contributions to interaction research methodology. *Studies in Second Language Acquisition* 28 (2), 301–338.

Rodgers, D. (2015) Incidental language learning in foreign language content courses. *The Modern Language Journal* 99, 113–136.

Salomone, A. (1992) Immersion teachers' pedagogical beliefs and practices: Results of a descriptive analysis. In E. Bernhardt (ed.) *Life in Language Immersion Classrooms* (pp. 9–44). Clevedon: Multilingual Matters.

Sinclair, J. and Coulthard, R.M. (1975) *Towards an Analysis of Discourse: The English Used by Teachers and Pupils.* Oxford: Oxford University Press.

Smit, U. and Dafouz, E. (2012) Integrating content and language in higher education: An introduction to English-medium policies, conceptual issues and research practices across Europe. *AILA Review* 25, 1–12.

Stern, H.H. (1983) *Fundamental Concepts of Language Teaching.* Oxford: Oxford University Press.

Stern, H.H. (1992) *Issues and Options in Language Teaching.* Oxford: Oxford University Press.

Swain, M. (1974) French immersion programs across Canada: Research findings. *The Canadian Modern Language Review* 31, 117–129.

Swain, M. (1985) Communicative competence: Some roles of comprehensible input and comprehensible output in its development. In S. Gass and C. Madden (eds) *Input in Second Language Acquisition* (pp. 235–253). Rowley, MA: Newbury House.

Swain, M. (1988) Manipulating and complementing content teaching to maximize second language learning. *TESL Canada Journal* 6, 68–83.

Swain, M. (1993) The Output Hypothesis: Just speaking and writing aren't enough. *The Canadian Modern Language Review* 50, 158–165.

Swain, M. (1995) Three functions of output in second language learning. In G. Cook and B. Seidlhofer (eds) *Principle and Practice in Applied Linguistics: Studies in Honour of H.G. Widdowson* (pp. 125–144). Oxford: Oxford University Press.

Swain, M. (1996) Integrating language and content in immersion classrooms: Research perspectives. *The Canadian Modern Language Review* 52, 529–548.

Swain, M. (1998) Focus on form through conscious reflection. In C. Doughty and J. Williams (eds) *Focus on Form in Classroom Second Language Acquisition* (pp. 64–81). Cambridge: Cambridge University Press.

Swain, M. (2013) Cognitive and affective enhancement among older adults: The role of languaging. *The Australian Review of Applied Linguistics* 36, 4–19.

Swain, M. and Lapkin, S. (1986) Immersion French in secondary schools: 'The goods' and 'the bads'. *Contact* 5 (3), 2–9.

Swain, M. and Carroll, S. (1987) The immersion observation study. In B. Harley, P. Allen, J. Cummins and M. Swain (eds) *Development of Bilingual Proficiency. Final Report. Volume II: Classroom Treatment* (pp. 190–316). Toronto, ON: Modern Language Centre, OISE/UT.

Swain, M. and Lapkin, S. (1995) Problems in output and the cognitive processes they generate: A step towards second language learning. *Applied Linguistics* 16, 370–391.

Swain, M. and Lapkin, S. (1998) Interaction and second language learning: Two adolescent French immersion students working together. *The Modern Language Journal* 82, 320–337.

Swain, M. and Lapkin, S. (2001) Focus on form through collaborative dialogue: Exploring task effects. In M. Bygate, P. Skehan and M. Swain (eds) *Researching Pedagogic Tasks: Second Language Learning, Teaching and Testing* (pp. 99–118). Harlow: Pearson Education.

Swain, M. and Lapkin, S. (2002) Talking it through: Two French immersion learners' response to reformulation. *International Journal of Educational Research* 37, 285–304.

Swain, M., Lapkin, S., Knouzi, I., Suzuki, W. and Brooks, L. (2009) Languaging: University students learn the grammatical concept of voice in French. *The Modern Language Journal* 93, 5–29.

Wajnryb, R. (1990) *Grammar Dictation*. Oxford: Oxford University Press.

Wong, J. and Waring, H.Z. (2009) 'Very good' as a teacher response. *ELT Journal* 63 (3), 195–203.

Wright, R. (1996) A study of the acquisition of verbs of motion by grade 4/5 early French immersion students. *The Canadian Modern Language Review* 53, 257–280.

2 Context Matters: Translanguaging and Language Immersion Education in the US and Canada

Tara W. Fortune and Diane J. Tedick

Introduction

In the US and Canada, bilingual and language immersion education – the practice of schooling in two or more languages as a means to develop advanced levels of bilingualism and biliteracy – emerged in the 1960s/1970s. Today, different program options are available to preK-12 learners from majority (English) and minority (non-English) linguistic backgrounds for a range of purposes.[1] These include (a) developmental bilingual programs[2] in the US, which have traditionally targeted minority language learners; (b) foreign/second language (L2) immersion, which has largely served majority language learners in the US and Canada; and (c) US two-way immersion programs, which intentionally enroll both majority and minority language students. Each of these program models makes use of the minority language as a medium of instruction for at least half of the elementary school day and offers literacy instruction in both program languages. Critical to the successful implementation of the two-way program model is the integration of linguistically diverse students during core academic and literacy instruction. Bilingual and immersion education in the 21st century aims for additive bilingualism[3] and biliteracy for *all* learners using 'strong' forms, described as those having bilingualism and biliteracy as intended outcomes (Baker & Wright, 2017). Our focus in this chapter is on two strong forms of immersion education: foreign/ L2 immersion and two-way immersion.

US and Canadian immersion programs hinge on a central characteristic, or keystone practice: the teaching of core subject matter in a second or minority language for extended periods of time. Immersion scholars routinely begin their discussions of research by referring to this keystone practice. Indeed, it is this practice within the context of the program's goals that gives rise to the need for language and content integration in curriculum, instruction and assessment as well as other essential instructional practices (e.g. Genesee, 1987; Lindholm-Leary, 2001; Lyster, 2007).

As straightforward as this distinguishing approach to classroom instruction appears on the surface, a number of critical 'how to' questions quickly emerge and must be addressed in practice: Who will use the minority language? How often? In what contexts? For what purposes? Complex questions concerning optimal language use practices in bilingual and immersion education have been discussed by researchers in the past and are increasingly the focus of intense debate today (García & Wei, 2014; Jacobson & Faltis, 1990; Turnbull & Dailey-O'Cain, 2009). This debate stems in part from new thinking about what language is and how bilinguals develop, process and communicate in their languages. Today, languages are described as ever-evolving, interrelated and interactive systems of meaning making. Capitalizing on the relationship between and among one's languages is now perceived as beneficial, even essential, to bilingual language acquisition, processing and communication (e.g. Cummins, 2014; García, 2009; García & Wei, 2014). We believe that these theoretical perspectives have merit and that bilingual learners need to be supported in making connections across languages. Yet, we raise questions about how best to enact this support pedagogically in immersion programs.

Although a comprehensive discussion of the classroom language use debate is beyond the scope of this chapter, we will begin with a literature review of three distinct stances that represent a continuum of practices: (1) separation of languages, (2) maximal minority language use and (3) translanguaging. Next, we present evidence-based counterarguments that invite a re-examination of the ubiquitous support for translanguaging practices in bilingual and immersion programs among scholars and educators today. We then challenge the increasingly divisive rhetoric about the intended audience and purpose of these programs. Finally, we call for the implementation of research-supported practices to realize the full range of program goals as well as the development of a rigorous research agenda prior to the universal adoption of radical changes to a keystone program practice.

Three Major Orientations to Bilingual and Immersion Classroom Language Use

Separation of languages

Within immersion programs, clear guidelines for separating languages emerged in the 1970s and 1980s amid a backdrop of widely diverse language use practices among teachers and students in various types of US bilingual programs (Wong Fillmore & Valadez, 1986) and a lack of research to guide bilingual program practice. On the one hand, there was some type of concurrent teacher use of English and the minority language; on the other, teachers systematically alternated use of the two instructional languages, a practice sometimes referred to as 'language separation' (Legaretta-Marcaida, 1981). In his volume on language use issues in bilingual schooling, Jacobson (1990) identified 10 distinct sub-categories of language distribution practices including variations on both concurrent language use and language separation. Concurrent language use practices ranged from concurrent translation – consistently repeating the message in the other language – to random switching between the two languages. Separating the use of the two languages typically occurred by pairing different languages with certain subject matter/topics, a lesson preview/review versus content presentation, a person, time and/or place.

It was within this context that the principle of language separation emerged and became a distinguishing hallmark of Canadian and US immersion education for majority language students (English first language [L1]). Programs sought to employ teachers from minority language-speaking homes who were highly proficient in the minority language. During interaction with students, teachers pretended to be able to speak only the minority language in order to serve as language models. Programs intentionally created minority language spaces buttressed by teacher language use, time of day, subject area and/or classroom environment. Such strategies were adopted in both Canadian and US foreign/L2 immersion classrooms (Genesee, 1987; Lambert, 1984). Teachers' singular use of a new language aimed to simulate majority language students' experiences of L1 learning. Students were encouraged to use the L2 as much and as soon as possible during instructional time in that language. However, it was understood that they would make use of English until they had sufficient exposure and productive abilities in the L2, typically by Grade 1 (Genesee, 1987). Young English-speaking children appeared to readily accept that their teachers understood them even though they only communicated with them in English. 'Monolingual' teaching and learning occurred during instruction in both the students' L1 and L2.[4]

In a 1974 report, Cohen (1974) juxtaposed his experiences as evaluator of a Northern California bilingual program and researcher for the first foreign language (Spanish) immersion program in the US in Culver City, California.[5] The bilingual program implemented mainly concurrent translation, whereas the immersion program used Spanish exclusively from the beginning. Cohen found stark differences in program outcomes relative to second language acquisition (SLA) and inter-ethnic relations. Anglo (majority language) students in the bilingual program were not functionally proficient in Spanish even after three years, whereas Anglo children in the Culver City program were acquiring proficiency in Spanish with stronger receptive skills. Anglo students in the bilingual program rarely interacted with Latino (minority language) peers. In contrast, Cohen observed that in the immersion program, Latino children were welcomed and admired as language models and treated as equals.

Meanwhile, two-way immersion programs also adopted the practice of language separation. In the first directory of these US programs, Lindholm (1987: 5) named four defining characteristics, among them 'periods of instruction during which only one language is used'. She listed a number of essential factors known to contribute to program efficacy, including sustained monolingual lesson delivery, found to promote SLA better than 'language mixing' (Lindholm, 1987: 6). While pointing out that language mixing was in itself not harmful, she mentioned US studies in bilingual classrooms that had reported it to be less effective for bilingual language development.

Legaretta (1977), for example, examined language use in five bilingual kindergarten classrooms. Four of the five teachers used the concurrent approach, whereas one separated languages by time of day. Data analysis showed more equitable distribution of languages (53% English/47% Spanish) when there was language separation. In contrast, teachers using concurrent translation were observed using English to a much greater extent, nearly 80% of the time in three of the classrooms, even though teachers perceived they were using both languages equally. Reflecting on these findings in a later report, Legaretta-Marcaida (1981) concluded:

> Instead of producing bilingual pupils, a language environment so heavily English-dominated discriminates against Spanish-speaking pupils and discourages Anglo pupils from learning Spanish as well. Rather than being bilingual education, capitalizing on the unique linguistic and cultural backgrounds of Latino children, the Concurrent Translation model studied is a rapid transition-to-English program. (Legaretta-Marcaida, 1981: 105)

In another study, Legaretta (1979) investigated the relationship between English and Spanish language outcomes of Spanish monolingual kindergarteners in six bilingual classrooms, of which only one implemented language separation. Pre- and post-test scores of students' comprehension, vocabulary, production and communicative competence showed greater gains in oral comprehension of English (L2) and communicative competence in both Spanish and English for the language separation group compared with groups experiencing the concurrent approach.

Wong Fillmore (1982) also observed bilingual kindergarten classrooms and found that notably higher percentages of Spanish or Cantonese L1 students had acquired at least some English in two of four classrooms investigated. Analysis of video-recorded observational data and field notes called attention to two factors in classrooms that promoted L2 learning: (a) sufficient opportunities for meaningful L2 input and production and (b) use of one language at a time with rare exceptions of language mixing. She reported that when teachers used the concurrent translation approach, their students were 'alternately attentive and inattentive as the teacher switched between languages in their lessons' (Wong Fillmore, 1982: 294).

Support for the separation of languages was also argued from a principle perspective. Swain (1983) identified three basic principles underlying linguistically and academically successful immersion programs: (a) 'First Things First' – explicit support and development of learners' L1; (b) 'Bilingualism Through Monolingualism' – separation of languages by teachers; and (c) 'Bilingualism as a Bonus' – belief in and communication of the benefits of bilingualism to students and stakeholders. She clarified her rationale for the language separation principle with the following research-based arguments:

- Learners may ignore input in an unfamiliar language if they know the teacher will repeat the message in a familiar language.
- Teachers and learners use more creativity, concentrated effort and 'work harder' to communicate meaningfully through a language that is new to students.
- Teachers' linguistic and online interpretation resources are not as taxed, resulting in less professional exhaustion.
- Teachers' and learners' tendency to (over)use the societally dominant majority language can be counteracted through periods of exclusive use of the minority language.

In sum, Swain cogently argued the benefits of language separation in relation to sound pedagogy, psychology and sociolinguistics based on the knowledge base of the early 1980s. Two decades later, Swain's voice became prominent in the literature again, arguing for a new stance toward language use in immersion classrooms – maximized minority language use with some L1 (English) use among students.

Maximal minority language use

The position of maximized minority language use holds that limited and principled L1 use can play an essential role in learning new content and acquiring another language (e.g. Swain & Lapkin, 2000, 2013; Turnbull & Dailey-O'Cain, 2009). Advocates of this position explicitly advise against the overuse of the L1 due to how it limits input in and acquisition of the L2. The emergence of the maximal minority language use position nearly 20 years ago resulted from Swain's and other scholars' shift in theoretical understandings of language and SLA away from a cognitive perspective toward a Vygotskian sociocultural view. Sociocultural theory radically reconsiders language as much more than simply a means to transmit ideas through a conduit of input and output (Swain & Lapkin, 2013). Instead, as Vygotsky (1986) argued, language is a human being's most important *psychological tool*. When used as a psychological tool, language becomes the vehicle and 'languaging' (Swain, 2006: 97–98) the means for actively constructing new knowledge by conceptualizing ideas and solving problems. Scholars therefore hypothesized that as a critical means for constructing new knowledge (including language knowledge), some use of the more developed L1 tool may be necessary and advantageous for learners.

Relative to studies supporting language separation, research carried out in immersion contexts that supports the maximal minority language use position is more limited. Swain and Lapkin (2013) reanalyzed an interaction between two Grade 7 early French immersion students who were rewriting a picture-based story in French after having received teacher feedback on an earlier draft. They argued that students' use of English (L1) during this task was 'essential' (Swain & Lapkin, 2013: 106) for extracting more nuanced meanings of select words and phrases in their story, suggesting that L1 use allowed the students to more effectively communicate their intended meaning in the L2.

Earlier, Swain and Lapkin (2000) investigated a larger group of Canadian Grade 8 early French immersion students' use of English (L1) during collaborative dialogue. They noted three communicative purposes for L1 use: (a) moving the task along, (b) focusing attention and (c) interpersonal interaction. In a separate analysis of these data, Swain and Lapkin (2013: 110) reported that 'students whose stories received lower ratings used more L1 in their collaborative dialogues'. This finding suggests that L1 use did not improve the final L2 product; alternatively, students' greater L1 use may simply be indicative of lower L2 proficiency in general.

Two other Canadian studies were designed and carried out in late French immersion classrooms to explore whether increased L1 use is positively associated with gains in the L2 and/or subject knowledge (Behan et al., 1995; Turnbull et al., 2011). In a late immersion context, we might anticipate a gap between the complexity of academic content and the L2 proficiency of learners and therefore an increased need or tendency to use the L1.

Behan et al. (1995) investigated Grade 7 students' small-group interaction as they worked to prepare an oral presentation. Two groups worked in the classroom with regular teacher encouragement to use French and two in the cafeteria without such encouragement. Data included transcribed one-hour group interactions, written notes from their dialogues and recordings of final presentations. The researchers reported (a) a relationship between greater L1 use for task organization and somewhat more favorable evaluations of the final oral presentation; (b) more 'evidence of learning' in the final product when there was more L1 use; and (c) L1-mediated meta-talk about language resulting in somewhat higher evaluations of French production during oral presentations. However, the study had significant limitations, for example, very few students ($n = 13$); a very limited time frame for data collection; and lack of attention to some results, such as differences in the amount and type of L1 use among groups *vis à vis* the quality of the final product.

In the second study, Turnbull *et al.* (2011) examined language use practices of Grade 7 late French immersion students to assess the relationship between students' increased use of the L1 when discussing complex science content in the L2 and gains in French and science knowledge. They hypothesized that as the complexity of the oral responses to questions in French increased, so too would the likelihood of students' L1 use. Using data from French-medium interviews conducted before and after the science unit, researchers coded students' oral responses for language (French, English or both) and level of content complexity. Quantitative study findings indicated a positive correlation between greater L1 use and more complex L2 utterances, more total words in written French and greater growth in science knowledge.

Swain and Lapkin (2013) suggested that the results from this study lend support to the Vygotskian notion that the use of one's L1 may be needed to mediate thinking and processing of more complex content. Nevertheless, in the same paper they also strongly stated the following: 'What we do not know is if any use of the L1 *by the students* is essential; if it expedites the learning process or is simply the easier route to take' (Swain & Lapkin, 2013: 110, emphasis original).

While discussions about maximal minority language use were taking place in some professional circles in the US and Canada, ideas about translanguaging began to surface in others.

Translanguaging

The term 'translanguaging' was coined by Cen Williams (1996) in the 1980s to refer to the planned, systematic use of two languages for teaching and learning within a lesson in Welsh–English bilingual programs. The idea was to enable students to engage in deeper, more complete processing of information and to support the use and status of Welsh in these bilingual classrooms by pushing students to develop more cognitively complex ideas in their weaker language (typically Welsh).

More recently, translanguaging has been adopted and its definition expanded by US and Canadian scholars.[6] Although Cummins (2007) did not use the term 'translanguaging' initially, he questioned the practice of language separation in classrooms serving minority language learners and in Canadian French immersion. Somewhat later, García (2009) argued that it was not natural for bilinguals to keep their languages separate and introduced the idea of 'translanguaging' as a typical social practice among bilinguals. According to García (2009; García & Wei, 2014), translanguaging refers to the use of two or more languages to make meaning, shape experience and gain understanding and knowledge. It reflects the notion that an individual's whole linguistic repertoire functions as one integrated system.

Much of the US and Canadian literature on translanguaging emphasizes learning by bilingual children who use a minority language in the
home in minoritized language situations where students' language use
practices are marginalized in school or society. It emphasizes the importance of supporting these students' socioemotional well-being and bilingual identities, as well as the promotion of social justice and educational
equity through schooling. These are long-standing, widely embraced
themes among scholars and educators in immersion education (see e.g.
Howard & Sugarman, 2007; Tedick & Björklund, 2014). Whereas a
thorough review of research on translanguaging is beyond the scope of
this chapter, here we describe a few studies conducted in US two-way
immersion programs.

Palmer *et al.* (2014) explored the translanguaging pedagogical practices of two classroom teachers in Texas (preK and Grade 1). Drawing
upon the concepts of positioning and investment associated with identity
theory, they described three translanguaging instructional strategies: the
teachers (a) modeled bilingualism by using 'hybrid' language practices
(mixing languages) during instruction in both languages to express meaning, ensure students' understandings and demonstrate natural bilingual
language use practices; (b) positioned students as bilingually competent, for example, by asking minority language students to translate for
classmates; and (c) celebrated students' bilingual language practices and
growing metalinguistic awareness. Palmer *et al.* (2014) concluded that
these pedagogies invited minority language students to discuss important
and sensitive themes (immigration, identity) and take risks in expressing
themselves in their developing languages. The authors did not link these
translanguaging pedagogies to academic learning or SLA.

García (2011) reported on a study done in a two-way immersion
kindergarten classroom that revealed how the children translanguaged.
She found that children (having a range of proficiencies in Spanish and
English) used translanguaging to carry out six metafunctions: to (a) mediate understandings, (b) co-construct meaning of what another is saying,
(c) construct meaning within themselves, (d) include others, (e) exclude
others and (f) demonstrate knowledge. García (2011: 52, emphasis original) concluded that students, particularly Latino students, '*appropriate*
the use of language as they use their entire linguistic repertoires flexibly'.

García-Mateus and Palmer (2017) summarized a study conducted
in a Grade 1 two-way immersion classroom in the Southwest. They
described and hypothesized about pair interactions between two students, 'Alejandro', a Spanish-dominant Latino immigrant and 'Ray', an
English-dominant African American student, both new to the program.
Alejandro used Spanish, English and a mixture of the two. In one interaction, Alejandro was assigned the role of 'Jorge', the teacher in a poem they
had just read, and he attempted to push Ray to use Spanish by demanding

that he call him '*maestra*'[7] (teacher), a sign of respect in Mexican class-rooms. Ray refused to even try to say *maestra*. The authors interpreted Alejandro's use of language as a display of his developing bilingual identity; Ray's refusal to use Spanish was viewed as an assertion of his identity as an English speaker. García-Mateus and Palmer (2017: 253) contended that because Ray heard *maestra* along with 'teacher' in this lesson where both languages were allowed, 'translanguaging could play a part in supporting Ray's development of a bilingual identity'. Nonetheless, they also reported that at no time during the six weeks of data collection was Ray observed speaking Spanish. We question whether Ray will ever develop a bilingual identity or any level of proficiency in Spanish at all if consistently allowed to use English only in this two-way program.

As reflected in these studies, much of the US research literature on translanguaging conducted in immersion contexts emphasizes the empowerment and identity development of minoritized emergent bilin-guals while generally failing to discuss the educational needs of majority language students or the effect of translanguaging practices on achieve-ment and SLA. Examples of translanguaging typically showcase minor-ity language students' use of Spanish (L1) while acquiring English (L2). The vast majority of research on this topic has been carried out with Spanish speakers rather than other minority languages and minoritized groups in the US. Moreover, this literature has not examined translan-guaging in foreign/L2 immersion, a context in which Canadian immer-sion researchers have recently questioned its appropriateness (Ballinger *et al.*, 2017).

Call for translanguaging practices in bilingual and immersion education

Despite the limitations and relative dearth of US and Canadian research on translanguaging in immersion settings, scholars are increas-ingly calling for overt support of translanguaging in all language class-rooms with little regard for learner background or program context (e.g. García & Wei, 2014; Palmer *et al.*, 2014). Moreover, recently published handbooks guide bilingual and immersion teachers in how to effectively implement translanguaging pedagogy (e.g. García *et al.*, 2017). Given robust research support for immersion education based on decades of achievement and proficiency outcomes in programs that have embraced language separation, such context-general recommendations and prac-tice guides seem to position the cart before the horse. In the next sec-tion, we review findings that suggest caution in advance of widespread implementation of translanguaging in immersion settings if program goals continue to target advanced levels of bilingualism, biliteracy and academic achievement for all learners.

Evidence-Based Counterarguments to Translanguaging

Decades of US and Canadian research has consistently shown that immersion programs lead to higher levels of SLA relative to more traditional language learning (Center for Applied Second Language Studies, 2013; Thomas & Collier, 2012). Additionally, immersion students from varied socioeconomic, ethnic, linguistic and developmental backgrounds demonstrate academic achievement commensurate with or above that of same-age peers in English-medium programs (Genesee & Fortune, 2014, for review; Steele *et al.*, 2017). Nonetheless, studies in immersion programs have also illustrated (a) the prevalence of English use and (b) the persistent challenge of underdeveloped minority language proficiency among learners.

Prevalence of English use

Both quantitative and qualitative research on student language use in foreign language (Broner, 2000; Fortune, 2001) and two-way immersion classrooms in the US (e.g. Ballinger & Lyster, 2011; Freeman, 1998; Hernández, 2015; Potowski, 2004) has consistently shown that students often prefer English during minority language instructional time *regardless of their home language background*. English use is especially prevalent and persistent as students advance in grade level. For example, Broner (2000), Fortune (2001) and Potowski (2004) each conducted in-depth studies with Grade 5 students in three different Spanish/English whole-school immersion contexts in the US: a foreign language immersion program, a foreign language immersion program that enrolled some Spanish L1 students and a two-way program, respectively. Although these researchers used different units of measure (e.g. utterance, turn), they reported that between 36% and 45% of student production occurred in English during Spanish instructional time. Notably, these findings emerged within whole-school immersion programs; this school context has evidenced relatively greater use of the minority language compared to strand programs, situated within English-medium elementary schools (see Doell, 2011, for review).

Minority language development challenges

Just as studies in Canada have revealed limitations in the French proficiency of majority language immersion students (Lyster, 2007, for review), so too has US research reported grammatical, lexical and complexity weaknesses in L2 proficiency for majority language immersion students acquiring various languages (Burkhauser *et al.*, 2016; Fortune & Ju, 2017; Lindholm-Leary, 2001; Tedick & Young, 2016). Further, majority language students appear to reach a plateau in their minority language development by upper elementary (Fortune & Tedick, 2015) and have difficulty exceeding upper intermediate levels by Grade 8 (Burkhauser *et al.*, 2016).

Studies involving Spanish-speaking students in two-way immersion have also pointed to underdeveloped Spanish (e.g. Potowski, 2004). Tedick and Young (2016) reported on students in a Grade 5 two-way classroom whose Spanish proficiency was judged to be at a low-intermediate level although they spoke Spanish at home and had been in the program since kindergarten. Minority language students also often become dominant in English over time. For example, Delia, a student in Fortune's (2001) study, was Spanish dominant in kindergarten, but tested English dominant in Grade 5. The vast majority of her instruction had occurred in Spanish and Spanish was used more often at home.

Re-examining the Call for Translanguaging in Immersion Education

The findings summarized above lead us to question the idea that increased use of English through translanguaging will lead to greater minority language proficiency among students. Indeed, these studies indicate that most students are already making extensive use of English even during those times of the day when use of the minority language is privileged by language separation. SLA research has clearly established that achieving high levels of L2 proficiency requires extensive exposure to and use of that language. Acquisition is driven by meaningful input, and immersion classroom exposure to the minority language is the primary (often only) source of input for all majority language and some minority language students. Language proficiency is further enhanced when students make extensive use of the minority language for authentic, purposeful communication. Findings on the underdeveloped nature of immersion students' minority language proficiency suggest insufficient opportunities for students to construct meaning with language, both in speaking and in writing. But does the level of proficiency attained in these languages really matter?

Research in two-way immersion programs finds that minority language Latino students develop higher levels of proficiency in English and Spanish compared to peers in other US programs (e.g. Lindholm-Leary & Howard, 2008; Thomas & Collier, 2012). They also develop higher levels of bilingual proficiency than majority language students in two-way programs, who remain English dominant. These higher bilingual proficiency levels co-occur with increased academic language proficiency and successful schooling experiences. For example, Latino students with higher bilingual proficiency levels are more likely to complete secondary school and have higher grade point averages and more positive attitudes toward school than their *monolingual* English-speaking Latino peers (for review, see Lindholm-Leary & Genesee, 2014).

Importantly, Thomas and Collier (2012) and others have emphasized that successful two-way bilingual programs adhere to certain non-negotiable practices, one of which is separation of languages.

In a recent review of studies exploring the advantages of bilingualism among Latinos and other immigrant groups in the US, Gándara (2015) highlights the significance of developing *balanced bilingualism* – the ability to speak, read and write the minority language and English well or very well. Balanced bilinguals were much less likely to drop out of school. Moreover, Gándara reported on a study that found a strong relationship between being a high-use bilingual (one who frequently uses the L1 within the family and community) and attending a four-year college. Young people with four-year college degrees increased their earnings potential; strong bilingual proficiency opened up employment possibilities in high-level, high-paying jobs in the global marketplace that increasingly requires such skills (Gándara, 2015).

There is a growing amount of compelling evidence that countries like the US and Canada need to advance the bilingual capacity *of all children*, regardless of home language, to meet the rising linguistic demands of the globalized world. Of course, having the potential to participate in a rapidly expanding global marketplace is but one of a wide range of cognitive, sociocultural, identity, educational and personal fulfillment benefits of becoming a highly proficient bilingual/biliterate individual.

Indeed, like us, other scholars also assert that it is critical to take the local context and program model into account when considering the appropriateness of translanguaging pedagogies. This is particularly important in societies where English is the majority language and co-exists with the minority or co-official language both inside and outside the classroom. In discussing Canadian French immersion programs, for example, Ballinger *et al.* (2017) warn researchers and educators about calling for an increase in English use during French instruction, maintaining instead that

> ... until empirical evidence supports increased use of English in immersion, crosslinguistic approaches that maintain a separate space for the majority language may represent ideal pedagogical practices in these contexts. (Ballinger *et al.*, 2017: 32)

Research Gaps and Questions for Future Inquiry

What is clear from this discussion of the literature on language use practices in immersion contexts is that more classroom-based, quasi-experimental, qualitative and longitudinal studies *in a range of program models* with a clear link to bilingual and biliteracy outcomes and content learning are needed. Questions deserving investigation include:

- What is the relationship between L1 languaging or translanguaging and the achievement of advanced levels of bilingualism, biliteracy and content learning?

- What is the relationship between (a) more advanced levels of bilingualism, biliteracy and academic achievement; and (b) students' socioemotional well-being, social justice consciousness and empowered bilingual identity development?
- Are there specific translanguaging teaching or learning strategies that are more effective than others for promoting advanced levels of bilingualism, biliteracy and content learning?
- Are there particular ages, proficiency levels or developmental levels at which minority language and majority language learners would most benefit from L1 languaging or translanguaging practices to further advanced levels of bilingualism, biliteracy and content learning?
- In what ways are immersion students able to use their developing language (L2) as a cognitive tool?
- In what ways can educators help students develop cross-linguistic connections while still offering protected spaces and support for minority language development?

Conclusion

The explosion of literature and discourse among US and Canadian researchers and educators on translanguaging as a new theoretical orientation toward language and classroom language use practice is impressive, indeed, unparalleled. It has refueled a long-standing, often impassioned, even polarizing debate about the keystone practice of language separation in immersion programming. Yet, many of the arguments being made about the nature of language and bilingualism by advocates of translanguaging are also fully supported by researchers and educators in favor of language separation. For example, as L2 education researchers, we uphold the view that languages other than English are assets to be nurtured and developed in schools and that doing so can and does result in academic, linguistic and personal advantages for learners. We agree that bilingualism is a dynamic practice that cannot and should not be reduced to the notion of two independent monolinguals co-existing in one person. We view the practice of shifting between one's languages as sophisticated, disciplined and natural practice among bilinguals and argue for the importance of utilizing the entirety of one's linguistic repertoire in schooling and elsewhere. Indeed, we readily accept the compelling evidence indicating that a bilingual's two languages are always available regardless of their use of one language versus another in any given moment (Kroll *et al.*, 2015). However, we question the context-blind rejection of immersion program implementation practices that have resulted in decades of successful achievement outcomes and higher levels of bilingual proficiency than any other school-based language program to date.

The literature on translanguaging in comparison to other discussions of language allocation in immersion programs often positions issues of social justice and educational equity as primary goals as well as addressing the socioemotional needs and affirming the bilingual identity of the minority language learner. We concur that these issues are critically important and worthy of researcher and educator attention. We are aware of the need to raise teachers' critical attentiveness to the potential for inequitable classroom discourse practices among peers in immersion classrooms that are prone to mirror persistent societal inequalities experienced by groups and individuals from a range of socioeconomic, racial, ethnic and linguistic backgrounds and diverse gender identities. We actively work toward addressing these issues in professional development with immersion educators.

At the same time, we argue that the long-range goals of social justice and educational equity may ultimately be best accomplished through the achievement of advanced levels of SLA and academic performance for *all* learners. Dichotomous juxtapositioning of minority language and majority language learners' needs and harshly worded attacks on programs that serve them (e.g. Flores & García, 2017) suggest limited, dualistic thinking. But, the success of immersion, as described earlier in this chapter, can be at least partially attributed to its non-dualistic integrated approach to (a) schooling linguistically diverse learners in one program and (b) teaching subject matter and language simultaneously.

In a similarly non-dualistic manner, we contend that the ultimate goal of creating a more socially just and educationally equitable world is held by *all* immersion educators, not just those who teach minority language learners. The intense focus on advanced levels of minority language and literacy development and the practice of privileging the minority language within specific periods of instructional time can also be viewed as *a critical means to the overarching mutually held end goals* of cultural empowerment, bilingual identity development and educational achievement for *all* learners.

These ambitious aims can be fostered through a variety of program design and implementation practices. For example, we favor the officially sanctioned use of the minority language in public schooling that currently occurs in immersion programs for set periods of time. We strongly support curriculum design that intentionally targets the teaching of cross-linguistic connections during instructional time in English or while using the minority language (e.g. Lyster *et al.*, 2013). We argue for program leadership that ensures partner teachers of each language have sufficient time to plan for and coordinate language and content development opportunities for students. We embrace a range of classroom practices that seek to validate and showcase students' bilingual identities and the use of various grouping and cooperative learning strategies that help rebalance inequitable classroom discourse. In short, we aim for the deeply transformational learning that transpires when children realize their full potential as academically and linguistically competent bi- and multilinguals. Such learning stimulates the very real sense of accomplishment, self-esteem, openness to difference and personal empowerment that often emerge in concert with acquiring strong capabilities in at least two languages and a deeper understanding of diverse peoples and cultures.

At present, research evidences the efficacy of immersion education in the US and Canada for a range of learners, including minority language students. While there is always a need to improve current educational practice, unquestioningly embracing a new approach to classroom language use in all bilingual and immersion contexts seems premature given the current state of research. We join with Merrill Swain and others and call for researchers and educators to collaborate on high-quality classroom-based research that explores the relationship between classroom language use practices and L2 and literacy acquisition. The field will benefit from investigations that further explore how to most effectively make use of minority and majority languages in ways that lead to the highest levels of bilingualism and biliteracy for all learners. Indeed, it is through enriched bilingual and immersion education and the development of empowered bilingual/biliterate individuals that these programs will be well-positioned to realize the social justice and educational equity goals that all bilingual and immersion educators seek.

Acknowledgments

We are grateful to the anonymous reviewers and editors for their insightful comments on earlier drafts.

Notes

(1) We acknowledge that French is not considered a minority language in Canada, but rather a second official language. Nevertheless, we chose to refer to English as the majority language and English speakers as majority language learners and non-English languages as minority languages and their speakers as minority language speakers. Such terminology is frequently encountered in US immersion literature.

(2) Bilingual education in the US has traditionally been associated with educational program options for minority language students. There are many types of bilingual programs, ranging from 'weak' models (Baker & Wright, 2017) that do not foster bilingualism, to 'strong' models like developmental bilingual education.

(3) We are aware that in translanguaging discourse the term 'additive bilingualism' is seen as espousing an outdated and indeed illegitimate view of language as an independent singular entity (García & Wei, 2014). We agree with Cummins' (2017) recent critique of this perspective. He argues that while bilingual processing as a cognitive act is dynamic and integrated, the construct of individual languages remains viable, as do associated terms that describe the nature of language on a continuum, e.g. home versus school language, L1 versus L2 and additive versus subtractive bilingualism.

(4) It is important to clarify that separation of languages *per se* does not mean that students' languages are separated in their brains. At a cognitive level, both teachers and

students process knowledge structures in both their languages, and the L1 and other languages are present even if they are not overtly used.

(5)   Although the Culver City program primarily served majority language students, it also included some minority language students (Spanish L1). Likewise, the bilingual program that Cohen evaluated enrolled some majority language (English L1) students.

(6)   Scholars from all over the world have contributed significantly to the conceptualization and research base on translanguaging, but we limit our discussion in this chapter as much as possible to the work of US and Canadian scholars.

(7)   Alejandro used the feminine form, *maestra*, instead of the masculine, *maestro*.

References

Baker, C. and Wright, W. (2017) *Foundations of Bilingual Education and Bilingualism* (6th edn). Bristol: Multilingual Matters.

Ballinger, S. and Lyster, R. (2011) Student and teacher oral language use in a two-way Spanish/English immersion school. *Language Teaching Research* 15 (3), 289–306.

Ballinger, S., Lyster, R., Sterzuk, A. and Genesee, F. (2017) Context-appropriate cross-linguistic pedagogy: Considering the role of language status in immersion education. *Journal of Immersion and Content-Based Language Education* 5 (1), 30–57.

Behan, L., Spek, J. and Turnbull, M. (1995) Can L1 use in collaborative dialogues help bridge the L2 proficiency gap? Ontario Institute for Studies in Education, Toronto, ON. Unpublished manuscript.

Broner, M. (2000) Impact of interlocutor and task on first and second language use in a Spanish immersion program. Unpublished doctoral dissertation, University of Minnesota.

Burkhauser, S., Steele, J.L., Li, J., Slater, R.O., Bacon, M. and Miller, T. (2016) Partner-language learning trajectories in dual-language immersion: Evidence from an urban district. *Foreign Language Annals* 49 (3), 415–433.

Center for Applied Second Language Studies (2013) What levels of proficiency do immersion students achieve? See https://casls.uoregon.edu/wp-content/uploads/pdfs/tenqu estions/TBQImmersionStudentProficiencyRevised.pdf (accessed 27 August 2018).

Cohen, A.D. (1974) The Culver City Spanish immersion program: The first two years. *The Modern Language Journal* 43 (3), 95–103.

Cummins, J. (2007) Rethinking monolingual instructional strategies in multilingual classrooms. *Canadian Journal of Applied Linguistics* 10, 221–241.

Cummins, J. (2014) Rethinking pedagogical assumptions in Canadian French immersion programs. *Journal of Immersion and Content-Based Language Education* 2 (1), 3–22.

Cummins, J. (2017) Teaching minoritized students: Are additive approaches legitimate? *Harvard Educational Review* 87 (3), 404–425.

Doell, L. (2011) Comparing dual-track and single-track French immersion programs: Does setting matter? *The ACIE Newsletter* 14 (2), 3, 12–15. See http://carla.umn.edu/imme rsion/acie/vol14/no2/may2011_bp.html (accessed 27 August 2018).

Flores, N. and García, O. (2017) A critical review of bilingual education in the United States: From basements and pride to boutiques and profit. *Annual Review of Applied Linguistics* 37, 14–29.

Fortune, T. (2001) Understanding immersion students' oral language use as a mediator of social interaction in the classroom. Unpublished doctoral dissertation, University of Minnesota.

Fortune, T.W. and Tedick, D.J. (2015) Oral proficiency development of English proficient K–8 Spanish immersion students. *Modern Language Journal* 99 (4), 637–655. doi: 10.1111/modl.12275

Fortune, T.W. and Ju, Z. (2017) Assessing and exploring the oral proficiency of young Mandarin immersion learners. *Annual Review of Applied Linguistics* 37, 264–287. doi: 10.1017/S0267190517000150

Freeman, R. (1998) *Bilingual Education and Social Change.* Clevedon: Multilingual Matters.

Gándara, P. (2015) Is There Really a Labor Market Advantage to Bilingualism in the U.S.? Policy Information Report. Princeton, NJ: Educational Testing Service. doi: 10.1002/ets2.12054. See www.ets.org/research/pic (accessed 27 August 2018).

García, O. (2009) *Bilingual Education in the 21st Century: A Global Perspective.* Malden, MA: Wiley-Blackwell.

García, O. (with Makar, C., Starcevic, M. and Terry, A.) (2011) Translanguaging of Latino kindergarteners. In K. Potowski and J. Rothman (eds) *Bilingual Youth: Spanish in English-Speaking Societies* (pp. 33–55). Amsterdam: John Benjamins.

García, O. and Wei, L. (2014) *Translanguaging: Language, Bilingualism and Education.* New York: Palgrave Macmillan.

García, O., Johnson, S.I. and Seltzer, K. (2017) *The Translanguaging Classroom: Leveraging Student Bilingualism for Learning.* Philadelphia, PA: Caslon Publishing.

García-Mateus, S. and Palmer, D. (2017) Translanguaging pedagogies for positive identities in two-way dual language bilingual education. *Journal of Language, Identity, and Education* 16 (4), 245–255. doi: 10.1080/15348458.2017.1329016

Genesee, F. (1987) *Learning through Two Languages: Studies of Immersion and Bilingual Education.* Cambridge, MA: Newbury House.

Genesee, F. and Fortune, T.W. (2014) Bilingual education and at-risk students. *Journal of Immersion and Content-Based Language Education* 2 (2), 196–209.

Hernández, A.M. (2015) Language status in two-way bilingual immersion: The dynamics between English and Spanish in peer interaction. *Journal of Immersion and Content-Based Language Education* 3 (1), 102–126.

Howard, E.R. and Sugarman, J. (2007) *Realizing the Vision of Two-Way Immersion: Fostering Effective Programs and Classrooms.* Washington, DC: Center for Applied Linguistics and Delta Publishing.

Jacobson, R. (1990) Allocating two languages as a key feature of bilingual methodology. In R. Jacobson and C. Faltis (eds) *Language Distribution Issues in Bilingual Schooling* (pp. 3–17). Clevedon: Multilingual Matters.

Jacobson, R. and Faltis, C. (eds) (1990) *Language Distribution Issues in Bilingual Schooling.* Clevedon: Multilingual Matters.

Kroll, J.F., Bobb, S.C. and Hoshino, N. (2014) Two languages in mind: Bilingualism as a tool to investigate language, cognition, and the brain. *Current Direction in Psychological Science* 23 (3), 159–163.

Lambert, W.E. (1984) An overview of issues in immersion education. In R. Campbell (ed.) *Studies on Immersion Education: A Collection for United States Educators* (pp. 8–30). Sacramento, CA: California State Department of Education.

Legaretta, D. (1977) Language choice in bilingual classrooms. *TESOL Quarterly* 11, 9–16.

Legaretta, D. (1979) The effects of program models on language acquisition by Spanish speaking children. *TESOL Quarterly* 13 (4), 521–534.

Legaretta-Marcaida, D. (1981) Effective use of primary language in the classroom. In Office of Bilingual Bicultural Education, California State Department of Education (ed.) *Schooling and Language Minority Students: A Theoretical Framework* (pp. 83–116). Los Angeles, CA: Evaluation, Dissemination, and Assessment Center, California State University, Los Angeles. ERIC ED 249 773.

Lindholm, K.J. (1987) *Directory of Bilingual Immersion Programs: Two-Way Bilingual Education for Language Minority and Majority Students.* Los Angeles, CA: University of California Center for Language Education and Research (CLEAR). ERIC ED 291-241.

Lindholm-Leary, K.J. (2001) *Dual Language Education.* Clevedon: Multilingual Matters.

Lindholm-Leary, K. and Howard, E. (2008) Language development and academic achievement in two-way immersion programs. In T.W. Fortune and D.J. Tedick (eds) *Pathways to Multilingualism: Evolving Perspectives on Immersion Education* (pp. 177–200). Clevedon: Multilingual Matters.

Lindholm-Leary, K. and Genesee, F. (2014) Student outcomes in one-way, two-way, and indigenous language immersion education. *Journal of Immersion and Content-Based Language Education* 2 (2), 165–180.

Lyster, R. (2007) *Learning and Teaching Languages through Content: A Counterbalanced Approach.* Amsterdam: John Benjamins.

Lyster, R., Quiroga, J. and Ballinger, S. (2013) The effects of biliteracy instruction on morphological awareness. *Journal of Immersion and Content-Based Language Education* 1 (2), 169–197.

Palmer, D.K., Martínez, R.A., Mateus, S.G. and Henderson, K. (2014) Reframing the debate on language separation: Toward a vision for translanguaging pedagogies in the dual language classroom. *Modern Language Journal* 98 (3), 757–772.

Potowski, K. (2004) Student Spanish use and investment in a dual immersion classroom: Implications for second language acquisition and heritage language maintenance. *Modern Language Journal* 88 (1), 75–101.

Steele, J.L., Slater, R.O., Zamarro, G., Miller, T., Li, J., Burkhauser, S. and Bacon, M. (2017) Effects of dual-language immersion programs on student achievement: Evidence from lottery data. *American Educational Research Journal* 54 (1S), 282S–306S.

Swain, M. (1983) Bilingualism without tears. In M.A. Clarke and J. Handscombe (eds) *On TESOL 82: Pacific Perspectives on Language, Learning and Teaching* (pp. 35–46). Washington, DC: TESOL.

Swain, M. (2006) Languaging, agency and collaboration in advanced second language learning. In H. Byrnes (ed.) *Advanced Language Learning: The Contributions of Halliday and Vygotsky* (pp. 95–108). London: Continuum.

Swain, M. and Lapkin, S. (2000) Task-based second language learning: The uses of the first language. *Language Teaching Research* 4, 251–274.

Swain, M. and Lapkin, S. (2013) A Vygotskian sociocultural perspective on immersion education: The L1/L2 debate. *Journal of Immersion and Content-Based Language Education* 1 (1), 101–129.

Tedick, D.J. and Björklund, S. (eds) (2014) Language immersion education: A research agenda for 2015 and beyond [Special issue]. *Journal of Immersion and Content-Based Language Education* 2 (2).

Tedick, D.J. and Young, A.I. (2016) Fifth grade two-way immersion students' responses to form-focused instruction. *Applied Linguistics* 37 (6), 784–807. doi: 10.1093/applin/amu066

Thomas, W.P. and Collier, V.P. (2012) *Dual Language Education for a Transformed World.* Albuquerque, NM: Dual Language Education of New Mexico and Fuente Press.

Turnbull, M. and Dailey-O'Cain, J. (eds) (2009) *First Language Use in Second and Foreign Language Learning.* Bristol: Multilingual Matters.

Turnbull, M., Cormier, M. and Bourque, J. (2011) The first language in science class: A quasi-experimental study in late French immersion. *Modern Language Journal* 95, 182–198.

Vygotsky, L.S. (1986) *Thought and Language* (rev. edn). Cambridge, MA: MIT Press.

Williams, C. (1996) Secondary education: Teaching in the bilingual situation. In C. Williams, G. Lewis and C. Baker (eds) *The Language Policy: Taking Stock* (pp. 39–78). Llangefni: CAI.

Wong Fillmore, L. (1982) Instructional language as linguistic input: Second language learning in classrooms. In L.C. Wilkinson (ed.) *Communicating in the Classroom* (pp. 283–294). New York: Academic Press.

Wong Fillmore, L. and Valadez, C. (1986) Teaching bilingual learners. In M. Wittrock (ed.) *Handbook of Research on Teaching* (3rd edn; pp. 648–685). New York: Macmillan.

3 Research Trends and Future Challenges in Swedish Immersion

Siv Björklund

Introduction

Inspired by the innovative way of teaching a second language (L2) in French immersion, in 1987 a research group in the city of Vaasa launched a Swedish immersion program for Finnish-speaking children. Vaasa is a bilingual city situated in the west of Finland with 67,000 inhabitants. Today, 69.5% of the city's population are registered as Finnish speakers and approximately 22.5% as Swedish speakers. Although Finnish has been the dominant language since the 1920s, Swedish is still used and heard daily in the center of the city as most of the rural municipalities surrounding the city are strongly dominated by Swedish. Alongside the relatively stable societal bilingualism of the city, other languages have been a natural part of the scene for centuries because of Vaasa's position as a lively center for trade and export. In addition, during the 2000s the city received many residents who use other languages than Finnish or Swedish. Currently, there are 120 nationalities speaking 94 different languages in Vaasa.

Starting from the city of Vaasa, Swedish immersion programs have spread to other cities, mostly in the western and southern parts of Finland, which are bilingual areas where both Finnish and Swedish are used daily. Though Swedish is officially one of the two national languages of Finland, there is a big variation both locally and regionally regarding the use and the status of Swedish as the non-dominant official language across the nation. In many respects, Swedish can be regarded as a minority language, since only approximately 5% of the population are registered as Swedish speakers.

In this chapter, I first introduce some of the core characteristics of Swedish immersion education and then describe how they parallel those of French immersion and other bilingual programs. I then describe the sociolinguistic and sociopolitical conditions of Swedish immersion in Finland and discuss how they relate to ongoing language ideological debates about Swedish as the other official language in Finland. I subsequently focus on research objectives and program evaluation in Swedish immersion research. I briefly outline research issues and then present a current research project. In the concluding section, I position current Swedish immersion in contemporary Finnish society and discuss the challenges to its future development.

My understanding of the development of Swedish immersion in Finland is largely built upon research conducted by the immersion research team at the University of Vaasa. This group of researchers has been a leading research group of Swedish immersion in Finland since the start of the first program in the city of Vaasa. I have had the privilege of belonging to this group since its establishment and, among other important activities, had the opportunity of participating in its first trip to Canada in the late 1980s. My first personal encounter with Professor Merrill Swain dates back to this trip.

Positioning Swedish Immersion in Relation to Other Bilingual Programs

In one of the first internationally widely read articles on French immersion in Canada, Lambert and Tucker (1972) presented an educational plan for French immersion and noted that this program should not, as it stands, be seen as *the* solution for all societies or countries that are looking for models of bilingual education. Nevertheless, from a sociological point of view they underlined that if a school wishes to implement a well-functioning bilingual program, it must give priority to the language that is less likely to develop in the environment outside school. Furthermore, to compensate for the imbalance between the two languages outside school, they recommended that the less used language should be widely used within the school.

> When applied to bilingual settings, this principle calls for the establishment of two elementary school streams, one conducted in language A and one in language B, with two groups of teachers who either are or who function as though they were monolinguals in one of the languages. If A is the more prestigious language, then native speakers of A would start their schooling in language B, and after functional bilingualism is attained, continue their schooling in both languages. (Lambert & Tucker, 1972: 216)

Societal language use and language prestige are thus presented as the cornerstones of French immersion, and these were later reconfirmed in further research on French immersion by other Canadian researchers as core characteristics. In 1982, Swain and Lapkin (1982: 85) defined majority group membership of the participating students and parents 'as one of the four major principles for French immersion', and, in 1997,

Swain and Johnson (1997: 6–8) noted that language immersion students mainly use their immersion language in school, where it is extensively used as the language of instruction. They add that there is explicit support for immersion students' first language (L1) outside school. These early features of immersion, though, were later revisited by these scholars (e.g. Swain & Lapkin, 2005; also see section titled 'Discussion and Implications for Future') to better meet the growing linguistic diversity in Canada and in French immersion.

At the outset of the first Swedish immersion program in 1987, the official bilingual English–French context in Canada corresponded significantly to the official bilingual Finnish–Swedish context in Finland. It was therefore quite straightforward to apply the recommendations for the structure of the French immersion program to Finnish conditions, where Swedish is clearly the non-dominant official language (for more information about the first implementations of Swedish immersion in Finland, see e.g. Björklund, 1997). At the time of implementation in Finland, Canadian research on French immersion showed that an early start in kindergarten led to communicative benefits in the immersion language (Genesee, 1987; Swain & Lapkin, 1982). For this reason, an early total immersion model was chosen in Finland, and this has been the prevailing model ever since. Unlike in Canada, there have been no delayed (middle) or late programs.

Though the structure of the early total Swedish immersion model was mostly inspired by the early total French immersion model, there are some differences between the two models. In Finland, early total immersion usually starts with children aged five even though some kindergartens allow enrolment from the age of three. The children mostly come from backgrounds where only Finnish has been used as the home language. During the kindergarten year(s) and the preschool year, Swedish (the students' L2) is mainly used as the language of instruction. Finnish (the students' L1) is introduced as the language of instruction in Grade 1, and during Grades 1 and 2 it comprises approximately 10% of total instruction time. From Grades 5 and 6 onward, instructional time is equally distributed between Finnish and Swedish until the program ends after Grade 9, when the students are 15 years old.

Despite the similarities between the Swedish immersion model and the French model, there are some differences. First, in Swedish immersion, Finnish is introduced earlier in the program than in the French model, but the instruction focuses on oral skills and strengthening students' cultural identity as Finnish speakers rather than on early literacy skills, which are formally taught in Swedish. Second, the language pair of the program, Finnish and Swedish, is not lexically or syntactically related. Finnish belongs to the Fenno-Ugrian language family and is structurally very different from Swedish, which is a Germanic language and shares many similarities with e.g. English and German. Third, given

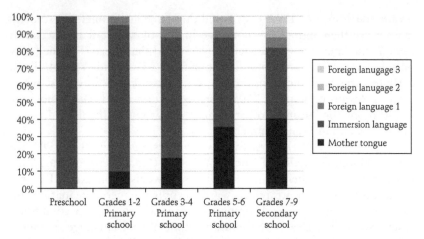

Figure 3.1   A typical program structure allowing for five languages in total within an early total Swedish immersion program (Modified version based on Björklund & Mård-Miettinen, 2011)

the European context of the Swedish program, more languages need to be included in the program, along the same lines as in other European language immersion programs (see e.g. Cenoz, 2009; Nissilä & Björklund, 2014). The inclusion of additional languages in the immersion program gives it a more multilingual than bilingual orientation, since the teaching of additional languages in many Swedish immersion programs in Finland starts earlier than in non-immersion schools. In many immersion programs, it is possible for students to learn three additional languages (see Figure 3.1 for a description of a typical program structure allowing for five languages in total within an early total program).

The first foreign language (L3 of the program) is almost always English, while French, German and Spanish are typically L4 and L5 languages of the program. Additional languages are not used as extensively as Swedish and Finnish as languages of instruction but are mostly planned as separate language lessons during regular school days. Most teachers in Swedish immersion (also teachers of additional languages) mainly use the target language as the language of instruction in the classroom and teach across subjects, using thematic units or a project-based teaching approach as a starting point for collaborative teaching. Even if teachers act as one-language models in the classroom, students will encounter all the languages used in the program on an almost daily basis. The Swedish immersion program ends after Grade 9 (15-year-old students) and immersion students can choose between entering either a Finnish-medium or a Swedish-medium upper secondary or vocational school. The students predominantly choose a Finnish-medium school, where Swedish is taught as a subject and not used as a language of instruction for other content teaching. However, the long-term effects of the program are still visible in the national matriculation examinations (18-year-old students), where the results of Swedish immersion students show that their competence in all languages of the program has developed very well in comparison with same-age, non-immersion students (Bergroth, 2006). All in all, the inclusion of several languages in Swedish immersion is highly appreciated by immersion parents and the learning of Swedish functions as a gateway to the efficient learning of the additional languages of the program as well (Björklund & Mård-Miettinen, 2011).

Following French immersion and its inception in the mid-1960s, not only have different language immersion programs been established but also a variety of adaptations, to such an extent that there are no longer necessarily any clear-cut differences between different programs. With changing conditions, definitions of language immersion also become blurred as the following quote illustrates:

> It [immersion] may be considered 'total' if the entire curriculum is taught in what is termed the target language, or 'partial' if that language is the language of instruction for just some subjects. (Eurydice, 2006: 7)

However, neither in French immersion nor in Swedish immersion can the entire curriculum be taught in the students' L2, as claimed in the quote, as this would render immersion programs subtractive rather than additive bilingualism. Regardless of the type of language immersion program, students have instructional time in their L1 to maintain and develop their L1 (see also the above description of the typical allocation of instructional time for each language in Swedish immersion).

As the quote illustrates, there is some dispute as to how much instructional time with the immersion language as the medium of instruction is sufficient to meet the expected linguistic and academic achievements associated with immersion programs (see also e.g. Genesee, 2004). In practice, it may be very difficult to find a consensus across all educational contexts about what constitutes an immersion program in relation to other types of bilingual programs. In the European context, there has been discussion about the similarities and differences between language immersion and content and language integrated learning (CLIL) programs (see Cenoz, 2015; Cenoz et al., 2013; Dalton-Puffer et al., 2014; Lasagabaster & Sierra, 2010). The acronym CLIL was coined in the mid-1990s even though the phenomenon was not a new one but based on language immersion (Mehisto et al., 2008). Today, CLIL is widely used in Europe, mainly due to the fact that the European Union has heavily promoted the use of the term with reference to teaching approaches that attend to both content and language. Because of the vast range of CLIL variations since its inception, one does not encounter as much discussion around the core characteristics of CLIL as is found in the language immersion debate. Both CLIL and immersion programs have a common interest in developing pedagogical approaches to implement and facilitate language learning within content-based lessons (see e.g. Genesee & Hamayan, 2016; Lyster, 2007; Nikula *et al.*, 2016).

Swedish Immersion within the Finnish Context

In this section, I present Swedish immersion and its position in public discourse in Finland during its 30 years of existence. It is impossible to contextualize the role of Swedish immersion without discussing the discourse surrounding the two national languages of Finland since Swedish immersion is closely intertwined with the status of Swedish in Finland. Therefore, I start by giving a short description of how Finnish and Swedish are generally taught in Finnish schools.

The constitutional status of the Finnish and Swedish languages means that both language groups learn the other national language as a subject in school. However, the language groups are kept separate and taught parallel in either Finnish- or Swedish-medium schools. It may be surprising, but in officially bilingual Finland there are no bilingual Finnish–Swedish schools. Parallel education systems for the two national languages have been established and designed to safeguard the Swedish language, which today still maintain its status as an official language but societally must be considered to be a minority language (there are 5.3% Swedish speakers as against 88.7% Finnish speakers and 6.0% speakers of other languages at the national level; Official Statistics of Finland, 2015). The education system supports the maintenance of Swedish-speaking schools for Swedish speakers, but the majority of Finnish-speaking students never really encounter the Swedish language in their daily lives. For Swedish-speaking students, Finnish, as the other domestic language, is the first 'foreign' language that they learn in school, but the Swedish language is not perceived as an equally important language by Finnish-speaking students. Consequently, more than 90% of the Finnish-speaking students choose English as their first 'foreign' language in school. However, at some point during their basic education, all students, both Finnish and Swedish speakers, must learn the other national language ('the other domestic language'): it is a mandatory school subject.

Since Swedish is not part of everyday life for most Finnish speakers in Finland, Swedish as a mandatory school subject has been vividly discussed and public debates tend to be polarized. On the one hand, it has been claimed that mandatory Swedish is artificial, demotivates Finnish-speaking students and hinders the learning of other languages. On the other hand, learning Swedish in school has been perceived as natural in Finland (as one of the Nordic countries), and it has been proposed that Finnish–Swedish bilingual schools should be established. In 2014, there was even a citizens' initiative to end the mandatory teaching of Swedish, but mandatory teaching was kept.

Given that public discourse is sometimes very negative about Swedish as a compulsory school subject, one might wonder what effects this debate has on Swedish immersion, where Swedish is used as the main instructional language throughout the program. However, Swedish immersion offers an alternative that parents can choose, but there is no pressure on them to make this choice for their children. Nearly all Swedish immersion programs are located in Finnish-speaking schools, i.e. in dual-track schools where parallel non-immersion classes are also available. Obviously, there are Finnish-speaking parents who consider the Swedish language to be important, as they choose to enroll their children in Swedish immersion. Until recently, however, language policy and language ideology have not been research topics addressed in immersion research in Finland (also see section titled 'Emerging Research Topics in Swedish Immersion').

When presenting how Swedish immersion has been viewed during its implementation in Finland, I draw on three different types of data that derive from three different public discourses: press data, debates about bilingual schools and the national core curricula. The press data are derived from analyses of articles published in the main Finnish and Swedish national newspapers. The debate data come from recent research discussions about the possibilities of establishing bilingual Finnish–Swedish schools in Finland. The educational data focus on how Swedish immersion is addressed in the national core curriculum. All three types of data have been collected as part of an ongoing research project titled 'The Interplay between Language Practices, Multilingual Identity and Language Ideologies in Language Immersion' (2016–2020) (also see section titled 'Emerging Research Topics in Swedish Immersion'). As the project has only recently started, at this stage I can only present some preliminary findings.

The press data. In order to develop an overview of how language immersion has been presented in the press during the past 30 years, headlines where the word 'immersion' (translated literally as 'language bath' in both Swedish and Finnish) were identified in the main Finnish daily newspaper (*Helsingin Sanomat*, HS) and in the main Swedish daily newspaper (*Hufvudstadsbladet*, Hbl) during three different time periods (1990–1993, 2000–2003, 2010–2013). Both newspapers are based in the capital, Helsinki, and are published seven days a week. The daily circulation of HS is approximately 313,000 and of Hbl only about 40,700. So far, quantitative results show that such headlines are very evenly distributed numerically between the two newspapers (Björklund, 2015). Because Swedish immersion programs are located in Finnish-speaking schools, I had expected more interest in the program in HS, but it seems that Hbl, which is read mainly by Swedish speakers, has taken an active role in following Swedish immersion. In both newspapers, the years 2000–2003 had the most headlines referencing immersion. This result was also somewhat unexpected since the public debate on immersion was most heated when the first immersion programs were established in the early and mid-1990s. However, the time period 2000–2003 coincided with the period of the establishment of many well-functioning such programs. Other results show that in both HS and Hbl, the term 'immersion' is also used to refer to out-of-school contexts (e.g. a visit to Sweden could be described as a language bath/immersion). In an educational context, the term 'immersion' is also used to refer to other situations such as summer camps in another language or language exchanges; this use of the term appeared more frequently in Hbl than in HS. In both newspapers, immersion was most frequently the main theme of an article during the first period (1990–1993). My impression is that there is little or no reference to the debate on mandatory Swedish, which seems not to be associated with Swedish immersion. However, further in-depth text analyses are needed to confirm this impression.

The debate data. Whereas the press data include three decades of language immersion in Finland, the scientific debate on how to define bilingual (Finnish–Swedish) schools and bilingual education has only arisen in recent years in the research literature. The debate was initiated by a politically active mother from Sweden who had moved with her bilingual Finnish–Swedish family to Finland. In 2011, she asked why there were no bilingual schools for simultaneous bilingual children in Finland. There are a growing number of bilingual Finnish–Swedish families in Finland, so this is, in many respects, a timely issue. First results of the analysis of the scientific debate on bilingual schools (for articles addressing the debate, see e.g. Boyd & Palviainen, 2014; Karjalainen & Pilke, 2012; Slotte-Lüttge et al., 2013) have shown that there is no single, uncontested definition of what constitutes a bilingual school in Finland. In the research literature, Swedish immersion is mostly mentioned as an excellent example of a bilingual education program in which students develop high language competence in the two languages. After these rather brief statements about how successfully Swedish immersion programs are functioning, Swedish immersion disappears from the debate, which centers on co-located schools and different suggestions on how Finnish–Swedish classes in future should be designed to allow for interaction between the language groups. The latter type of bilingual program has not yet been set up in Finland, but such sketched programs have many traits that resemble those of a two-way immersion program. 'Two-way immersion' is a term used in the United States to refer to immersion programs that are intended for both English-speaking students and students who speak a minority language at home (see e.g. Christian, 2011; Fortune & Tedick, 2008). Along these lines, a recent report on future bilingual education possibilities in Finland suggests a two-way immersion model (90:10) for establishing classes including both Swedish-speaking and Finnish-speaking students (Sundman, 2013).

The educational data. A preliminary analysis of the three most recent national core curricula shows how Swedish immersion is gradually being integrated into the core curriculum. In the 1994 national core curriculum, published seven years after the first Swedish immersion programs had opened, there is no mention of language immersion. However, it is stated that the Swedish language can also be used as a tool for learning in Finnish-speaking schools. The next national core curriculum was published in 2004, and in this version both the terms 'language immersion' and 'CLIL' are used without any clear definitions of the two programs. It should be noted that the organizers of bilingual programs, i.e. schools themselves, were given the right to decide what labels to use for them (cf. see section titled 'Positioning Swedish Immersion in Relation to Other Bilingual Programs'). The most recent national core curriculum published in 2014 (Finnish National Board of Education, 2016) and implemented in the fall of 2016 in basic education, gives bilingual education a chapter of its own. There are now guidelines and restrictions to definitions, points of departure for the organization of instruction, and assessment. Definitions are given of large-scale and small-scale bilingual education programs. Language immersion is used to refer to large-scale programs for the national languages of Finland, whereas CLIL is used to label both large-scale and small-scale programs, depending on their length and scope. A more detailed description of the discourses surrounding the actual writing of the bilingual education chapter in the most recent national core curriculum is provided by Bergroth (2016).

Research on Swedish Immersion: In Brief

In the following section, I will focus on the main research objectives with respect to Swedish immersion. As has been characteristic of French immersion in Canada (see e.g. Cummins, 1998), so too in other contexts research forms an essential part of program evaluation. The use of a second or foreign language as the language of instruction across subjects for a major part of the program is still regarded as unusual and thus calls for substantial research. The timeline for Swedish immersion research (Figure 3.2) can be generalized to include three different phases, in each of which there is some major component that is particular to that period, although there may also be studies that concentrate on elements that occur during the whole time period.

The first studies on Swedish immersion education (1987–2000) followed the same research design as in Canada, with a clear focus on immersion students' L1 and L2 development and/or academic achievement. Of special interest was the development of Swedish as an L2, research on which (see e.g. Björklund, 1996; Buss, 2002) was inspired by the studies of communicative competence and L2 acquisition by Merrill Swain and her colleagues (Canale & Swain, 1980; Harley *et al.*, 1990; Swain, 1985, 1988). During

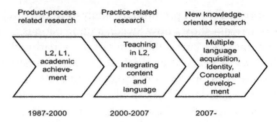

Figure 3.2 Main research objectives within Swedish immersion research from 1987 to present (Translated to English from Björklund, 2017)

this first phase of research, studies confirmed the effectiveness of Swedish immersion. In the next research phase (2000–2007), practice-related research on teaching in an L2 and the efficient integration of content and language were the dominant research topics in immersion research in Finland. Based upon research conducted by Swain (1996, 2000, 2001), the dialogue between teacher and students in immersion classrooms and its learning potential were salient research issues. In particular, studies focused on the early years of immersion (see e.g. Björklund *et al.*, 2013b; Södergård, 2008). In general, process-oriented research that seeks to find effective methods to teach in an L2 and to integrate content and subject efficiently has been a major research objective throughout the history of Swedish immersion research. I have defined the present research phase as a new knowledge-oriented phase. Considering that, in Canada, French immersion started more than 50 years ago, and that in Finland, Swedish immersion celebrated 30 years in 2017, it is time to re-examine and refine the established perspectives on immersion research in order to better meet changing multilingual and multicultural education settings (for the situation in Finland, see e.g. Björklund *et al.*, 2013a) and to explore newly emerging aspects in language immersion research. This third phase of research on Swedish immersion is also closely related to research conducted by Swain and her colleagues (see e.g. Swain *et al.*, 2010; Swain & Lapkin, 2005, 2013). For her continued engagement in the local development of language immersion programs in different countries as well as for her inspiring pioneer research on language immersion, which has also served as the basis for research in Swedish immersion in Finland, Swain received an honorary doctorate from the University of Vaasa, Finland, in 2011. The award acknowledges her outstanding research on L2 acquisition and language immersion over multiple decades.

Emerging Research Topics in Swedish Immersion

The new knowledge-oriented research agenda (see previous section) targets three research areas: multiple language acquisition, identity and conceptual development. In this section, I will briefly address multilingualism, multiple language acquisition and language identity, as these are the key concepts that have emerged over time and are now studied from different perspectives in research on Swedish immersion. These key concepts are central in the ongoing project 'The Interplay between Language Practices, Multilingual Identity and Language Ideologies in Language Immersion'. The press, debate and educational data I presented in the section titled 'Swedish Immersion within the Finnish Context' to contextualize Swedish immersion in Finnish society, are part of this project and are intended to serve as identifiers of societal discourses that are likely to impact on how students, their parents and teachers in immersion perceive the Swedish language within the framework of Swedish immersion.

However, the starting point of this project is not only the Swedish language, but also (re)constructions of language identities and multiple language use in Swedish immersion. Both multilingualism and identity are multifaceted concepts with no unanimously accepted clear or concise definitions. Several approaches are needed to cover most aspects of both concepts. Nevertheless, they have expanded quickly as research areas, which suggests that they correspond to the needs of a globalizing world. Research on both language identity and multilingualism shares a shift in conceptualization: earlier they were viewed as rather static and linear while now they are conceptualized as more dynamic and socially constructed phenomena that are also context dependent. As for immersion research, identity-related research issues concerning students as representatives of majority speakers have received almost no attention (see e.g. Cummins, 1998) since identity studies tend to focus on minority and heritage language learners.

Early Canadian immersion research tended to stress that the L1 language and culture of immersion students will develop as expected even though an L2 is used in immersion classrooms (Swain & Johnson, 1997; Swain & Lapkin, 1982). In a more recent Canadian study (Roy & Galiev, 2011), students in French immersion were asked how they viewed the relationship between their L1 (English) and L2 (French). The results show that the immersion students in the study did not perceive themselves to be 'truly' bilingual, even though they had spent several years in French immersion. The students did not believe that their proficiency in the immersion language would be accepted by native speakers of French. Roy and Galiev conclude that educators should be more aware of, and sensitive to, the multiple language resources of the students and find ways to show them that monolingual native speakers do not have a monopoly as far as the correct way to speak French is concerned.

As described earlier in this chapter, Swedish immersion programs have gradually developed a multilingual orientation that includes the earlier introduction of additional languages into the programs, even though Swedish remains the main language. Because of the multilingual orientation of Swedish immersion, it was natural for the project 'The Interplay between Language Practices, Multilingual Identity and Language Ideologies in Language Immersion' to start from a multilingual rather than a bilingual perspective. In the current project, language identity is defined

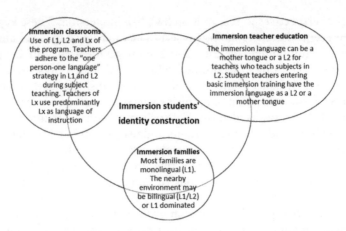

Figure 3.3 Agents related to Swedish immersion students' identity construction (Adapted from Björklund, 2017)

by membership of a shared speech community. Therefore, it is assumed that the immersion program has a considerable influence on how originally language-majority pupils position themselves as individuals and members of groups in a school context where several languages are used. Further, language identity is seen as socially and dynamically (re)constructed in relation to the languages shared within the community, in this case especially the school. Immersion students' views and beliefs about their multilingualism and their language identity may differ with age and with different interlocutors/agents (Figure 3.3).

One starting point for the project was the responses to one item on a questionnaire, in which 75% of Swedish immersion students in Grades 7–9 (*n* = 114) perceived themselves as multilingual (Björklund *et al.*, 2015) (cf. results by Roy & Galiev, 2011). In light of this response, the project is now heading toward a more dialogical analysis, in which it is assumed that the individual and the social interact and that each individual's perspectives have a social origin. Although the project members have an interest in immersion students as a group, it is recognized that every individual has a unique life history that they can choose to accept or not, to repeat, reject or affirm different ways of constructing their own language identity. The aim of the project is to study beliefs (for research on beliefs, see e.g. Barcelos & Kalaja, 2011) about multiple language use and language identities as a research field in a language immersion context. To achieve this goal, immersion students are invited to participate as active social agents in the data generation. Student reflections are complemented by students' self-reported visualizations of their linguistic environment and of their personal visual language inventories (photographs) in informal school spaces and in outside-of-school spaces. Currently, this type of data is being analyzed and, in the next phase, the students' multilingualism, their multiple language use and their reflections on languages will be investigated in light of language identity construction.

Discussion and Implications for Future

Because Swedish immersion celebrated 30 years as a bilingual education program in Finland in 2017, it is a suitable moment to look both backward and forward. Since the start of Swedish immersion in 1987, other types of programs aiming at bilingualism have emerged both outside and inside Finland. New ways of acting bi- and multilingually in different school contexts offer fresh and different perspectives that can both identify the essential core characteristics of language immersion programs and inspire the development of other bilingual enrichment programs. In the Finnish context, the definition of small-scale and large-scale bilingual education in the new national core curriculum can be a useful tool for developing future programs. The proposal for a two-way immersion program for mixed Finnish- and Swedish-speaking student groups is another initiative, but legally not possible due to the Finnish constitution (cf. see section titled 'Swedish Immersion within the Finnish Context').

Over 30 years, Swedish immersion has gradually become a well-established program that stands on its own. Press data show that Swedish immersion is not explicitly associated with the parallel, often negatively tuned discourse on mandatory Swedish in Finnish-speaking schools. Debates on bilingual education in Finland showcase Swedish immersion as a successful program and the new national core curriculum explicitly identifies language immersion as a type of bilingual teaching with its own characteristics.

At the same time, there are also changes in society that indicate the need to further develop Swedish immersion in Finland. First, there is a growing target group of students who are newcomers to Finland and whose languages have not yet been taken into consideration but who should also have access to bilingual programs such as language immersion (for this issue in French immersion, see e.g. Swain & Lapkin, 2005). Second, although Swedish immersion is mostly presented positively, references to it as 'only Swedish' can potentially be a drawback in that the multilingual nature of the program is not explicitly stated. The more multilingual framework in Swedish immersion brings an added value to students who perceive themselves as multilingual. Bringing several languages into the program seems to offer a smooth transition from a focus on only two languages to a more flexible and dynamic perspective, where languaging in several languages is natural. Multiple language use makes it easier to get away from the 'two language solitudes', often referred to in the literature on bilingualism (see e.g. Cummins, 2008), where bilingualism is conceptualized as two parallel monolingual languages. It is quite easy to revert to thinking in terms of two separate languages when only two languages are involved, but when three or more languages are involved there seems to be a more pragmatic view on how one's different languages are acquired and used.

References

Barcelos, A.M.F. and Kalaja, P. (2011) Introduction to beliefs about SLA revisited. *System* 39, 281–289.

Bergroth, M. (2006) Immersion students in the matriculation examination. Three years after immersion. In S. Björklund, K. Mård-Miettinen, M. Bergström and M. Södergård (eds) *Exploring Dual-Focussed Education. Integrating Language and Content for Individual and Societal Needs* (pp. 123–134). Vaasa: Vaasa University.

Bergroth, M. (2016) Reforming the national core curriculum for bilingual education in Finland. *Journal of Immersion and Content-Based Language Education* 4 (1), 86–107.

Björklund, M., Björklund, S. and Sjöholm, K. (2013a) Multilingual policies and multilingual education in the Nordic countries. *International Electronic Journal of Elementary Education* 6 (1), 1–21.

Björklund, S. (1996) Lexikala drag och kontextualisering i språkbadselevers andraspråk [Lexical traits and contextualisation in immersion students' second language]. Acta Wasaensia 46, PhD dissertation, University of Vaasa.

Björklund, S. (1997) Immersion in Finland in the 1990s: A state of development and expansion. In R.K. Johnson and M. Swain (eds) *Immersion Education: International Perspectives* (pp. 85–101). Cambridge: Cambridge University Press.

Björklund, S. (2015) Språkbad i finländska tidningstexter: Analys av uppfattningen om språkbad under tre decennier [Language Immersion in Finnish newspaper texts: Analysis of Swedish immersion during three decades]. In C. Sandström, I. Cantell, E-R. Grönroos, P. Nuolijärvi and E. Sommardahl (eds) *Perspektiv på lexikografi, grammatik och språkpolitik i Norden [Perspectives on Lexicography, Grammar and Language Policy in the Nordic Countries]* (pp. 359–372). Helsinki: Institutet för de inhemska språken.

Björklund, S. (2017) Språkmöten inom undervisningen [Language encounters in education]. In L-E. Edlund and M. Nordman (eds) *Språkmöten i Västerbotten och Österbotten [Language Encounters in Westrobothnia and Ostrobothnia]* (pp. 130–142). Bottniska studier 4. Vaasa: University of Vaasa.

Björklund, S. and Mård-Miettinen, K. (2011) Integration of multiple languages in immersion: Swedish immersion in Finland. In D. Tedick, D. Christian and T. Fortune (eds) *Immersion Education: Practices, Policies, Possibilities* (pp. 13–35). Bristol: Multilingual Matters.

Björklund, S., Mård-Miettinen, K. and Savijärvi, M. (2013b) Swedish immersion in the early years in Finland. Special Issue: Immersion education in the early years. *International Journal of Bilingual Education and Bilingualism* 17 (2), 197–214. doi: 10.1080/13670050.2013.86662

Björklund, S., Pakarinen, S. and Mård-Miettinen, K. (2015) Är jag flerspråkig? Språkbadselevers uppfattning om sin flerspråkighet [Am I multilingual? Immersion students' beliefs about their multilingualism]. In J. Kalliokoski, K. Mård-Miettinen and T. Nikula (eds) *Kieli koulutuksen resurssina: vieraalla ja toisella kielellä oppimisen ja opetuksen näkökulmia [Language as an Educational Resource: Perspectives on Learning and Teaching in a Second or a Foreign Language]* (pp. 153–167). AFinLA-e. Soveltavan kielitieteen tutkimuksia 8. See http://ojs.tsv.fi/index.php/afinla/article/view/53 777/16874 (accessed 23 August 2018).

Boyd, S. and Palviainen, Å. (2014) Building walls or bridges? A language ideological debate about bilingual schools in Finland. In M. Halonen, P. Ihalainen and T. Saarinen (eds) *Language Policies in Finland and Sweden* (pp. 57–89). Bristol: Multilingual Matters.

Buss, M. (2002) Verb i språkbadselevers lexikon – En sociolingvistisk studie i andraspråket [Verbs in immersion students' lexicon – A sociolinguistic study in the second language]. Acta Wasaensia 105, PhD dissertation, University of Vaasa.

Canale, M. and Swain, M. (1980) Theoretical bases of communicative approaches to second language teaching and testing. *Applied Linguistics* 1, 1–47.

Cenoz, J. (2009) *Towards Multilingual Education. Basque Educational Research from an International Perspective*. Bristol: Multilingual Matters.

Cenoz, J. (2015) Content-based instruction and content and language integrated learning: The same or different? *Language, Culture and Curriculum* 28 (1), 8–24. doi: 10.1080/07908318.2014.1000922

Cenoz, J., Genesee, F. and Gorter, D. (2013) Critical analysis of CLIL: Taking stock and looking forward. *Applied Linguistics* 1–21. doi: 10.1093/applin/amt011

Christian, D. (2011) Dual language education. In E. Hinkel (ed.) *Handbook of Research in Second Language Teaching and Learning*, Vol. II (pp. 3–20). New York: Routledge.

Cummins, J. (1998) Immersion education for the millennium: What have we learned from 30 years of research on second language immersion? In M.R. Childs and R.M. Bostwick (eds) *Learning through Two Languages: Research and Practice, Second Katoh Gakuen International Symposium on Immersion and Bilingual Education* (pp. 34–47). Japan: Katoh Gakuen.

Cummins, J. (2008) Teaching for transfer: Challenging the two solitudes assumption in bilingual education. In N. Hornberger (ed.) *Encyclopedia of Language and Education* (pp. 1528–1538). New York: Springer. doi: 10.1007/978-0-387-30424-3_116

Dalton-Puffer, C., Llinares, A., Lorenzo, F. and Nikula, T. (2014) 'You can stand under my umbrella': Immersion, CLIL and bilingual education. *Applied Linguistics* 35 (2), 213–218.

Eurydice (2006) *Content and Language Integrated Learning (CLIL) at School in Europe*. Brussels: European Commission, Eurydice.

Finnish National Board of Education (2016) *National Core Curriculum for Basic Education 2014*. Helsinki: Finnish National Board of Education.

Fortune, T. and Tedick, D. (2008) One-way, two way and indigenous immersion: A call for cross-fertilization. In T. Fortune and D. Tedick (eds) *Pathways to Multilingualism: Evolving Perspectives on Immersion Education* (pp. 3–21). Clevedon: Multilingual Matters.

Genesee, F. (1987) *Learning through Two Languages: Studies of Immersion and Bilingual Education*. Rowley, MA: Newbury House.

Genesee, F. (2004) What do we know about bilingual education for majority language students? In T. Bhatia and W. Ritchie (eds) *Handbook of Bilingualism and Multiculturalism* (pp. 546–576). Malden, MA: Blackwell.

Genesee, F. and Hamayan, E. (2016) *CLIL in Context. Practical Guidance for Educators*. Cambridge: Cambridge University Press.

Harley, B., Allen, P., Cummins. J. and Swain, M. (eds) (1990) *The Development of Second Language Proficiency*. Cambridge: Cambridge University Press.

Karjalainen, K. and Pilke, N. (2012) Samlokalisering, samarbete eller kanske sammansmältning? Analys av begreppet 'tvåspråkig skola' i en dagstidning [Co-located, cooperation of fusion? Analysis of the concept 'bilingual school' in a daily newspaper]. In N. Nissilä and N. Sipoonkoski (eds) *Kielet liikkeessä, Språk i rörelse, Languages in Motion, Sprachen in Bewegung [Co-location, Cooperation or Maybe Consolidation? Analysis of the Concept 'Bilingual School']* (pp. 58–69). Vaasa: Vakki.

Lambert, W. and Tucker, R. (1972) *Bilingual Education of Children: The St. Lambert Experiment*. Rowley, MA: Newbury House.

Lasagabaster, D. and Sierra, J.M. (2010) Immersion and CLIL in English: More differences than similarities. *ELT Journal* 64, 376–395.

Lyster, R. (2007) *Learning and Teaching Languages through Content: A Counterbalanced Approach*. Amsterdam: John Benjamins.

Mehisto, P., Marsh, D. and Frigols, J. (2008) *Uncovering CLIL: Content and Language Integrated Learning in Bilingual and Multilingual Education*. Melbourne: Macmillan Education.

Nikula, T., Dafouz, E., Moore, P. and Smit, U. (eds) (2016) *Conceptualising Integration in CLIL and Multilingual Education*. Bristol: Multilingual Matters.

Nissilä, N. and Björklund, S. (2014) One-way immersion in Europe: Historic, current, and future perspectives on program implementation and student population. Special issue: Language Immersion Education. A Research Agenda for 2015 and Beyond (edited by D. Tedick and S. Björklund). *Journal of Immersion and Content-Based Language Education* 2 (2), 288–302.

Official Statistics of Finland (2015) Population structure (e-publication). ISSN=1797-5395. 2015. See http://www.stat.fi/til/vaerak/2015/vaerak_2015_2016-04-01_tau_002_en.h tml (accessed 23 August 2018).

Roy, S. and Galiev, A. (2011) Discourses on bilingualism in Canadian French immersion programs. *The Canadian Modern Language Review* 67 (3), 351–376.

Slotte-Lüttge, A., From, T. and Sahlström, F. (2013) Tvåspråkiga skolor och lärande – en debattanalys [Bilingual schools and learning: A debate analysis]. In L. Tainio and H. Harju-Luukkainen (eds) *Kaksikielinen koulu – tulevaisuuden monikielinen Suomi. Tvåspråkig skola – ett flerspråkigt Finland i framtiden [Bilingual Schools: A Multilingual Finland in Future]* (pp. 221–244). Helsinki: Suomen kasvatustieteellinen seura.

Södergård, M. (2008) Teacher strategies for second language production in immersion kindergarten in Finland. In T. Fortune and D. Tedick (eds) *Pathways to Multilingualism: Evolving Perspectives on Immersion Education* (pp. 152–176). Clevedon: Multilingual Matters.

Sundman, M. (2013) *Tvåspråkiga skolor? En analys av fördelar och risker med införandet av skolor med svenska och finska som undervisningsspråk [Bilingual Schools? An Analysis of Advantages and Risks in Schools with Swedish and Finnish as Languages of Instruction]*. Magma-studie 4/2013. Helsinki: Tankesmedjan Magma. See http://magma.fi/images/stories/reports/ms1304_webb.pdf (accessed 23 August 2018).

Swain, M. (1985) Communicative competence: Some roles of comprehensible input and comprehensible output in its development. In S. Gass and C. Madden (eds) *Input in Second Language Acquisition* (pp. 235–253). Rowley, MA: Newbury House.

Swain, M. (1988) Manipulating and complementing content teaching to maximize second language learning. *TESL Canada Journal* 68–83.

Swain, M. (1996) Integrating language and content in immersion classrooms: Research perspectives. *Canadian Modern Language Review* 52, 529–548.

Swain, M. (2000) The Output Hypothesis and beyond: Mediating acquisition through collaborative dialogue. In J.P. Lantolf (ed.) *Sociocultural Theory and Second Language Learning* (pp. 97–114). Oxford: Oxford University Press.

Swain, M. (2001) Integrating language and content teaching through collaborative tasks. *Canadian Modern Language Review* 58 (1), 44–63.

Swain, M. and Johnson, K. (1997) Immersion education. A category within bilingual education. In K. Johnson and M. Swain (eds) *Immersion Education: International Perspectives* (pp. 1–16). Cambridge: Cambridge University Press.

Swain, M. and Lapkin, S. (1982) *Evaluating Bilingual Education: A Canadian Case Study*. Clevedon: Multilingual Matters.

Swain, M. and Lapkin, S. (2005) The evolving sociopolitical context of immersion education in Canada: some implications for program development. *International Journal of Applied Linguistics* 15 (2), 169–186.

Swain, M. and Lapkin, S. (2013) A Vygotskian sociocultural perspective on immersion education: The L1/L2 debate. *Journal of Immersion and Content-Based Education* 1 (1), 101–129.

Swain, M., Kinnear, P. and Steinman, L. (2010) *Sociocultural Theory in Second Language Education: An Introduction Through Narratives*. Bristol: Multilingual Matters.

Part 2
Languaging

4 The Role of Languaging in Collaborative and Individual Writing: When Pairs Outperform Individuals

Yuko Watanabe

Merrill Swain (2006a: 98) defines languaging as the 'process of making meaning and shaping knowledge and experience through language'. I still remember vividly when I first *languaged* with Merrill. It was 2003 when I visited her office to share the first sketch of my research idea. At that time, I was a master's student with little research experience. There was something I wanted to explore but was unsure how to explain my thoughts. I was very nervous. As I unconfidently shared my thoughts, Merrill smiled and said, 'That's very interesting'. She was very positive and encouraging, open to my ideas and listened to me with respect. She then asked me some questions and as I formulated answers, my vision became clearer. We talked it through and by the time I left her office, I knew my research direction. It was very powerful. The first of many insightful learning experiences that I would have through languaging with Merrill.

In this chapter, I explore the role of languaging in second language (L2) writing by examining how university English learners *language* when interacting with a peer (collaborative dialogue) and when interacting with themselves (*speech for self*). I also examine how interaction affects the students' languaging and writing. Swain (2006a, 2010) argues that the act of using language mediates solutions to a cognitively complex problem. The concept of languaging is rooted in Vygotsky's (1978, 1987) sociocultural theory that highlights the critical role language plays in mediating learning.

In the past decade, Swain's (2000) work on the significance of languaging as collaborative dialogue for L2 development has inspired research on the benefits of peer mediation as an aspect of L2 classroom practices. A number of studies have shown how interaction among peers provides L2 learners with opportunities to engage in languaging as they seek out and provide assistance with language-related problems, and in this way, languaging mediates L2 learning (see Swain & Watanabe, 2013 for a review).

Despite a substantial body of research supporting the benefits of collaborative dialogue, the question as to whether working with a peer is more effective than working individually remains unclear. Studies that have compared the effectiveness of collaborative and individual tasks to date have demonstrated mixed findings (e.g. Fernández Dobao, 2012; Shehadeh, 2011; Storch, 1999, 2005). Of particular interest for the current study is the research comparing collaborative and individual writing. Whereas some researchers have claimed that peers together produced a better text than writing individually, others have reported no differences between them. While the benefits of peer–peer collaborative dialogue are well-researched and supported, an unanswered question is whether working with a peer provides more affordances for L2 learning than working individually, or vice versa, whether working individually is more conducive to learning than working collaboratively. If so, *when* do peers (languaging with a peer) outperform or underperform individuals (languaging with oneself)? The present study addresses this question.

Literature Review

Studies to date have explored whether peer mediation is more effective than working individually in learning L2 grammar, vocabulary, listening comprehension, pragmatics and writing. In these studies, although students were engaged in oral languaging, the performance measures were related to the written product.

In terms of learning grammar, Storch's (1999) study provided partial support for the benefits of peer work. In her study, university-level English learners completed three different grammar-focused tasks in pairs and individually. The results showed the positive effect of working with a peer on the overall grammatical accuracy of the resulting written text, although the effect varied depending on the grammar items. However, Kuiken and Vedder (2002) reported conflicting findings. In their study, high school English learners completed a dictogloss task with peers and individually. The post-test results indicated no differences between the two groups.

Similarly, research focusing on vocabulary learning has demonstrated mixed findings. Whereas Borer (2007) reported that both pair and individual conditions were effective in promoting L2 learners' vocabulary learning, Kim's (2008) findings favored the pair condition. In Kim's study, those L2 learners who completed dictogloss tasks in pairs performed significantly better on the vocabulary test than those who worked individually. In the area of listening (Garcia & Asención, 2001) and pragmatics (Taguchi & Kim, 2016), the findings supported the pair condition, confirming Kim's (2008) results.

Research comparing collaborative and individual writing alike demonstrated varying findings. For example, Storch (2005) compared the quality of texts produced by English learners in pairs and individually and found that pairs produced shorter but more superior texts in terms of grammatical accuracy and complexity. In a larger scale study, Storch and Wigglesworth (2007) compared the text produced by pairs and individuals. Like Storch (2005), they found that pairs produced texts with greater grammatical accuracy than individuals, despite little differences in complexity and fluency.[1] Wigglesworth and Storch (2009) confirmed these results. In a longitudinal study, Shehadeh (2011) compared two university English writing classes. One class carried out individual writing while the other wrote in pairs for 16 weeks. The analysis of the text quality after 16 weeks revealed that collaborative writing had positive effects on content, organization and vocabulary but not on grammatical accuracy or mechanics. Similarly, Nixon (2007) compared pair and individual writing produced by university L2 learners and found no significant difference in grammatical accuracy between the two groups. Fernández Dobao (2012) compared L2 Spanish learners' text produced by groups of four, pairs and individuals. The analysis demonstrated that the texts produced by groups were more grammatically accurate than those written individually and in pairs. However, no significant differences in accuracy were found between pairs and individuals, although pairs received better scores than did individual learners on most of the accuracy measures.

In the area of computer-mediated communication, Elola and Oskoz (2010) examined how L2 Spanish learners write essays using wiki and chats in pairs and individually. The analysis indicated no statistically significant differences in terms of accuracy, fluency and complexity between the two groups. Similarly, Strobl (2014) compared the quality of texts produced by university L2 learners in pairs and individuals using Google Docs. The results showed that while the joint texts scored significantly higher on content, no differences were found in accuracy.

To summarize, previous studies have not agreed on the effects of peer and individual work in L2 learning. There are some possible reasons for this discrepancy. For example, each study used different measurement instruments for written texts, different time limits for the writing tasks and different student populations. However, one important reason for the discrepancy may be a lack of attention to the nature of interaction. Past studies comparing peer and individual work have seldom considered how the nature of peer interaction affects language learning.

Storch's (2002) study underscored the importance of attending to group dynamics during peer mediation. Using the dimensions of mutuality (i.e. level of engagement with each other's contributions) and equality (i.e. the degree of control over the task), Storch distinguished four types of patterns of pair interaction: collaborative, dominant/dominant,

dominant/passive and expert/novice. The study revealed that more instances of knowledge transfer took place in pairs with a collaborative stance (collaborative and expert/novice) than occurred in pairs with a non-collaborative stance (dominant/dominant and dominant/passive). Furthermore, the data from the latter two patterns displayed a greater number of instances showing either no transfer of knowledge or missed opportunities. Researchers who applied Storch's framework have confirmed her findings that the nature of interaction significantly affects L2 learning (e.g. Li & Zhu, 2017; Storch & Aldosari, 2013; Watanabe & Swain, 2007).

To my knowledge, studies comparing peer and individual tasks have not applied Storch's framework thus far. Moreover, while researchers highlight the importance of peer–peer dialogue during peer-mediated tasks, individual tasks are often regarded as 'a silent process' that seems to involve no talk or oral languaging (but, see e.g. Negueruela, 2008; Swain et al., 2009). With these issues in mind, the current study examined whether peer mediation enhances L2 writing more than writing individually through an analysis of the nature of interaction and languaging. The research questions addressed were as follows.

(1) How does the quality of text produced differ when university English learners write in pairs and individually?
(2) What is the relationship, if any, between the nature of interaction and the quality of the text produced in pairs and individually?

Method

The data came from a larger project (Watanabe, 2014), which was conducted in an intact Freshman-level English course for English-major students in a Japanese university. The course involved 20 students (8 males and 12 females) who were placed based on a placement test.[2] They were between 18 and 20 years old and were all native speakers of Japanese. All 20 students volunteered to participate in the study and signed an informed consent form.

At my request, the course instructor assigned pair and individual writing tasks as out-of-class assignments, which the students carried out in a seminar room over a two-week period. Each student attended two writing sessions. I counterbalanced the two writing conditions (pair vs. individual) as well as the two writing prompts (see Appendix) across participants to control the order effect of the writing conditions and prompts. In Week 1, half of the participants worked individually either on Prompt A (Group 1) and B (Group 2), while the remaining students worked as a pair on either Prompt B (Group 3) or A (Group 4). The following week, they switched the task and prompt. Table 4.1 describes the distribution of the writing conditions and prompts.

Table 4.1 Distribution of writing conditions and prompts

	Week 1	Week 2[a]
Group 1 (n = 6)	Individual (Prompt A, 30 min)	Pair (Prompt B, 30 min)
Group 2 (n = 4)	Individual (Prompt B, 30 min)	Pair (Prompt A, 30 min)
Group 3 (n = 6)	Pair (Prompt A, 30 min)	Individual (Prompt B, 30 min)
Group 4 (n = 4)	Pair (Prompt B, 30 min)	Individual (Prompt A, 30 min)

[a] The students also received stimulated recall and post-task interviews; however, these are not discussed in this chapter.

To ensure equivalence, I used two different writing prompts from the Educational Testing Service (ETS) website for the Test of English as a Foreign Language (TOEFL), which the original test designers had deemed to be approximately equivalent to each other for this standardized English test.

Researchers examining collaborative writing have generally assigned either no time limit (e.g. Storch, 2005; Watanabe, 2008) or assigned a longer timeframe for pairs than for individuals (e.g. Storch & Wigglesworth, 2007) based on the finding that pairs take longer to produce a joint text than when writing independently (Storch, 2005). Nevertheless, one could argue that differences in the text quality in the two writing conditions may be attributed to the uneven completion time allotted. In order to circumvent this argument, I enforced equal conditions by allocating the same amount of time for both collaborative and individual tasks.[3]

Due to familiarity among the classmates and scheduling difficulties, I formed the pairs based on the participants' availability rather than have them self-select their partner. Because this intact class met at least five times a week during their required courses for more than two months before the beginning of the data collection, the class appeared to have built a friendly atmosphere when I visited the class for recruitment.

At the beginning of each session, I described the upcoming writing task and clarified any unclear points. For the individual writing sessions, while I would have liked to have my participants produce sufficient private speech for analysis, it was equally important to minimize intervention so that the verbal data elicited would be comparable to pair dialogue. My compromise was to encourage the participants to talk to themselves aloud during the task but unlike a think-aloud technique, they were not required to do so. Moreover, I did not model the verbalization process for them nor did I provide them with a practice session. Since this 'encouraged private speech' should be distinguished from spontaneous private speech and also from think-aloud, I call it *speech for self*.

The participants' writing process was audio-recorded for later analysis. During the collaborative writing tasks, I sat at the back of the room and noted the task completion time and any salient features of the interactions. For the independent writing tasks, however, I left the room after giving instructions and waited outside while the participants recorded themselves to provide a comfortable setting to produce *speech for self* without my presence. The participants recorded themselves by operating a voice recorder continuously throughout the task.

Data Analysis

To rate the essays, I used Hamp-Lyons' (1991) 9-point global scale and communicative profile scale (consisting of the five traits of communicative quality, organization, argumentation, linguistic accuracy and linguistic appropriacy).[4] Each of the sub-scales was scored on a 9-point scale with 1 being the lowest and 9 the highest score. The rationale for using Hamp-Lyons' scales is, in addition to its explicitness and validation (Hamp-Lyons & Henning, 1991), because some of the other researchers who investigated the same issue also employed the same scales (Nixon, 2007; Suzuki, 2008). Moreover, Hamp-Lyons and Henning (1991) reported high reliabilities for these scales in relation to assessments in the TOEFL independent writing essays.

Two raters who have experience teaching university-level academic English writing independently scored all the essays. I trained them on the rating scales and handed them a typed and randomly ordered copy of the essays without explaining the research purpose so as to avoid them having preconceived ideas about the essays. Inter-rater reliability between the two raters for the *global scale* was 33% agreement (exact match); however, an additional 67% of the decisions were within 1 point difference. That is to say, all the decisions were within 1 point difference among the total of 9 points. I considered this proportion to be acceptable. As for the communicative profile scale, inter-rater reliability ranged from 27% to 43% (exact match) while an additional 50%–63% were within a 1 point difference and 0%–17% were within a 2 point difference. I set up a meeting for the two raters to discuss the differences, during which all disagreements were resolved.

I also analyzed the transcribed pair talk, using Storch's (2002) model, which classifies four distinct patterns of interaction mentioned previously. Collaborative pairs worked together throughout the task and displayed high levels of mutuality and equality, whereas dominant/ dominant pairs showed an unwillingness to value each other's contribution. Dominant/passive pairs involved one learner taking control of the task while the other participant assumed a subservient role. In expert/ novice pairs, a more knowledgeable participant actively encouraged the less knowledgeable partner to contribute to the task. In order to ensure reliability, a second coder[5] independently coded 50% of the unmarked copies of the transcripts. Inter-rater reliability was 90%. We discussed and resolved any disagreements.

Findings

Text quality

The first research question addressed how the quality of texts differs when the same learner writes in pairs and alone. Table 4.2 summarizes the essay scores using Hamp-Lyons' (1991) 9-band *global* and the *communicative profile* scales. Median scores for each of the traits rated ranged between 5.0 and 6.0 under pair writing and under individual writing conditions. Indeed, all median scores were the same in both writing conditions.

When looking at the individual differences on the global scale, only one pair and one individual received a score of 8, and one pair and two individuals obtained a score of 7, while the rest of the pairs and individuals were all given 5 or 6. Given that these students were grouped together in a single English course based on the placement test results, the small score difference among the students was to be expected. Nine students received a greater score on their joint writing text than their individual one, whereas six students attained a higher score for their independently written texts. Five students received the same score for both.

Nature of interaction and the text quality

The second research question examined the relationship between the nature of interaction and the quality of text produced by pairs and individuals. I first present the analysis of the pattern of interaction, followed by the analysis of the relationship between the patterns of interaction and the writing scores for pair and individual texts.

Among 10 pairs, I identified 4 collaborative, 4 expert/novice, 1 dominant/dominant and 1 dominant/passive patterns of interaction. The following excerpts show examples of each of the four patterns of interaction. I also provide some excerpts from individual writing in order to highlight the differences or similarities in the nature of languaging

Table 4.2 Global and communicative profile scores for pairs and individuals

	Pair (*n* = 10)			Individual (*n* = 20)		
	M	Mdn	SD	M	Mdn	SD
Global	6.1	6.0	0.9	6.0	6.0	0.8
CP[a] (of the five traits)	6.1	5.8	0.8	5.9	5.8	0.7
Communicative quality	6.4	6.0	0.8	6.0	6.0	0.8
Organization	6.2	6.0	0.9	6.2	6.0	0.8
Argumentation	5.4	5.0	0.5	5.3	5.0	0.9
Linguistic accuracy	6.3	6.0	0.8	6.0	6.0	0.7
Linguistic appropriacy	6.2	6.0	0.9	6.0	6.0	0.5

[a] An average of the five traits of the communicative profile scale.

between the two task conditions. In addition, most of the peer–peer dialogue and *speech for self* were in their first language, Japanese. Text in *italics* shows that it was said in Japanese and translated by the researcher.

Excerpt 1 presents an example of a collaborative pattern of interaction from the data of Nami and Sho.

Excerpt[6] 1: Nami and Sho (collaborative)

242	Sho:	Knowing his
243	Nami:	His lifestyle?
244	Sho:	Lifestyle, *yes*. In America
245	Nami:	America. *And then* First.
246	Sho:	*About his* celebrity, *right? So* he is very
247	Nami:	Very … famous, *again?*
248	Sho:	*Mmm. Can we say* familiar with?
249	Nami:	*Yeah. We have enough* 'famous'. [laughing]
250	Sho:	[laughing] *Is it* [familiar] *to or* with?
251	Nami:	*Isn't it* with?

As the excerpt shows, Nami and Sho worked together throughout the process of writing, and each of them added to and built on each other's contributions. Overall, their languaging involved a high frequency of requests (Turn 248), questions (Turn 250), other-repetitions (Turns 243, 244, 245, 247) and confirmations (Turns 244, 249) as well as many instances of collaborative completions.

Excerpt 2 illustrates an example of an expert/novice pattern of interaction from the data of Lisa and Hana.

Excerpt 2: Lisa and Hana (expert/novice)

313	Lisa:	Efforts. I have never seen someone like her … before?
314	Hana:	Before [writing]
315	Lisa:	*You missed* 'e' [in your spelling of 'before'].
316	Hana:	Before
317	Lisa:	*Then what do we want to say?*
318	Hana:	… *therefore?*
319	Lisa:	*Yes, therefore. So* … that's why.
320	Hana	[writing]
321	Lisa:	*Anything else you would like to add?*
322	Hana:	*For example?*
323	Lisa:	… When I knew her
324	Hana:	*Yeah.* When I knew her … impress?

In this excerpt, Lisa was leading the task as the expert while Hana seemed to assume the novice role. As an expert, Lisa encouraged Hana to contribute to the task by inviting her to participate (Turns 317, 321) and providing a model (Turn 323). Although Hana seemed submissive at the beginning and generally accepted Lisa's suggestions (Turns 314, 316, 320), her level of involvement increased during this episode (and over time) (Turns 322, 324) as Lisa invited Hana to participate in the task and provided scaffolded assistance.

Excerpt 3 presents an example of a dominant/dominant pair from the data of Aya and Yuka.

Excerpt 3:   Aya and Yuka (dominant/dominant)

412	**Aya:**	Gandhi is
413	**Yuka:**	Known, known as? *Yes,* known as.
414	**Aya:**	Is known for?
415	**Yuka:**	Known as?
416	**Aya:**	*Ahm,* is known for, known for.
417	**Yuka:**	Known as.
418	**Aya:**	Known for … *and add a quotation mark, then no violence, no obedience.*

Although Aya and Yuka were both highly involved in the task, they often disagreed and rejected each other's ideas, spending many turns insisting on their own idea with little discussion. As a result, they had little time to discuss and complete the essay. In Excerpt 3, Aya thought 'known for' was the correct form (Turns 414, 416, 418) while Yuka suggested to use 'known as' (Turns 413, 415, 417). They both claimed that they were correct with little attempt to negotiate. In the end, Aya wrote down her idea rather strongly and moved on without Yuka's approval (Turn 418). In addition, although not seen in Excerpt 3, their talk involved many uses of 'but' for disagreement.

While Yuka and Aya's pair dialogue seemed to be impeded by their frequent conflicts and difficulty in solving problems, both of their *speech for self* appeared to facilitate their individual writing. Excerpt 4 indicates how Aya used languaging to mediate her writing.

Excerpt 4:   Aya

Since … *when the sentence starts with* since … *I need to use … the present perfect tense? Or can it to be the past tense?* Since … *he has become* famous. *Present perfect, right? Yes, present perfect* [while writing] Represent? *No?* Japanese team? Represent? [checking the dictionary] Delegation … delegation … *doesn't sound right …* Soccer team? *Can I say* Japanese soccer team? [writing]

As the excerpt illustrates, Aya directed many questions to herself and explored alternative ideas. Unlike her languaging with Yuka, her decision-making appeared to be much smoother as she did not have to deal with the difficult process of reaching a consensus with her peer partner.

Another interesting difference between Aya and Yuka's pair dialogue and their *speech for self* was the absence of using languaging for affective purposes when working together. There were several instances where pairs and individuals used languaging for affective functions such as reducing stress, controlling frustration and keeping motivated (Watanabe, 2014). While it was also evident in Aya and Yuka's individual *speech for self*, such examples were not observed in their pair dialogue. Excerpt 5 shows how Yuka uses *speech for self* for affective purpose.

Excerpt 5: Yuka

[After reading the prompt that asks them to write about a famous athlete or entertainer] ... *Be decisive, be decisive, be decisive, make a decision without hesitating ... be decisive ... if you hesitate your decision ... if you hesitate ...* [writing]

In this excerpt, Yuka talked to herself repeatedly in order to decide on a writing topic as quickly as possible. It seems that she talks to herself as a way to encourage and push herself to be decisive.

Excerpt 6 shows an example of a *dominant/passive* pattern of interaction from the data of Ema and Hiro.

Excerpt 6: Ema and Hiro (dominant/passive)

96	Ema:	I think this is good. Let's start writing. Writing takes time, you know. Okay ... hook, hook, [writing] Have you ever? Ahm ...
97	Hiro:	*Ahm like*
98	Ema:	*It's good to use* 'have you ever' *at the beginning of* [an essay].
99	Hiro:	Yeah.
100	Ema:	[writing] *Because one essay for two, I think it should be* 'we'.
101	Hiro:	We.
102	Ema:	[while writing] Never ... *and then* topic [sentence].
103	Hiro:	Topic *oh.*
104	Ema:	Topic. *This is* thesis, thesis sentence. *So what should I write?* What ... no. It is possible to ... *what can I say?*

As the excerpt presents, Ema took control of the process of writing while Hiro's utterances tended to be limited to simple acknowledgment (Turn 99) or echoic repetition of what Ema said (Turns 101, 103).

Much of her speech was seemingly directed to herself (Turns 96, 100, 102, 104), suggesting that she might have been treating the task as an independent one. She seemed to make little attempt to invite Hiro's participation or contribution to the decision-making process (Turns 98, 100, 102). When Hiro tried to make suggestions, they were hesitant (Turn 97) and often rejected by Ema. Hiro's attempt to participate in the task diminished over time and thus he was making minimal contributions to the task.

Excerpt 7 shows Ema's languaging while writing alone.

Excerpt 7:   Ema

First, he … he has, he was, he is … *because people still say* [that he is handsome], I should use 'he is' … *still say it so* … he has been, he has been, he is been said? *No, he has been said, right? Right? Being said, being said,* he has been said, he, he has been said … that he was very handsome, he was, he was very handsome.

In this excerpt, Ema asked questions to herself and repeated herself to arrive at the solution, which appeared to be comparable to her languaging when writing with Hiro. In other words, even during pair writing, Ema often appeared to be writing by herself. Conversely, the nature of Hiro's languaging during individual writing was much different than during pair writing with Ema.

Excerpt 8:   Hiro

How do you say having unique ideas? Can I use 'creative?' *Yes.* He has? He was, *right? He was so creative … yes.* First, he was so creative. *For example, he established a co-op company owing to his creativity … I don't think I need this example. It's too specific.*

As Excerpt 8 shows, Hiro talked himself through the problems as they arose. He asked questions, confirmed the answer and justified his decision. It is clear that he had more opportunities to language in order to facilitate his writing process than his joint writing with Ema.

Table 4.3 presents the relationship between the patterns of interaction and the writing scores for their pair and individual texts. Due to space limitation and the fact that the scores were similar, Table 4.3 only shows the scores for the global scale and not for the communicative profile scale. The letter in brackets indicates the first initial of the student in that role.

The first four pairs are identified as having a collaborative pattern of interaction. Among the eight participants in these pairs, five (Fumi, Waka, Sho, Nami and Ichiro) received a higher score for their collaborative text than their individual one. Ichiro scored 2 points higher while the

Table 4.3 Pattern of interaction and writing scores (global scale)

Name	Individual	Name	Individual	Pair	Patterns of interaction
Fumi	5.0	Waka	5.0	6.0	Collaborative
Sho	6.0	Nami	6.0	7.0	Collaborative
Ichiro	6.0	Sala	8.0	8.0	Collaborative
Ryo	6.0	Jo	6.0	6.0	Collaborative
Aya	6.0	Yuka	6.0	5.0	Dominant/dominant
Ema	6.0	Hiro	6.0	5.0	Dominant (E)/passive (H)
Lisa	7.0	Hana	6.0	6.0	Expert (L)/novice (H)
Miwa	6.0	Kana	5.0	6.0	Expert (M)/novice (K)
Kojiro	7.0	Chika	5.0	6.0	Expert (K)/novice (C)
Tomo	6.0	Go	6.0	6.0	Expert (T)/novice (G)

other three scored 1 point higher. The remaining three students (Ryo, Jo and Sala) received an identical score for both joint and individual texts. The next two are the pairs with a non-collaborative stance – dominant/dominant and dominant/passive. Both students in each pair received a lower score, 5 for their joint text, whereas they each received a 6 for their individual one.

The last four dyads are an expert/novice pair. The trend for these pairs is less straightforward than the other three patterns of interaction. As for the participants who played the role of expert, Lisa and Kojiro received a score that was a 1 point lower score on their joint text than that of their individual text, whereas Miwa and Tomo received an identical score for both texts. Regarding the participants who acted as the novice, while Kana and Chika achieved a 1 point higher score on their joint text than their individual text, Hana and Go received the same score for both pieces of writing.

To summarize, in the collaborative pairs, both students received higher or similar scores for their joint text than their individual text. Conversely, in the dominant/dominant and dominant/passive pairs, both students received lower scores for their joint text than their independent one. In the expert/novice pair, the 'expert' student received the same or a lower score on their joint text, while the 'novice' student received the same or a higher score on their joint text than their individual one.

Discussion

In the present study, I examined two research questions. The findings for the first research question demonstrated that the students in this study produced similar quality texts whether writing with a peer or individually, which partially supported previous studies (e.g. Elola & Oskoz, 2010; Nixon, 2007; Shehadeh, 2011; Strobl, 2014).

This finding led to my second research question – the potential relationship between the nature of interaction and the students' writing. The findings indicated that not all pairs worked in a collaborative manner. More importantly, the trend suggested that the nature of interaction affected the students' opportunities for and quality of languaging and thus the quality of text that they produced. The analysis revealed that in collaborative pairs, both students received a higher or the same score for pair writing as compared with individual writing. In non-collaborative pairs, both students received a lower score for pair writing than they did on their individual writing. These findings supported previous research that the pattern of interaction affects language learning (e.g. Li & Zhu, 2017; Storch, 2002; Watanabe & Swain, 2007). This means that students benefit more from peer-mediated work than working individually when they interact in a collaborative manner, that is, when peer–peer interaction is mediated by more opportunities to engage in better quality languaging. In other words, when students fail to maximize the potential of peer languaging opportunities, an individual task may mediate their learning more than that of peer tasks.

However, one may ask whether the three students (Jo, Ryo and Sala) in the collaborative pair who achieved the same score for both pair and individual writing tasks benefited from working with their peer partner, or it did not influence them whatsoever. In their one-on-one follow-up interviews,[7] all three students expressed that they learned more from writing with their peer than writing individually. They stated that they learned different expressions and ideas (Ryo, Jo and Sala) as well as grammar and vocabulary (Jo) from their partner. Their languaging transcripts also support their interview comments. Nevertheless, further studies tracing students' writing development using a post-test are needed in order to confirm whether the students retained what they languaged.

In terms of the expert/novice pairs, the expert received the same or lower scores for pair writing while the novice received the same or higher scores for pair writing than individual writing. This contradicts the findings of Watanabe and Swain (2007). They found that only the expert students seemed to benefit from working with their novice partner. In the current study, at least half of the novice partners received better scores when working with the expert partner, while conversely, half of the expert partners got lower scores when working with the novice partner. One explanation for this discrepancy may be the use of a different task and research design. For example, the current exploratory study did not explore whether the expert student might achieve a higher score on later writing tasks using a post-test as was the case in Watanabe and Swain (2007). Future research should consider addressing these issues.

Overall, the data demonstrated that all the participants in this study *languaged* with their peer and with themselves to facilitate their writing process, which lends further support for Swain's (2006a, 2010) argument that languaging plays a critical role in mediating L2 learning. However, the findings also suggested that just providing an opportunity to talk through language-related problems does not automatically result in higher quality writing outcomes. Learners have to *language*. And just languaging is not enough as it is the quality of languaging that enhances learning opportunities.

By focusing on the nature of interaction and languaging during the task performance, the current study yielded an explanation as to when peers outperform individuals and why. Therefore, future studies would benefit from examining the *process* of task performance (i.e. languaging) and not just the product (i.e. written text, post-test results). Moreover, a unique aspect of the current study is that I explored how the same learner uses language to facilitate their L2 task with a peer and individually. While a number of studies have explored the effects of collaborative dialogue, studies on the roles of (the intentional use of) *speech for self* in L2 learning have received less attention (Swain, 2006b). Therefore, more studies investigating the roles and effects of *speech for self* as a source for L2 learning are called for.

Pedagogically, it is essential for L2 teachers to be aware of the mediational role that languaging plays in L2 learning (Swain *et al.*, 2009) and consider providing students with the opportunity to verbalize their thoughts whether working with a peer or independently. However, simply introducing a task is not sufficient. As shown in this study, the nature of languaging influences the affordances for learning. In their research examining self-directed languaging, Swain and her colleagues found that not all learners seemed able to language efficiently (Knouzi *et al.*, 2010; Swain *et al.*, 2009). This may be the case for both peer and individual tasks. Not all students are aware of ways in which to enhance the quality of languaging or how to create a collaborative pattern of interaction, and why these are important to their L2 learning. Kim and McDonough (2011) found that young English learners in Korea who viewed videotaped models of collaborative interaction prior to the task demonstrated greater collaboration than those who did not receive the pre-task modelling. Given this finding, it would seem useful that, upon implementing the task, the teacher shows pre-task models or explains the facilitative way of talking about language-related problems – whether with a peer or individually.

Finally, the findings of the current study need to be treated with caution. In terms of the students' overall writing scores, there was a 1 or 2 point difference out of 9 with no statistical analysis. Moreover, the research was conducted within a short timeframe; however, it may take weeks or months of writing and learning, rather than just performing a couple of tasks for development in English writing to occur in ways that can be measured by holistic assessments of written compositions. Despite these limitations, I hope the findings of this study have contributed to our understanding of the role of languaging in facilitating collaborative and individual tasks and provided ways to maximize the opportunity and quality of languaging.

Acknowledgments

This study is based on an analysis of additional data from my doctoral research. I am grateful to Alister Cumming, Merrill Swain and Clare Brett for their guidance and encouragement throughout my doctoral study, and Lindsay Brooks and Neomy Storch for their insightful comments on the dissertation draft. My appreciation also goes to Chris Brown, Hyeyoon Cho, Ibtissem Knouzi, Merrill Swain and the anonymous reviewers for their constructive feedback on an earlier draft of this chapter. I am thankful to my participants for their willingness to share their time and insights, and the course instructor for her support.

Notes

(1) Storch (2005) measured fluency in terms of the total number of words in each text.
(2) The placement test was a paper-based TOEFL and an average score was 508.
(3) All the pairs and individuals used almost the entire 30 minutes.
(4) I also analyzed fluency of the text produced in pairs and individually; however, this is not discussed within the scope of the current study.
(5) The second coder was a Japanese-speaking, university-level L2 instructor and researcher who is familiar with Storch's (2002) framework.
(6) Transcription conventions (adapted from Watanabe, 2008):
   [ ] Words or phrases that were omitted from the speech or clarification of the information unclear to the reader (i.e. transcriber's commentary)
   … Short pause, between 0.5 and 3 seconds
(7) In a larger study (Watanabe, 2014), I conducted one-on-one stimulated recall and follow-up interviews after the task performance; however, it is not explored in the current study.

References

Borer, L. (2007) Depth of processing in private and social speech: Its role in the retention of word knowledge by adult EAP learners. *The Canadian Modern Language Review* 64, 269–295.

Educational Testing Service (n.d.) Writing topics. See http://www.ets.org/Media/Tests/TOEFL/pdf/989563wt.pdf (accessed 2 March 2012).

Elola, I. and Oskoz, A. (2010) Collaborative writing: Fostering foreign language and writing conventions development. *Language Learning and Technology* 14, 51–71.

Fernández Dobao, A. (2012) Collaborative writing tasks in L2 classroom: Comparing group, pair and individual work. *Journal of Second Language Writing* 21, 40–58.

Garcia, P. and Asención, Y. (2001) Interlanguage development of Spanish learners: Comprehension, production, and interaction. *The Canadian Modern Language Review* 57, 377–401.

Hamp-Lyons, L. (1991) Reconstructing 'academic writing proficiency'. In L. Hamp-Lyons (ed.) *Assessing Second Language Writing in Academic Contexts* (pp. 127–153). Norwood, NJ: Ablex.

Hamp-Lyons, L. and Henning, G. (1991) Communicative writing profiles: An investigation of the transferability of a multiple-trait scoring instrument across ESL writing assessment contexts. *Language Learning* 41, 337–373.

Kim, Y. (2008) The contribution of collaborative and individual tasks to the acquisition of L2 vocabulary. *Modern Language Journal* 92, 114–130.

Kim, Y. and McDonough, K. (2011) Using pretask modelling to encourage collaborative learning opportunities. *Language Teaching Research* 15, 183–199.

Knouzi, I., Swain, M., Lapkin, S. and Brooks, L. (2010) Self-scaffolding mediated by languaging: Microgenetic analysis of high and low performers. *International Journal of Applied Linguistics* 20, 23–49.

Kuiken, F. and Vedder, I. (2002) The effect of interaction in acquiring the grammar of a second language. *International Journal of Educational Research* 37, 343–358.

Li, M. and Zhu, W. (2017) Good or bad collaborative wiki writing: Exploring links between group interactions and writing products. *Journal of Second Language Writing* 35, 38–53.

Negueruela, E. (2008) Revolutionary pedagogies: Learning that leads development in the second language classroom. In J.P. Lantolf and M. Poehner (eds) *Sociocultural Theory and the Teaching of Second Languages* (pp. 189–227). London: Equinox Publishers.

Nixon, R.M. (2007) Collaborative and independent writing among adult Thai EFL learners: Verbal interactions, compositions, and attitudes. Unpublished doctoral dissertation, University of Toronto.

Shehadeh, A. (2011) Effects and student perceptions of collaborative writing in L2. *Journal of Second Language Writing* 20, 286–305.

Storch, N. (1999) Are two heads better than one? Pair work and grammatical accuracy. *System* 27, 363–374.

Storch, N. (2002) Patterns of interaction in ESL pair work. *Language Learning* 52, 119–158.

Storch, N. (2005) Collaborative writing: Product, process and students' reflections. *Journal of Second Language Writing* 14, 153–173.

Storch, N. and Wigglesworth, G. (2007) Writing tasks: The effects of collaboration. In M.P. Garcia Mayo (ed.) *Investigating Tasks in Formal Language Learning* (pp. 157–177). Clevedon: Multilingual Matters.

Storch, N. and Aldosari, A. (2013) Learners' use of first language (Arabic) in pair work in an EFL Class. *Language Teaching Research* 14, 355–375.

Strobl, C. (2014) Affordances of web 2.0 technologies for collaborative advanced writing in a foreign language. *CALICO Journal* 31, 1–18.

Suzuki, M. (2008) Japanese learners' self-revisions and peer revisions of their written compositions in English. *TESOL Quarterly* 42, 209–233.

Swain, M. (2000) The output hypothesis and beyond: Mediating acquisition through collaborative dialogue. In J.P. Lantolf (ed.) *Sociocultural Theory and Second Language Learning* (pp. 97–114). Oxford: Oxford University Press.

Swain, M. (2006a) Languaging, agency and collaboration in advanced language proficiency. In H. Byrnes (ed.) *Advanced Language Learning: The Contribution of Halliday and Vygotsky* (pp. 95–108). London: Continuum.

Swain, M. (2006b) Verbal protocols: What does it mean for research to use speaking as a data collection tool? In M. Chaloub-Deville, M. Chapelle and P. Duff (eds) *Inference and Generalizability in Applied Linguistics: Multiple Research Perspectives* (pp. 97–113). Amsterdam: John Benjamins.

Swain, M. (2010) 'Talking-it-through': Languaging as a source of learning. In R. Batstone (ed.) *Sociocognitive Perspectives on Language Use and Language Learning* (pp. 112–130). Oxford: Oxford University Press.

Swain, M. and Watanabe, Y. (2013) Languaging: Collaborative dialogue as a source of second language learning. In C. Chapelle (ed.) *The Encyclopedia of Applied Linguistics*. (pp. 3218–3225). Hoboken, NJ: Wiley Blackwell.

Swain, M., Lapkin, S., Knouzi, I., Suzuki, W. and Brooks, L. (2009) Languaging: University students learn the grammatical concept of voice in French. *The Modern Language Journal* 93, 5–29.

Taguchi, N. and Kim, Y. (2016) Collaborative dialogue in learning pragmatics: Pragmatics-related episodes as an opportunity for learning request-making. *Applied Linguistics* 37, 416–437.

Vygotsky, L.S. (1978) *Mind in Society: The Development of Higher Psychological Processes*. Cambridge, MA: Harvard University Press.

Vygotsky, L.S. (1987) *Thinking and Speech*. In R.W. Reiber, A.S. Carton and N. Minik (eds) *The Collected Works of L.S. Vygotsky. Volume 1: Problems of General Psychology* (pp. 37–285). New York: Plenum Press.

Watanabe, Y. (2008) Peer–peer interaction between L2 learners of different proficiency levels: Their interactions and reflections. *Canadian Modern Language Review* 64, 605–636.

Watanabe, Y. (2014) Collaborative and independent writing: Japanese university English learners' processes, texts and opinions. Unpublished doctoral dissertation, University of Toronto.

Watanabe, Y. and Swain, M. (2007) The effects of proficiency differences and patterns of pair interaction on second language learning: Collaborative dialogue between adult ESL learners. *Language Teaching Research* 11, 121–142.

Wigglesworth, G. and Storch, N. (2009) Pairs versus individual writing: Effects on fluency, complexity and accuracy. *Language Testing* 26, 445–446.

Appendix

Writing Prompt A

If you could meet a famous entertainer or athlete, who would that be, and why? Use specific reasons and examples to support your choice.

Writing Prompt B

If you could travel back in time to meet a famous person from history, what person would you like to meet? Use specific reasons and examples to support your choice.

Taken from *writing topics* of the TOEFL
(Educational Testing Service, n.d.)

5 Effect of Languaging Activities on L2 Learning Motivation: A Classroom-Based Approach

Tae-Young Kim

The present study provides an empirical validation of the beneficial effect of languaging (Swain, 2006a, 2006b, 2010, 2013a) on students' second/foreign language (L2) learning motivation. Languaging, or 'the activity of mediating cognitively complex ideas using language' (Swain & Lapkin, 2011: 105), emphasizes the power of expressing one's ideas in a variety of cognitively demanding contexts. Languaging activities, such as recounting one's life history, an uncommon form of narrative, have been implemented in applied linguistics by Swain and colleagues (e.g. Knouzi *et al.*, 2010; Swain, 2006a, 2010; Swain & Lapkin, 2011; Swain *et al.*, 2009). The findings of previous studies indicate that languaging can boost cognitive abilities and can also result in an enhanced sense of self (e.g. Lapkin *et al.*, 2010; Lenchuk, 2009; Lenchuk & Swain, 2010; Swain, 2013a). As Vygotsky (1978) pointed out, language is not merely a passive vehicle for conveying our thoughts. Instead, it changes the very structure of the mind through the act of expressing thoughts in either an oral or written manner. Swain's (1995, 2005) early works on L2 output conceptualized this as a metacognitive function of language. Emphasizing the unique power of language, Clark (1998: 178) stated that language 'enables us to stabilize very abstract ideas in working memory'. Swain and Lapkin (2011: 106) also stated that language 'enables us to inspect and criticize our own reasoning in ways that no other representational modality allows'.

However, to date, languaging has not been studied in the area of L2 learning motivation, a major contributing factor to differences in performance among L2 students. In this chapter, it is argued that languaging activities can bridge the gap between L2 motivation theories and L2 teachers' concerns regarding student learning outcomes, as many students are susceptible to demotivation in the L2 classroom (Falout *et al.*, 2009; Song & Kim, 2017). Although there are exceptions, such as Dörnyei (2001) and Hadfield and Dörnyei (2013), who provided useful tips for enhancing students' L2 learning motivation, and Lear (2013), who examined the effect of reflective journals on students' motivation to improve their L2 pronunciation, the majority of L2 (de)motivation research still focuses on identifying and describing the major (de)motivational (sub-)factors in specific national or regional contexts (e.g. Kim, 2006, 2010).

Within this context, the present study compares the effects of three different languaging activities on learners' English as a foreign language (EFL) learning motivation and L2 selves by adopting a classroom-based research design. The effect of languaging on students' L2 learning motivation has not been sufficiently studied, and to my knowledge, a comparative study on the effects of different languaging activities on L2 learning motivation has not yet been undertaken. By administering languaging activities with EFL students in elementary and junior high schools in Korea, the present study examined the following research questions:

(1) Among the three types of languaging activities tested, which one is the most effective in enhancing students' L2 learning motivation?
(2) Among the subcomponents of L2 learning motivation, which one is most affected by the implementation of languaging activities in class?

Languaging and its Potential to Enhance L2 Learning Motivation

Although studies on languaging and its potential to improve participants' learning outcomes are becoming increasingly common (Lapkin *et al.*, 2010; Swain, 2013b), studies examining the effects of languaging on L2 learning motivation are rare. An example L2 class activity in which languaging can be used to improve students' L2 learning motivation is for students to verbalize or write about their career or personal aspirations related to the L2; through such an activity, they will be able to recognize the gap between their current level of L2 proficiency and their desired level. That is, once given the opportunity for critical self-reflection through verbal or written languaging, students may be better able to envision the need for L2 proficiency for their futures, which can serve as a motivational catalyst.

The field of psychology offers insights from relevant literature on motivation. Levav and Fitzsimons (2006: 207) investigated the cognitive involvement of participants when responding to intent questionnaires having items 'asking people about their intent to engage in a certain behavior'. They found that intent questions that helped participants to visualize their future behavior were shown to increase the likelihood of the participants engaging in that behavior. Morwitz and Fitzsimons (2004: 64) coined this phenomenon the *mere-measurement effect*, meaning 'measuring general intentions increases the salience of thoughts about engaging in the general behavior'.

These findings from psychology can be applied to the L2 learning context, in which we can expect self-reflection activities to result in improved learner motivation. Speaking and writing in either the first language (L1) or L2 can shape and reshape our thinking, and this process of self-reorganization is an essential aspect of human learning (Vygotsky, 1978, 1987). Likewise, while engaged in languaging activities in which learners formulate and solidify their future aspirations, they can make an accurate assessment of where they are currently at in terms of their L2 proficiency and where they would like to be, and thus establish a clear plan of action concerning how to get there. Thus, languaging can assist L2 learners in developing and maintaining a high level of motivation that will support the general L2 learning process.

Addressing the L2 Motivational Self System through to Languaging

With the advent of the internet, international travel and global economic exchange, communication in English with speakers of other languages is now a required aspect of successful participation in a globalizing world. Reflecting on this recent global shift in English language usage, while criticizing Gardner's (1985, 2001) integrativeness as 'a myth' in applied linguistics, Dörnyei (2009) proposed *the L2 motivational self system* as an alternative framework. This system comprises three core elements: the ideal L2 self, the ought-to L2 self and the L2 learning experience. Dörnyei (2009) describes these elements as follows:

> *Ideal L2 Self*, which is the L2-specific facets of one's 'ideal self': if the person we would like to become speaks an L2, the *'ideal L2 self'* is a powerful motivator to learn the L2 because of the desire to reduce the discrepancy between our actual and ideal selves. ... *Ought-to L2 Self*, which concerns the attributes that one believes one *ought to* possess to meet expectations and to *avoid* possible negative outcomes. ... *L2 Learning Experience*, which concerns situated, 'executive' motives related to the immediate learning environment and experience (e.g., the impact of the teacher, the curriculum, the peer group, the experience of success). (Dörnyei, 2009: 29, emphasis in original)

Compared with the concepts of integrativeness and instrumentality in Gardner's (1985) socioeducational model, Dörnyei (2009) emphasized L2 learners' self-image as perceived by themselves. The L2 motivational self system is based on earlier studies by Markus and Nurius (1986) and Higgins (1998). If an L2 learner can create positive future outcomes after successful L2 learning, they are said to have created an ideal L2 self. On the other hand, an ought-to L2 self is created when the learner is afraid of being unsuccessful (i.e. losing a job, not being promoted to a better position in the workplace or failing to be admitted to a university because of their lack of adequate L2 proficiency). This also occurs when the learner studies the L2 simply to meet perceived social responsibilities or family obligations (Taguchi *et al.*, 2009).

As outlined above, the use of various types of languaging activities in L2 classrooms can foster higher levels of self-awareness among learners. The purpose of this study stems from current classroom practices in South Korea (which are similar to those used in L2 classroom environments in many other nations), where a considerable number of EFL learners in both primary and secondary schools experience demotivation and amotivation (Kim & Seo, 2012). According to Dörnyei and Ushioda (2011: 139), demotivation concerns 'specific external forces that reduce or diminish the motivational basis of a behavioral intention or an ongoing action', whereas amotivation is defined as 'a lack of motivation caused by the realization that "there is no point…" or "it's beyond me"'. By adopting a mixed methods approach, Kim and Seo (2012) identified three major reasons for Korean students' demotivation: dislike for their English teacher or the teaching methods used, excessive social expectations concerning English proficiency and the widening English proficiency gap among students. In this challenging learning context, a variety of languaging activities can boost students' low motivational levels. By providing students with the opportunity to critically recollect their previous and current English learning behavior, the students can concretize their future L2 goals and visions. In this sense, languaging activities conducted in either verbal or written modes are termed 'motivational languaging activities' (MLAs). As evidenced in Swain and colleagues' previous research (e.g. Lenchuk & Swain, 2010; Swain, 2013a), cognitive and affective functions are enhanced when participants are engaged in languaging activities. The present study is thus an academic endeavor to connect the efficacy of MLAs to the domain of L2 learning motivation.

Methods

To investigate the impact of MLAs on student motivation, a questionnaire comparing students' motivational changes at two different points in time (i.e. at the beginning and end of the semester) was used. The questionnaire data were analyzed using a series of paired-samples *t*-tests.

Research context: Participants and instructors

A total of 837 Korean elementary and junior high school students participated in the present study. In Korea, although most students begin learning English in private language schools when they are in kindergarten, public English education begins in Grade 3. Grades 3 and 4 receive two 40-minute classes per week, and Grades 5 and 6 receive three

Table 5.1 Student information based on school grade

School level	Grade	No. of students	Percentage (%)
Elementary school	5	420	50.2
Junior high school	7	417	49.8
Total		837	100.0

40-minute classes per week. In the case of junior high school students, they receive four to five 45-minute classes per week. The participants of the present study were students from three different public schools in the Seoul metropolitan area (one elementary and two junior high schools). The number of elementary school students was 420 (50.2%), and that of junior high school students was 417 (49.8%). Table 5.1 displays the participant information for each grade level.

Data collection method: EFL learning motivation questionnaire

To measure changes in the participants' levels of L2 learning motivation, the same questionnaire was administered twice, first at the beginning of the spring semester of 2012 (March) and then at the end (July). Before beginning the study, a pilot test was conducted in June 2011 to modify the questionnaire items. A total of 69 students (i.e. 26 elementary and 43 junior high school students) participated in the pilot study. The subcomponents included in the questionnaire were based on Taguchi *et al.*'s (2009) items used in their study investigating the English learning motivation of Japanese, Chinese and Iranian students. In addition, Kim's (2012) motivation questionnaire items were also considered in the formulation of the present study's questionnaire. The constructs included were: (1) ideal L2 self (8 items; $\alpha = 0.936$), (2) ought-to L2 self (8 items; $\alpha = 0.846$), (3) instrumental (promotion) motivation (7 items; $\alpha = 0.855$), (4) instrumental (prevention) motivation (7 items; $\alpha = 0.877$), (5) family influence (8 items; $\alpha = 0.851$), (6) motivated behavior (5 items; $\alpha = 0.894$), (7) attitude toward English learning (5 items; $\alpha = 0.886$), (8) integrativeness (3 items; $\alpha = 0.715$), (9) attitude toward the English-speaking community (3 items; $\alpha = 0.844$) and (10) cultural interest (4 items; $\alpha = 0.646$) (see Appendix for sample questionnaire items and definitions of constructs).

All students who participated in the pilot study were excluded from the main study. After checking the internal consistency of the items for each construct, the items that lowered the consistency coefficient were either deleted or modified. A 5-point Likert scale was used, and additional items asking about students' previous English learning experience were also included. To analyze students' motivational changes throughout the course of the semester, a matched-pair *t*-test was used.

Motivational languaging activity design

As stated above, the MLAs used in this study were based on the belief that students' explicit efforts to think critically about their previous English learning, current proficiency level and their desired L2 proficiency level in either a verbal or written manner would enhance their motivation levels. This may contribute to boosting demotivated learners' motivation to learn English and thus alleviate classroom management problems stemming from unmotivated students while creating better learning conditions in EFL classrooms. In this section, the application of MLAs in EFL classrooms in Korea will be explained in two consecutive stages: the preparation and implementation stages.

Preparation stage

In this stage, I endeavored to develop languaging activities with high ecological validity in the classroom context. According to Thorne (2013: 3), ecological validity is based on 'the idea that instructed language education might be more adaptively aligned with contemporary conditions of superdiversity and better integrated with the broader intellectual efforts of educational institutions and cultures'. Thus, in my collaborative efforts with EFL teachers at the participating schools to devise useful languaging activities, the most crucial criteria included the (1) ease of use for teachers and (2) students' interest in the activity. To fulfill these criteria, activities requiring less time for both preparation and implementation were preferred. Students' maximal opportunity to critically reflect on their previous English learning experiences was also considered. Given that English teachers have an enormous administrative workload in Korea, which is often cited as a major challenge concerning English lesson preparation (cf. Kim, 2004; OECD, 2014), it was decided that the MLAs should not take much time to implement; for this reason, the activities were implemented seven times (every other week) over a course of 14 weeks, with each session lasting for 15–20 minutes out of the allotted 40 minutes (elementary school) or 45 minutes (junior high school) of regular class time.

Table 5.2 lists the MLAs implemented in three different experimental conditions plus one control condition: (1) an English learning diary, (2) opinion writing after watching and reading about exemplary cases of famous Koreans who speak fluent English and (3) peer discussion after watching and reading about the exemplary cases. All MLAs were conducted in Korean, the participants' L1.

In the opinion writing and peer discussion groups, a series of short video clips was shown to the students. In the video clips, which lasted 3–5 minutes, Korean celebrities (e.g. a famous sports star, a diplomat)

Table 5.2 Motivational languaging activities

	Control group	Experimental group		
		(1) English-learning diary (written in Korean)	(2) Opinion writing after watching and reading exemplary cases	(3) Peer discussion after watching exemplary cases
Activity contents	Distribution of exemplary cases and students' individual reading materials (all written in Korean)	Individual writing activity (English learning diary reflecting on what the learner did last week during English class) after reading exemplary cases	After watching a short video clip and reading an exemplary case, students record their feelings	After watching a short video clip and reading an exemplary case, students engage in peer discussion
Types of languaging	None	Written languaging	Written languaging	Spoken languaging
Teacher's role	Have students read the exemplary cases	Check the diary	Check for assignment completion and provide feedback	Encourage active student discussion
Interaction between teacher and students	No	No	Yes	Yes

delivered lectures, made public speeches or conducted interviews in English. For example, Ban Ki-Moon, the former UN secretary general, and Yuna Kim, the 2010 woman's Olympic figure skating gold medalist, made a public speech or conducted an interview in English. It was assumed that by watching such video clips, the students could reflect on their own L2-related future aspirations, which would have a beneficial effect on their English learning motivation.

For all three experimental groups, a special notebook named *Dream Notebook* (hereafter referred to as simply 'the Notebook') was created and distributed to the students. In the Notebook, exemplary cases of Koreans with high English proficiency levels were introduced, and their methods of English learning were systematically compiled in Korean. Moreover, sections asking about the students' learning methods and those of the celebrities were provided. The students had ample opportunities to compare the different EFL learning methods. The contents of the Notebook were used as the basis for individual opinion writing or peer discussion in the MLAs; a sample page is shown in Figure 5.1.

Implementation stage

Three participating teachers adopted the three MLA conditions and control conditions in their classrooms, constituting 12 classes (i.e. three teachers teaching students in four English classes with different

Figure 5.1 Dream Notebook sample page

conditions). Each teacher used the MLAs for one semester and investigated the changes in their students' English learning motivation.

In the case of the control group, the teacher distributed handouts on exemplary cases of Korean celebrities with high English proficiency levels and had the students read them. These handouts consisted of the reading section of the Notebook. Without conducting verbal or written languaging, the students read the cases silently. In the control group, written or spoken languaging either individually or collaboratively was not allowed by the instructor. However, students' voluntary silent speech not identified by the instructor was not discouraged in class.

As explained above, in all three experimental groups, the Notebook was provided to each student. For the English learning diary group, after reading about the exemplary cases of the English-speaking Koreans, they wrote a diary reflecting on their English learning during the week. It was hypothesized that through self-reflection, the students would notice the gap between their current English proficiency level and that of the Korean celebrities. This recognition was expected to enhance their L2 learning motivation. In this regard, the English learning diary is a type of written languaging activity. Figure 5.2 shows the students engaging in the English learning diary activity.

In the case of the opinion-writing group, together with their English teacher, the students first watched video clips of famous Korean celebrities, read the related reading materials in the Notebook and recorded

Figure 5.2 English learning diary group

Figure 5.3   Opinion-writing group

their feelings and reflections in the diary. To guide their thinking process, several prompting questions were included in the Notebook. For example, after students watched Mr Ban's UN speech, questions such as 'Why did Mr Ban Ki-Moon study English?' or 'Which part of Mr Ban's English learning method did you like the most and which did you like the least?' were provided as prompting questions. Further, students were asked to think about their life in 20 years and write down their ideal self-image. The students' conscious efforts in critical self-reflection regarding their English learning and proficiency level provided cognitively challenging conditions. Like the English learning diary, opinion writing was categorized as one specific type of written languaging. Figure 5.3 shows the students engaged in the opinion-writing activity utilizing the Notebook. Some students also asked the instructor (wearing a black suit) questions regarding what they needed to do during this activity.

Figure 5.4   Peer discussion group

For the last group, peer discussion instead of opinion writing was implemented. They first watched the same video clips, and under the supervision of their English teacher, they conducted peer discussions. Each group comprised three to four members, and each member was given an individual role in the discussion. The discussion topics were the same as the writing prompts used with the opinion-writing group: the same prompts were used to facilitate discussion among group members. Thus, the peer discussion condition is a type of verbal languaging. Figure 5.4 shows the junior high school English teachers explaining the discussion topic after watching the video clips.

Results

The effect of MLAs on students' English learning motivation

This section describes the results of the analysis on the MLAs' effectiveness in enhancing students' English learning motivation over a semester. The results for the elementary school students are reported first and those of the junior high school students follow.

Elementary school students' results

Table 5.3 shows that the periodical administration of MLAs over a semester had a positive effect on the students' L2 learning motivation. Compared with the control group, in which the students did not show any significant improvements in any subcomponents of L2 learning motivation, the opinion-writing condition in the experimental groups demonstrated a statistically significant increase in the three subcomponents: the ideal L2 self, attitude toward English learning and integrativeness. However, in the two different experimental groups (i.e. English learning diary and peer discussion conditions), students did not exhibit statistically significant motivational changes.

Table 5.3   Elementary school students' changes in L2 learning motivation

| | | Control group | | English learning diary | | Experimental group | | | |
| | | | | | | Opinion writing after watching and reading exemplary cases | | Peer discussion after watching exemplary cases | |
		Mean	t-score	Mean	t-score	Mean	t-score	Mean	t-score
Ideal L2 self	pre	3.71	-0.279	3.09	-1.369	3.46	-2.727*	3.63	-0.359
	post	3.78		3.36		3.96		3.72	
Ought-to L2 self	pre	2.91	-1.113	2.89	-0.083	3.11	-1.238	3.09	-1.358
	post	3.22		2.9		3.35		3.35	
Instrumentality (promotion)	pre	3.65	-0.043	3.31	0.253	3.76	-0.413	3.7	-0.579
	post	3.65		3.27		3.82		3.79	
Instrumentality (prevention)	pre	3.11	-0.831	3.06	0.451	3.37	-0.445	3.13	-0.738
	post	3.35		2.97		3.43		3.3	
Family influence	pre	3.04	-1.293	2.86	-0.740	3.06	-1.274	3.31	0.000
	post	3.41		2.97		3.26		3.31	
Motivational behavior	pre	3.44	-0.189	3.28	1.213	3.54	-0.597	3.67	-0.472
	post	3.5		3.02		3.65		3.75	
Attitude toward English learning	pre	3.52	-0.424	3.23	-0.603	3.64	-3.642**	4.05	0.626
	post	3.62		3.4		4.39		3.86	
Integrativeness	pre	3.66	0.55	3.24	-0.118	3.53	-2.320*	3.85	0.703
	post	3.5		3.26		4.13		3.64	
Attitude toward English community	pre	3.49	-0.081	3.11	0.000	3.71	-1.673	3.81	-0.065
	post	3.5		3.11		4.15		3.83	
Cultural interest	pre	3.23	-0.701	3	0.216	3.38	-1.382	3.57	-0.165
	post	3.41		2.95		3.68		3.62	

Note: ** p = 0.000, * p ≤ 0.05.

Junior high school students' results

Table 5.4 shows the results of implementing the same MLAs with junior high school students. As shown in Table 5.4, the junior high school students' ought-to L2 self increased when they participated in the English learning diary activity, in contrast to the results of the elementary school students. Interestingly, for those who participated in English learning diary activities, their attitude toward English learning worsened in a statistically significant manner ($t = 2.495$; $p < 0.05$). This seems related to the nature of diary writing. As Dörnyei (2009: 13) explained, the ought-to self refers to 'the representation of attributes that one believes one ought to possess (i.e. representation of someone else's sense of duties, obligations or moral responsibilities)'. While critically reflecting on their previous English learning activities, students in the English learning diary group might have internalized the necessity of English learning. Many students often wrote 'I will do my best to learn English because I heard that English is a must if I want to become a successful person' or 'I will be scolded by my parents if I don't study English'. Such self-awareness may have resulted in the increase in the ought-to L2 self.

Having an externally mandated ought-to L2 self has negative consequences, and as shown in Table 5.4, this is represented by the decrease in the students' positive attitudes toward English learning. This attitude is closely linked to the enjoyment of learning English, which reflects learners' intrinsic motivation (Ryan & Deci, 2000). While repeatedly internalizing the obligation to learn English and imagining possible, negative consequences of failing to do so, students in the English learning diary group sacrificed their positive attitude toward English learning at the expense of strengthening the ought-to L2 self.

Discussion

It is noteworthy that despite receiving the same treatment (i.e. watching the video clips and participating in the languaging activity), the peer discussion groups in both the elementary and junior high school groups did not reveal statistically significant increases in their L2 learning motivation levels. This demonstrates that a languaging activity involving opinion writing seems more effective than a group languaging activity involving oral discussion in terms of motivational enhancement. This implies that while engaging in the opinion-writing MLA, particularly in the case of the elementary school students, the students were better able to recognize the discrepancy between their current English proficiency level and that of the Korean celebrities speaking English fluently when they watched the short video clips and wrote about their opinion on the Korean celebrities' English learning and use. By participating in the written languaging activities held every other week, the elementary school students' sense of ideal L2 self, attitude toward English learning, and

Table 5.4 Junior high school students' changes in L2 learning motivation

| | | Control group | | Experimental group | | | | | |
| | | | | English learning diary | | Opinion writing after watching and reading about exemplary cases | | Peer discussion after watching exemplary cases | |
		Mean	t-score	Mean	t-score	Mean	t-score	Mean	t-score
Ideal L2 self	pre	3.55	0.919	3.43	1.361	3.36	-0.145	3.45	0.012
	post	3.47		3.33		3.38		3.45	
Ought-to L2 self	pre	2.75	-0.682	2.58	-2.408*	2.86	0.273	3	0.447
	post	2.81		2.84		2.83		2.96	
Instrumentality (promotion)	pre	3.69	0.776	3.6	1.313	3.66	1.521	3.74	1.315
	post	3.62		3.48		3.52		3.63	
Instrumentality (prevention)	pre	3.19	0.039	3.15	-0.552	3.44	1.889	3.45	0.703
	post	3.18		3.2		3.24		3.38	
Family influence	pre	2.85	-1.65	2.83	-0.325	3.08	1.238	3.07	0.199
	post	3.02		2.85		2.97		3.05	
Motivational behavior	pre	3.07	0.541	3.25	1.987	3.06	1.046	3.16	0.167
	post	3.01		3.06		2.93		3.15	
Attitude toward English learning	pre	3.15	-0.499	3.21	2.495*	2.82	-0.052	2.84	-0.062
	post	3.21		2.99		2.83		2.84	
Integrativeness	pre	3.33	0.556	3.31	0.507	3.06	-1.312	3.13	-0.265
	post	3.27		3.27		3.23		3.16	
Attitude toward English community	pre	3.5	0.721	3.24	0.000	3.01	-1.617	3.19	0.338
	post	3.41		3.24		3.21		3.15	
Cultural interest	pre	3.25	0.605	2.95	0.088	2.77	-2.517*	2.99	-1.21
	post	3.17		2.95		3.05		3.13	

Note: **p = 0.000, *p ≤ 0.05.

integrativeness increased and reached statistically significant levels. In the case of the junior high school students, their cultural interest increased at a statistically significant level.

Although the junior high school group also exhibited a statistically significant increase in their ought-to L2 selves when completing an English diary MLA, this requires further investigation because the same MLA resulted in a statistically significant decrease in positive attitudes toward English learning. This may be related to the nature of self-reflective diary writing, in which students should contemplate their learning behavior and decide to spend more time studying English. In this process, learners may have perceived a heightened level of obligation to learn English that was externally imposed upon them and thus related to their ought-to L2 self. Thus, such a sense of obligation may have exerted a negative influence on their attitude toward EFL learning. This, however, is speculation and requires further inquiry.

To summarize the results identified in Tables 5.3 and 5.4, although small changes were identified in both the elementary and junior high school groups, it seems that the most effective MLA among the three different types was the opinion-writing condition, even though for the junior high school students, only cultural interest showed a statistically significant increase. In this condition, the students first watched exemplary cases of English proficiency in the short video clips and then recorded their feelings after watching it. The results of this study indicate that this activity was more effective with the elementary school students than the junior high school students. This may be because elementary school students' self-awareness is fragile and still in the developing stage (Anderman & Anderman, 2010; Hamre & Pianta, 2005); therefore, the students may be more sensitive to this instructional approach (i.e. MLAs). As indicated above, for the elementary school opinion-writing group, it is noteworthy that the post-test results represented by the mean scores showed increases in all subcomponents of L2 learning motivation; furthermore, ideal L2 self, attitude toward English learning and integrativeness showed statistically significant increases. This indicates that elementary school students are more willing to emulate exemplary Koreans and aspire to become like them by improving their English proficiency levels. This desire might have been crystalized through the act of written languaging in opinion writing, which resulted in positive changes in L2 learning motivation. For the junior high school participants, the same MLA also demonstrated a positive increase in students' cultural interest toward English-speaking communities (see Table 5.4).

Summary and Future Directions

The present study investigated the effect of verbal and written languaging activities on EFL students' L2 learning motivation. Addressing the research questions, the findings are as follows. First, among the three types of MLAs, the opinion-writing condition, a type of written languaging activity, proved to be the most effective in improving elementary and junior high school students' English learning motivation. Second, in terms of the changes in the subcomponents of L2 learning motivation, for elementary school students, the opinion-writing MLA exerted positive influences on all subcomponents of L2 learning motivation; in particular, ideal L2 self, attitude toward English learning and integrativeness reached statistically significant levels of motivational enhancement. In the case of the junior high school students, their cultural interest in English-speaking communities increased in a statistically significant manner.

Swain's (2006a, 2013b) reconceptualization of output into languaging is now expanding its scope from cognitive human functioning to affective enhancement. To date, research on L2 learning motivation from a languaging perspective has not been conducted, and in this sense, the present study represents a first step in assessing its positive effects on L2 learning motivation. In future research, more diverse sets of MLAs should be implemented with students. In the present study, the same type of MLA was used with the same group to compare the effects of each MLA on the students' L2 learning motivation; thus, some participants expressed boredom resulting from repeating the same type of MLA. Furthermore, to improve the opinion-writing MLA, more interesting exemplary cases and video clips need to be compiled. In addition, a contextualized and localized Dream Notebook needs to be prepared by the practitioners. Furthermore, the study also needs to be replicated with high school. As the study results showed, after administering the MLAs over the course of one semester, the elementary school students' motivation increased much more than that of the junior high school students. This may be because elementary school students are more sensitive to educational treatment than their junior high school counterparts. For this reason, implementing MLAs with high school students and examining their effects are required, as they may be even less effective with this older age group than with the junior high school students. This speculation, however, will only be confirmed after conducting further research on the effect of MLAs on student L2 learning motivation.

References

Anderman, E.M. and Anderman, L.H. (2010) *Classroom Motivation*. Upper Saddle River, NJ: Pearson.

Clark, A. (1998) Magic words: How language augments human computation. In P. Carruthers and J. Boucher (eds) *Language and Thought: Interdisciplinary Themes* (pp. 162–183). Cambridge: Cambridge University Press.

Dörnyei, Z. (2001) *Motivational Strategies in the Language Classroom*. Cambridge: Cambridge University Press.

Dörnyei, Z. (2009) *The Psychology of Second Language Acquisition*. Oxford: Oxford University Press.

Dörnyei, Z. and Ushioda, E. (2011) *Teaching and Researching Motivation* (2nd edn). Harlow: Pearson.

Falout, J., Elwood, J. and Hood, M. (2009) Demotivation: Affective states and learning outcomes. *System* 37 (3), 403–417.

Gardner, R.C. (1985) *Social Psychology and Second Language Learning: The Role of Attitudes and Motivation.* London: Edward Arnold.

Gardner, R.C. (2001) Integrative motivation and second language acquisition. In Z. Dörnyei and R. Schmidt (eds) *Motivation and Second Language Acquisition* (pp. 1–19). Honolulu, HI: University of Hawaii Press.

Hadfield, J. and Dörnyei, Z. (2013) *Motivating Learning.* London: Pearson.

Hamre, B.K. and Pianta, R.C. (2005) Can instructional and emotional support in the first-grade classroom make a difference for children at risk of school failure? *Child Development* 76 (5), 949–967.

Higgins, E.T. (1998) Promotion and prevention: Regulatory focus as a motivational principles. *Advances in Experimental Social Psychology* 71 (6), 1062–1083.

Kim, J.-W. (2004) Education reform policies and classroom teaching in South Korea. *International Studies in Sociology of Education* 14 (2), 125–145.

Kim, T.-Y. (2006) Motivation and attitudes toward foreign language learning as socio-politically mediated constructs: The case of Korean high school students. *The Journal of Asia TEFL* 3 (2), 165–192.

Kim, T.-Y. (2010) Socio-political influences on EFL motivation and attitudes: Comparative surveys of Korean high school students. *Asia Pacific Education Review* 11, 211–222.

Kim, T.-Y. (2012) The L2 motivational self system of Korean EFL students: Cross-grade survey analysis. *English Teaching* 67 (1), 29–56.

Kim, T.-Y. and Seo, H.-S. (2012) Elementary school students' foreign language learning demotivation: A mixed methods study of Korean EFL context. *The Asia-Pacific Education Researcher* 21 (1), 160–171.

Knouzi, I., Swain, M., Lapkin, S. and Brooks, L. (2010) Self-scaffolding mediating by languaging: Microgenetic analysis of high and low performers. *International Journal of Applied Linguistics* 20 (1), 23–49.

Lapkin, S., Swain, M. and Psyllakis, P. (2010) The role of languaging in creating zones of proximal development (ZPDs): A long term care resident interacts with a researcher. *The Canadian Journal on Aging* 29 (4), 477–490.

Lear, E. (2013) Using guided reflective journals in large classes: Motivating students to independently improve pronunciation. *The Asian EFL Journal* 15 (3), 113–137.

Lenchuk, I.V. (2009) Languaging as a mediator of positive cognitive and affective change: A case study of Jane's small stories. Unpublished master's thesis, Ontario Institute for Studies in Education, University of Toronto.

Lenchuk, I.V. and Swain, M. (2010) Alise's small stories: Indices of identity construction and of resistance to the discourse of cognitive impairment. *Language Policy* 9, 9–28.

Levav, J. and Fitzsimons, G.J. (2006) When questions change behavior: The role of ease of representation. *Psychological Science* 17 (3), 207–213.

Markus, H. and Nurius, P. (1986) Possible selves. *American Psychologist* 41, 954–969.

Morwitz, V.G. and Fitzsimons, G.J. (2004) The mere-measurement effect: Why does measuring intentions change actual behavior. *Journal of Consumer Psychology* 14 (1/2), 64–74.

OECD (2014) *Education at a Glance 2014: OECD Indicators.* Paris: OECD Publishing.

Ryan, R.M. and Deci, E.L. (2000) Intrinsic and extrinsic motivations: Classic definitions and new directions. *Contemporary Educational Psychology* 25, 54–67.

Song, B.-S. and Kim, T.-Y. (2017) The dynamics of demotivation and remotivation among Korean high school EFL students. *System* 65, 90–103.

Swain, M. (1995) Three functions of output in second language learning. In G. Cook and B. Seidlhofer (eds) *Principle and Practice in Applied Linguistics: Studies in Honour of H. G. Widdowson* (pp. 125–144). Oxford: Oxford University Press.

Swain, M. (2005) The output hypothesis: Theory and research. In E. Hinkel (ed.) *Handbook of Research in Second Language Teaching and Learning* (pp. 471–484). Mahwah, NJ: Lawrence Erlbaum.

Swain, M. (2006a) Languaging, agency and collaboration in advanced language proficiency. In H. Byrnes (ed.) *Advanced Language Learning: The Contribution of Halliday and Vygotsky* (pp. 95–108). London: Continuum.

Swain, M. (2006b) Verbal protocols: What does it mean for research to use speaking as a data collection tool? In M. Chalhoub-Deville, C.A. Chapelle and P.A. Duff (eds) *Inference and Generalizability in Applied Linguistics: Multiple Perspectives* (pp. 97–114). Amsterdam: John Benjamins.

Swain, M. (2010) 'Talking-it-through': Languaging as a source of learning. In R. Batstone (ed.) *Sociocognitive Perspectives on Language Use and Language Learning* (pp. 112–129). Oxford: Oxford University Press.

Swain, M. (2013a) Cognitive and affective enhancement among older adults: The role of languaging. *Australian Review of Applied Linguistics* 36 (1), 4–19.

Swain, M. (2013b) The inseparability of cognition and emotion in second language learning. *Language Teaching* 46 (2), 195–207.

Swain, M. and Lapkin, S. (2011) Languaging as agent and constituent of cognitive change in an older adult: An example. *Canadian Journal of Applied Linguistics* 14 (1), 104–117.

Swain, M., Lapkin, S., Knouzi, I., Suzuki, W. and Brooks, L. (2009) Languaging: University students learn the grammatical concept of voice in French. *Modern Language Journal* 93 (1), 5–29.

Taguchi, T., Magid, M. and Papi, M. (2009) The L2 motivational self system among Japanese, Chinese and Iranian learners of English: A comparative study. In Z. Dörnyei and E. Ushioda (eds) *Motivation, Language Identity and the L2 Self* (pp. 66–97). Bristol: Multilingual Matters.

Thorne, S.L. (2013) Language learning, ecological validity, and innovation under conditions of superdiversity. *Bellaterra Journal of Teaching & Learning Language & Literature* 6 (2), 1–27.

Vygotsky, L.S. (1978) *Mind in Society: The Development of Higher Psychological Processes*. Cambridge, MA: Harvard University Press.

Vygotsky, L.S. (1987) *The Collected Works of L.S. Vygotsky. Volume 1. Thinking and Speaking*. New York: Plenum Press.

Appendix: Sample Motivation Questionnaire Items (5-Point Likert Scale)*

(1) Ideal L2 self (L2-specific facets of one's ideal self)

I can imagine myself living abroad and having a discussion in English with local people.
I can imagine myself speaking English with foreign friends or acquaintances.
I can imagine myself studying in a university where all my courses are taught in English.

(2) Ought-to L2 self (the attributes that one believes one ought to possess)

Learning English is necessary because people surrounding me expect me to do so.
My parents tell me that I must study English to be an educated person.
Studying English is important to me to bring honor to my family.

(3) Instrumentality promotion (the regulation of personal goals to become successful, such as attaining high proficiency in English to make money or find a better job)

Studying English is important to me because I think it will someday be useful for me in getting a good job.

Studying English is important to me because with a high level of English proficiency, I will be able to make a lot of money.

The things I want to do in the future require me to use English.

(4) Instrumentality prevention (the regulation of duties and obligations, such as studying English to pass an examination)

Studying English is necessary for me because if I don't have a good knowledge of English, I'll be considered a weak student.

Studying English is necessary for me because if I don't have a good knowledge of English, I think it will be difficult for me to get a job.

Studying English is necessary for me because if I don't have a good knowledge of English, I think I will fall behind my friends.

(5) Family influence (active and passive parental roles)

My parents encourage me to take advantage of every opportunity to use my English.

My parents encourage me to attend extra English classes after school.

My parents believe that I must study English to be an educated person.

(6) Motivated behavior (the learner's intended efforts toward English learning)

If I have more opportunities to learn English in the future, I will take advantage of them.

I think that I am doing my best to learn English.

If English were not a mandatory subject in school, I would still like to study it.

(7) Integrativeness (having a positive attitude toward the L2, its culture and native speakers of the L2)

Do you think learning English is important in order to learn about the culture and art of its speakers?

Would you like to become similar to a native English-speaking teacher?

Do you like English a lot?

(8) Attitude toward learning English (situation-specific motives related to the immediate learning environment and experience)

Do you think your English classes are interesting?

Do you always look forward to your English classes?

Would you like to have more English lessons at school?

(9) Attitude toward the L2 community (the learner's attitudes toward the community of the target language)

Do you like people who live in English-speaking countries?
Do you like meeting people from English-speaking countries?
Would you like to know more about people from English-speaking countries?

(10) Cultural interests (the learner's interest in cultural products of the L2 culture, such as TV, magazines, music and movies)

Do you enjoy reading English magazines, newspapers and books?
Do you enjoy watching TV programs (e.g. American TV drama series) produced in English-speaking countries?

* Note: The definitions of constructs are based on Taguchi *et al.* (2009: 74–75).

6 Second Language Concept-Based Pragmatics Instruction: The Role of Languaging

Rémi A. van Compernolle and Celeste Kinginger

Introduction

Expanding on her work on collaborative dialogue and language learning in the zone of proximal development (ZPD), Swain has explored the role of 'languaging' in developing students' understanding of complex grammatical concepts (e.g. active, middle and passive voice in French; Swain *et al.*, 2009). Languaging involves articulating one's understanding of the concept to be learned – or *externalization* in Vygotskian terms – so that it can become an object of conscious reflection and modification in internalization. Swain *et al.* (2009: 5) describe languaging as 'a form of verbalization used to mediate the solution(s) to complex problems and tasks'. This might involve private, or self-directed, speech, written reflections or social-communicative speech between interlocutors or even whole classrooms. The point is that learners use language to reflect on, work through, question and propose solutions to problems relevant to their learning. The concept is informed by Vygotsky's (1986) theory of the relationship between thinking and language use. Briefly put, language is not merely a conduit through which thought can be transmitted; instead, language use shapes the thinking process in real time. Languaging, then, is a form of thinking and, as Swain has argued, it is a fundamental process involved in learning and development, especially with regard to developing conscious control over new resources (e.g. language forms, concepts) that in turn mediate our thinking.

In this chapter, we discuss some of the ways the notion of languaging has been extended to the teaching of second language (L2) pragmatics. We focus on the notoriously challenging address form system in French as an additional language (i.e. *tu* vs. *vous*, or T/V). We first outline the difficulties of the T/V system before describing the integration of languaging in a Vygotskian approach to teaching called 'concept-based instruction'. We then present and discuss examples of different forms of languaging in concept-based pragmatics instruction (CBPI) to illustrate how the concept has been extended and adapted for use in various educational contexts.

Tu and *vous* in French

The ability to use second-person singular pronouns in social interaction (i.e. to say 'you') may initially appear to be a fairly straightforward matter. However, these pronouns of 'power and solidarity' (Brown & Gilman, 1970) are in fact fraught with complexity for all speakers of languages endowed with a T/V system. Even very expert speakers may encounter misunderstanding due to the multiple levels of indexicality inherent within these systems, and resultant ambiguity in specific communicative events (Silverstein, 1996). The choice of *tu* versus *vous* may point to the formality or informality of social settings, or to the distribution of power in relationships of respect, deference or solidarity. Additionally, address form choice may index a speaker's desired social identity, with the use of *vous* corresponding to conservatism, high social status or respect for tradition, and the use of *tu* pointing to youth, progressive political ideologies or egalitarianism. At a third level, these forms also point to stereotypical representations of their users, for example, an association between *vous* use and bourgeois snobbery. Morford's (1997) research demonstrated that speakers of French are strongly attached to the subtleties of this system, and will readily interpret errors in its use as gaffes, with consequences for social relationships. Thus, Dewaele (2004) characterizes the T/V system as a 'sociolinguistic tightrope' to be crossed by all users of French. Unfortunately, the complexities of the T/V system in French and other languages with such a system (e.g. German, Spanish) are not typically represented in pedagogical materials, which instead enjoin students to learn oversimplified rules of thumb (Dewaele & Planchenault, 2006; Kinginger & Belz, 2005).

As part of a larger study, Kinginger (2008) examined reported use and perceptions of the T/V system in French among 23 American college students prior to and following a semester-long sojourn in France. Kinginger hypothesized that exposure to everyday social encounters would enhance the students' awareness and use of these forms. A language awareness interview was designed for the study, which included a series of *tu/vous* choice situations in which students were asked to select an address form appropriate for the situation and explain their choice. Situations varied in the level of ambiguity they displayed. The most ambiguous 'bakery daughter' situation is embedded in the following example:

You have been frequenting the same bakery for several weeks and the lady at the counter now recognizes you and often exchanges pleasantries

*with you when you visit the bakery. She is about 50 years old and has a
daughter your age who sometimes works at the bakery. What do you call
the older woman? What do you call the younger woman?*

Results indicated that overall the students' choices became more
appropriate in principle at the end of their sojourn in France, with a
trend toward more liberal use of *tu* among younger interlocutors (e.g.
addressing the daughter in the situation above). At the same time, the
bakery daughter situation provoked far more uncertainty following
study abroad, even though students' choices had begun to align with
French sociolinguistic expectations. Students' explanations of their
decision-making in this situation included considerably more hesitation
and expression of doubt and considerably less assertiveness when compared to pre-study abroad responses. More importantly for the case we
wish to present here, the findings also showed that even when students
were able to choose an appropriate form, they were often unable to provide a coherent explanation for this choice. 'Bill', for example, was one of
the most successful language learners in the cohort who made dramatic
gains in both academic and colloquial French. However, his explanation
of T/V choices in Excerpt 1 illustrates an unsystematic understanding of
the T/V system and reveals behavior that would likely be perceived as
inappropriate in his real-life encounters with university personnel.

**Excerpt 1: Bakery daughter tu/vous choice (source: unpublished data)
(transcription conventions provided in Appendix B)**

B:	I dunno that's a call + that's a tough call with the chick I'd probably + I'd probably vous her.
I:	ok.
B:	yeah I'd probably vous her. uh simply because I'm ++ espe-cially because I'm an American I don't know exactly. so i'm gonna vous her til they tell me to shut up—until I hear them use tu with me,
I:	ok.
B:	then that's my + that's my signal, but like with the old woman definitely til she uses tu with me like whatever like I mean I know plenty of people that –like I tu all my admin-istrators, cuz they've +i've heard them tu me like=
I:	=if somebody says tu to you then + that's older than you + you think that that means that it's ok for you to call them tu.
B:	yeah.

Bill's pronoun choices could be considered 'correct' to the extent that
address form use can be viewed as right or wrong – most textbooks
instruct learners to use *vous* in case of doubt, and to use *tu* if a native
speaker does so first. However, his explanation invokes only his everyday

experiences, making no references to any broader, more systematic concepts, such as social distance, that might underlie norms of use. As we describe below, this example – and others like it – points to the value of explicit instruction centered around conceptual categories of meaning to enhance pragmatic awareness.

Languaging in Concept-Based Pragmatics Instruction

Responding to the consistent finding that learners have difficulty developing systematic understandings of *tu/vous* systems as described above, van Compernolle (2012, 2014) developed a novel approach to teaching pragmatics through conceptual categories of meaning, or CBPI. The framework centers on the concept of social indexicality (i.e. how communicative choices point to various levels of social meaning) and three subconcepts: self-presentation, social distance and power. The approach provides learners with a systematic semiotic orientation to making pragmatic choices, like *tu/vous* distinctions. Concept explanations are provided along with a series of pedagogical diagrams depicting the core meanings of the concepts imagistically (see Appendix A).

Concept-based instruction draws on Vygotsky's (1986) analysis of concept formation – especially the distinction between everyday and scientific concepts – and extensions of the theory to the domain of instruction by Davydov (2004) and Galperin (1989, 1992). Everyday concepts are developed through empirical experience and the process of abstraction. For example, children typically develop the concepts of 'square', 'triangle' and 'circle' as they encounter exemplar objects in the everyday world (e.g. the side of a box, a pizza slice, a coin). By contrast, scientific – or academic – concepts are developed starting with the abstraction (e.g. a definition or scientific explanation of a phenomenon). Thus, in school, older children are taught that a square is a two-dimensional figure with four equal sides that connect at 90° angles. This conception of 'square' requires no concrete referent or experience with square things. Importantly, the academic concept also provides a means for producing a square, which the everyday concept does not (see Davydov, 2004). In addition, while the scope of the everyday concept of 'square' is limited to a single category of similar objects, the academic concept of 'square' connects to other concepts – figures, sides, angles and so on – that recur elsewhere in mathematics. The argument, then, is that academic concepts are more useful than everyday concepts because they are more systematic (i.e. not tied to specific objects or experiences) and are therefore more easily recontextualized for use in circumstances that one has never encountered.

In L2 instruction, this line of reasoning has been extended as a rationale for teaching language through holistic academic concepts in contrast to what may be seen as more unsystematic form-focused instruction exemplified by the teaching of rules of thumb. As outlined by Negueruela's (2003) extension of concept-based instruction to L2 pedagogy, the focus is on teaching categories of meaning that orient learners to appropriate communicative practices. Thus, in Negueruela's study, rather than teaching rules of thumb for how to use past tenses (i.e. use preterit for a complete action in the past, use imperfect to describe past states, the weather and so on), learners were taught how to think through the academic concept of aspect as a means for choosing which past tense was effective for construing the intended meaning. For instance, the same event – say, a person going to the grocery store – could be construed as a bounded event, focusing on discrete starting and end points, through the use of preterit, or as an unbounded event with no discrete beginning or end. These two different construals in turn are pragmatically motivated, which is not described in rule-based pedagogy: a bounded event involves foregrounded information that moves a narrative forward whereas an unbounded event is backgrounded and contextualizes bounded events (e.g. *I went to the store* [=bounded event] *while you were watching tv* [=unbounded event] vs. *I was going to the store* [=unbounded event] *when you called me* [=bounded event]). In this way, concept-based instruction pushes learners to think through meanings as they can be encoded in linguistic signs.

A central feature of concept-based approaches to pedagogy is conscious reflection on language and meaning. This is achieved through verbalization (Negueruela, 2003), or *languaging* (Swain, 2006; Swain *et al.*, 2009), which involves speaking and/or writing to externalize one's conceptual knowledge and understanding of language so that it can become an object of conscious reflection. It is important because 'Languaging completes our thoughts/cognition/ideas and transforms them into artifacts that allow for further contemplation, which, in turn, transforms thought' (Swain *et al.*, 2009: 5). In concept-based instruction, learners are prompted to engage in languaging in two ways: (1) self-explanation of, and/or dialogue about, the concepts under study; and (2) verbalization of processes underlying communicative performance.

In what follows, we show how Swain's concept of languaging has been adapted and expanded for use in CBPI contexts. We wish to make clear from the start that in all of the examples, we consider languaging to be the key concept. Variations on the theme reflect the goals, affordances and constraints inherent in the various contexts in which the research presented below was conducted. Thus, while the kinds of tasks vary, the overarching principle is that language use was intended to elicit language-mediated thinking leading to learning and the internalization of relevant concepts, as noted in the introduction to this chapter. In other words, the point is that learners were talking themselves into an understanding of the concepts as such and how to use them in communication.

Languaging as verbalized reflection

Drawing on Swain's (2006) concept of languaging, and especially Swain *et al.*'s (2009) analysis of French learners' languaging behavior in relation to learning outcomes, van Compernolle (2012, 2014) designed materials and tasks aiming to elicit *inferencing* (i.e. going beyond instructional materials and generating hypotheses) and *self-assessment* (i.e. evaluating one's understanding and/or performance) forms of languaging. The concept-based materials included written explanations of concepts, pedagogical diagrams and think-aloud questions prompting learners to apply the concept to personal experiences, to extend their understandings to hypothetical situations and to evaluate their understanding of the concepts through speech (i.e. languaging). Learners engaged in such languaging activity first in a private task (i.e. monologic verbalized reflection [MVR]) and second in dialogue with a tutor (i.e. dialogic verbalized reflection [DVR]).

MVRs offer learners opportunities to get in touch with what they do and don't know as they are appropriating pragmatic concepts. For example, Excerpt 2 shows part of an MVR completed by Leon (all names are pseudonyms). Previously, Leon had been discussing a personal experience in which his high school French teacher had begun using and asked for *tu* in their interactions. Leon's MVR was focused on the concept of social closeness as expressed by the reciprocal use of *tu* between people, following a prompt given in the materials. The example was initially difficult for Leon to interpret because it contradicted the ingrained rule of thumb that students should use *vous* with teachers, especially given the age difference (cf. the 'rule' that one should use *vous* with adults/persons older than oneself).

Excerpt 2:   MVR example (source: van Compernolle, 2014: 108)

1	Leon:	°uh° + yeah. + uh although obviously yeah. sometimes
2		I'm like a + tee-shirt-and-tie, kind of guy, um ++
3		and it can be very difficult. for example in the classroom
4		where + you know. obviously I need to uh show my
5		teacher respect. but at the same time + um w-
6		we've become very familiar with each other::,
7		I can joke around with them, + we're:: + not friends.
8		at all. not friends per se. but + you know. + we uh:
9		++ we're familiars. ++ um ++ and f- and for that reason.
10		I think that's why + like uh: + there can be confusion.
11		+ and there has been. in the classroom. ++ where it needs
12		to be: explicitly said. you know. we can use:: + at least
13		the *te*. + uh the *tu* form.

This example is interesting because it shows Leon's thinking process externalized in languaging activity as he was considering the concepts under study. This is to say that the content of Leon's MVR was constituted in the act of speaking, rather than simply being communicated 'ready made' through the conduit of speech. Evidence for this interpretation of the data includes the numerous hesitant pauses and discourse markers (e.g. uh, yeah, um), which are used in private speech to regulate one's thinking processes (Gánem-Gutiérrez & Roehr, 2011) and false starts, self-repairs and disjointed speech (e.g. 'although obviously yeah. sometimes I'm like a' in Lines 1–2). These speech features suggest that Leon was attempting to make sense of an experience that he did not necessarily understand, or at least that he had not previously reflected on in a systematic way, through languaging.

Excerpt 3 provides an example of a DVR. In this instance, the student, Stephanie, was having difficulty understanding why social closeness, as indexed through the use of *tu*, may not always be considered friendly or appropriate. The example shows how, following monologic reflection, DVR can create a context in which languaging can become an inter-psychological activity, a tool for 'thinking together'.

Excerpt 3:   DVR example (source: van Compernolle, 2014: 115–116)

39	Tutor:	right, + cuz you- can you think of maybe of
40		a context where creating closeness + might not
41		be so friendly. or might not be interpreted as a
42		good thing. like friendliness.
43	Steph:	um:: + like when you wouldn't wanna be friendly?
44		I guess is a::
45	Tutor:	well go back to your professor situation.
46	Steph:	well yeah. that's true. you wouldn't wanna
47		be like- you wouldn't speak to them the way
48		their child would or something like that.
49	Tutor:	and: probably + in a lot of situations + that
50		professor wouldn't see that as friendliness,
51	Steph:	they would see it as disrespectful.
52	Tutor:	yeah. + because closeness for that relationship
53		is not maybe appropriate.
54	Steph:	mhm okay.

Note that the tutor's question initiated in Line 39 prompted Stephanie to consider when showing closeness might not be seen as friendly, or 'interpreted as a good thing' (Lines 41–42). However, her confusion about the concept is apparent when she equated closeness with friendliness (Line 43) as opposed to understanding that the latter is one possible interpretation of the former. The tutor intervened at Line 45, instructing

Stephanie to reconsider a previous example she had mentioned earlier (i.e. using *vous* to create distance when speaking with her professor), which created an opportunity for Stephanie, in cooperation with her tutor, to connect the example with the concept she was reflecting on at the moment through languaging. This is apparent at Line 51, where Stephanie provided a completion to the tutor's unfinished explanation from Lines 49 to 50: 'they would see it [closeness] as disrespectful'.

Verbalized reflection is an important form of languaging in CBPI. It pushes learners to externalize their thinking processes, thereby rendering them visible and open to conscious inspection either privately (i.e. MVR) or inter-psychologically (i.e. DVR). This creates opportunities for growth because thinking is carried out 'in the open' and may be revised as learners encounter difficulties or misunderstandings. In the next session, we examine an extension of this idea in the context of pragmatics problem-solving tasks.

Languaging as cooperative dialogue in problem-solving

Cooperative dialogue plays a crucial role in guiding learners to recontextualize their emerging conceptual knowledge of pragmatics to solve communicative problems. Appropriateness judgment tasks (AJTs) prompt learners to select appropriate pragmatic forms in a series of social interactive situations and then to verbalize in speech or writing their rationale for their choices. In the van Compernolle (2014) study, this was done in cooperation with the tutor. Excerpt 4, which was originally reported in van Compernolle and Kinginger (2013), shows the microgenesis of a synthetic concept in Nikki's thinking, which emerged in the languaging that occurred in collaboration with her tutor (see also van Compernolle, 2013). As we see, Nikki extended her understandings of the individual concepts in a way that conceived of them as part of a functional system, especially with regard to the relationship between social distance and power.

Excerpt 4:   Cooperative dialogue during an appropriateness judgment task (source: van Compernolle & Kinginger, 2013: 297)

56	Nikki:	I would use ++ wait. + ugh. + like I don't necessarily
57		want to show that I have power over her. But like +++
58		I w- + I'd use *vous*.
59	Tutor:	okay,
60	Nikki:	cuz +++ I don't ++ want to +++ cuz
61	Tutor:	mhm,
62	Nikki:	cuz I don't want a close relationship with this person.
63		so I'm like distancing myself from her.
64	Tutor:	okay,

65	Nikki:	but + and I don't want to show that I have power,
66		over the person, but ++ so I wanna (3.5) use ++
67		I think we should use vous with each other. + like
68		to show that like ++ it's an equal relationship. but
69		distance equal? Distant equal.=
70	Tutor:	=ah.

Leading up to this exchange, Nikki had been having difficulty choosing between *tu* and *vous* when addressing a grocery store clerk who was a near-age peer. She had changed her mind several times because she was unable to overcome the unsystematic rules of thumb that had been guiding her thinking: for example, *tu* seemed appropriate because the clerk was the same age as Nikki, but *vous* could also be appropriate because they did not know each other well or at all. The tutor instructed Nikki to consider the consequence of using *tu* but receiving *vous* in return, which would be expected in such service encounters. Asymmetrical use would result in an imbalance of power. As the data in Excerpt 4 show, Nikki eventually came to the conclusion that she could use *vous* and expect *vous* in return, which would create a 'distant equal' relationship.

Languaging in cooperative problem-solving tasks pushes learners not only to externalize their understandings of relevant concepts, but it also renders their recontextualization of their understandings visible so that a teacher can intervene. Although this works well in one-on-one tutoring contexts (van Compernolle, 2014), it is not scalable to the classroom. We address an adaptation of the approach to the classroom in the following section.

Languaging in classroom discourse

Van Compernolle and Henery (2014, 2015) extended CBPI to the French classroom. In so doing, they made several modifications to the approach so that it could be easily integrated into the existing curriculum and in a teacher-led, whole-class format. Here, we will discuss AJTs and how languaging was integrated into the course.

AJTs were first completed by students at home and submitted via their web course management system (Blackboard). The task was set up as an online quiz, with multiple-choice responses for choosing appropriate forms and text boxes for completing written explanations of their choices (i.e. monologic written languaging). The following day, the teacher, Mrs Hanks, would lead a whole-class instructional conversation (Tharp & Gallimore, 1988) in which students would share their responses and dialogue about the reasons for choosing *tu* versus *vous* for the various situations. Excerpt 5 shows one example. (The transcript is copied from the original publication, which used a columnar format with students on the left, and Mrs Hanks on the right.)

Excerpt 5: Instructional conversation in a French classroom (source: van Compernolle & Henery, 2015: 366)[1]

Turn	Students	Mrs Hanks
1		Alright. So I want us just to talk through some of these questionnaires, er some of the situations. And talk about again these concepts ((gesturing to screen)) and how we are going to make our choices about using *tu* and *vous*. And I want us to really um systematically use these concepts to make our decisions. Okay? So the first one... says ((reads situation)) So would you expect to use *tu* or *vous*? And would you expect to receive *tu* or *vous*? And let's be sure to think about these three concepts. So um what do you guys think? L.
2	L: Um I would expect to use *vous* and to receive *tu* because she's putting herself above me since I did something wrong and she's probably very upset, and there's a... sh- she- there's kind of a status differences /because/ it's my fault	/okay/
3		Okay. A status difference because it's my fault. Right. So you relied a lot on... on the power hierarchy one, right? Okay. Great. So um let's talk through this one and use all three. That was a great example, using the power one, but let's start with this first one ((pointing to self-presentation)). If we're just looking at this first one, what would you gu- what would you... how would you explain this situation using this first one. ((pointing to S?))
4	S?: I would use *vous* because I would try to present myself... to show that I'm conscientious and that I'm you know professional. Especially since she's professional, and I wouldn't intentionally try to hurt her, I'm a trustworthy person.	
5		Mkay. Right, so right now our choice is *vous* because we wanna try to be suit-and-tie. Alright? And then, for the second one ((adjusting concept diagrams on projector)), woops! These are in a funny order. Yeah, we want the distance one. This is the power one. Um ((puts distance diagram on projector)) so now with social distance. Who can talk about social distance with this situation?

What we see in this example is that Mrs Hanks avoided overtly correcting students or explaining the concepts in order to push them to think through the problem in social speech (i.e. a form of languaging). Instead, she focused on guiding them to use the pedagogical diagrams depicting self-presentation, social distance and power as a way of talking themselves through the decision-making process. Indeed, the idea of mediating students through this kind of metacognitive strategy was discussed extensively by Mrs Hanks and her more experienced co-researcher, as shown in the van Compernolle and Henery (2015) publication. In this way, students languaged not only to come to an understanding of the content of the concepts under study, but more importantly, they were developing a way of languaging privately that they could appropriate as a tool for thinking (i.e. thinking through the concepts in order – self-presentation, social distance and power – and how the demands of one might outweigh the demands of another).

The van Compernolle and Henery (2014, 2015) study showed that CBPI and a modified version of verbalized reflection and other languaging tasks were possible in the classroom (see van Compernolle *et al.* [2016] for an extension to Spanish). In our final example, we return to a tutoring context, but this time Henery's (2014) adaptation of the CBPI framework for use in study abroad.

Languaging in study abroad

Henery (2014) modified the CBPI framework for use with French students studying abroad in Aix-en-Provence. As in previous studies, languaging was a central feature of the enrichment program she designed for participants. One aspect of the study that Henery identified as particularly important was the interface between journal entries (written verbalization) and subsequent journal discussion sessions with an expert. Henery's participants were prompted to journal about salient or interesting language experiences in their day-to-day activities, and then to dialogue about them with the expert in relation to the concepts of self-presentation, social distance and power.

Excerpt 6 shows one example of a journal discussion. The participant, Kristina (K in the transcript), had been talking about *tu* and *vous* choices in a French elementary school where she had begun teaching English part time. In her journal entry, she had remarked that being called *madame* and *vous* by her students, who were 10 to 11 years old, was something she was not used to, and it made her feel old. At the same time, the main teacher for the class, a French woman, also called her *vous*, which she did not understand because Kristina 'emphasized that she was both too young and the teacher's subordinate and therefore expected the teacher to use *tu* with her instead of *vous*' (Henery, 2014: 103). The researcher (R in the transcript) responded by turning Kristina's attention to the pedagogical diagrams.

Excerpt 6: Journal discussion in study abroad (source: Henery, 2014: 104–105)[2]

164 R: ok so let's look at that situation then and talk about how it fits

165		into these diagrams
166	**K:**	**ok**
167	**R:**	**so if she [the teacher] is using vous with you,** what kind of meanings is
168		that expressing?
169	**K:**	well it it is more professional
170	**R:**	mhm
171	**K:**	and we're in a professional situation
172		um so it's not not t-shirt-and-jeans it's more the suit thing
173	**R:**	mhm
174	**K:**	so that does make sense
175		also it is maintaining distance because we're not going to get close
176	**R:**	((laughs))
177	**K:**	I mean that'd be weird
178		u::m but the power thing
179		like I said I do feel like she has more or I would think more power
180		than me so I was surprised when she didn't try to assert that power
181		you know by using vous in that way
182	**R:**	is there a reason for her to assert power in that situation?
183	**K:**	well I mean it's still her classroom
184		I'm just a guest and you know she:: you know she at any time could
185		tell me what to do I mean you know
186	**R:**	((laughs))
187	**K:**	she doesn't really have to, you know, she just wants to get out of
188		there and eat lunch
189	**R:**	right
190	**K:**	so she doesn't really care what I do but I mean she could if she
191		wanted to like alright tell me today you have to teach the kids this
192		and give me something
193	**R:**	mhm
194	**K:**	so I'm still below her technically
195	**R:**	mhm
196	**K:**	but I think I think it is more of her her trying to maintain a
197		professional relationship which I respect but it's just it's just
198		funny
199	**R:**	mhm yeah so I think the thing that's important to remember is that

200		um that there is a really strong preference for this égalité
201	K:	yeah
202	R:	to be equal and to be on an equal level with people and that that's
203		way of um of maintaining respect also is to use vous but on an
204		equal
205		like I respect you as another human being but we're not close
206	K:	yeah
207	R:	and and you know that kind of thing
208		and as a professional like you've you've obviously at least been
209		entrusted to take care of the kids
210	K:	yeah
211	R:	for this 45 minutes or however long it is and um and so there's a
212		lot of reasons
213		so there's not really
214		I mean even though she has the power to:: tell you what to do or
215		change things
216		it's also there's not it doesn't sound like there is anything that
217		you've like done wrong or that you know that you've that there is a
218		reason for her to be like hey you need to chill out ((laughs))
219	K:	yeah
220	R:	or you know whatever
221		there is not a real reason for her to assert her power

This lengthy discussion resulted in Kristina realizing that the teacher in the school may not have been orienting to power at all, but to the establishment and maintenance of an equal, though distant, social relationship (cf. Nikki's 'distant equal' concept in Excerpt 4). It is interesting to note that Kristina had no experience of being positioned in this way: she had always been positioned as a less powerful student in relation to teachers, and apparently had not understood that in the current context, she was seen as a colleague. Henery's (2014) student in general showed that journaling and languaging such as this helped learners to develop an interpretive framework for understanding the new language and culture they were participating in by challenging many of their assumptions and, even more importantly, heightening their sensitivity to the possibility that language forms can index important social meanings.

Concluding Remarks

In this chapter, we have explored how the concept of languaging (Swain, 2006) has been extended within concept-based pragmatic instruction for French as an additional language, focusing on the notoriously complex French address forms *tu* versus *vous*. The examples we have given illustrated different task types (e.g. MVR and DVR, collaborative problem-solving, instructional conversation) that, in our view, draw on and extend Swain's conception of languaging as the use of language to externalize thinking processes so that they can be objects of conscious reflection, revision and development. Research on CBPI and the role of languaging in driving pragmatic development is promising but admittedly rather limited. We believe that such work can and should be extended to additional languages, especially non-European languages, as well as related topics such as register and genre. Future research in this domain has the potential to contribute to our understanding of pragmatic development in instructed contexts as well as to knowledge of the relationship between development and languaging more generally.

Notes

(1) The transcript appears as published in the original version. The columnar format was used to highlight student vs. teacher turns, which tended to be long in these data, as opposed to the more common line-based linear format, which is helpful for interactions in which turn-taking occurs frequently and after relatively shorter utterances.

(2) Henery (2014) used a basic transcription convention focused on content (i.e. the words uttered) rather than delivery and timing issues, although some additional notation is included (e.g. elongation at Line 178; transcriber notes at Lines 186 and 218 for non-verbals).

References

Brown, R. and Gilman, A. (1970) The pronouns of power and solidarity. In R. Brown (ed.) *Psycholinguistics* (pp. 302–335). New York: The Free Press.

Davydov, V.V. (2004) *Problems of Developmental Instruction: A Theoretical and Experimental Psychological Study* (trans. P. Moxay). Moscow: Akademyia Press.

Dewaele, J.-M. (2004) Vous or tu? Native and non-native speakers of French in a sociolinguistic tightrope. *International Review of Applied Linguistics* 42, 383–402.

Dewaele, J.-M. and Planchenault, G. (2006) 'Dites-moi tu!' La perception de la difficulté du système des pronoms d'adresse en Français ['Say tu to me' Perceptions of difficulty in the French system of address pronouns]. In M. Faraco (ed.) *La classe de langue: Théories, méthodes, pratiques [The Language Classroom: Theories, Methods, Practices]* (pp. 153–171). Aix-en-Provence: Publications de l'Université de Provence.

Galperin, P.I. (1989) Organization of mental activity and the effectiveness of learning. *Soviet Psychology* 27 (2), 65–82

Galperin, P.I. (1992) Stage-by-stage formation as a method of psychological investigation. *Journal of Russian and East European Psychology* 30 (4), 60–80.

Gánem-Gutiérrez, G.A. and Roehr, K. (2011) Use of L1, metalanguage, and discourse markers: L2 learners' regulation during individual task performance. *International Journal of Applied Linguistics* 21, 297–318.

Henery, A. (2014) Interpreting 'real' French: The role of expert mediation in learners' observations, understandings, and use of pragmatic practices while abroad. PhD thesis, Carnegie Mellon University.

Kinginger, C. (2008) Language learning in study abroad: Case studies of Americans in France. *Modern Language Journal* 92, Supplement.

Kinginger, C. and Belz, J. (2005) Sociocultural perspectives on pragmatic development in foreign language learning: Case studies from telecollaboration and study abroad. *Intercultural Pragmatics* 2, 369–421.

Morford, J. (1997) Social indexicality in French pronomial address. *Journal of Linguistic Anthropology* 7, 3–37.

Negueruela, E. (2003) A sociocultural approach to teaching and researching second language: Systemic-theoretical instruction and second language development. Unpublished doctoral dissertation, The Pennsylvania State University.

Silverstein, M. (1996) Indexical order and the dialectics of sociolinguistic life. In J. Rasako, R. Parker and Y. Sunaoshi (eds) *Proceedings of the Third Symposium about Language and Society – Austin [SALSA]* (pp. 266–295). Austin, TX: University of Texas.

Swain, M. (2006) Languaging, agency and collaboration in advanced second language proficiency. In H. Byrnes (ed.) *Advanced Language Learning: The Contribution of Halliday and Vygotsky* (pp. 95–108). London: Continuum.

Swain, M., Lapkin, S., Knouzi, I., Suzuki, W. and Brooks, L. (2009) Languaging: University students learn the grammatical concept of voice in French. *Modern Language Journal* 93, 5–29.

Tharp, R.G. and Gallimore, R. (1988) *Rousing Minds to Life: Teaching, Learning, and Schooling in Social Context*. New York: Cambridge University Press.

van Compernolle, R.A. (2012) Developing sociopragmatic capacity in a second language through concept-based instruction. PhD thesis, The Pennsylvania State University.van Compernolle, R.A. (2013) From verbal protocols to cooperative dialogue in the assessment of second language pragmatic competence. *Intercultural Pragmatics* 10, 71–100.

van Compernolle, R.A. (2014) *Sociocultural Theory and L2 Instructional Pragmatics*. Bristol: Multilingual Matters.

van Compernolle, R.A. and Kinginger, C. (2013) Promoting metapragmatic development through assessment in the zone of proximal development. *Language Teaching Research* 17 (3), 282–302.

van Compernolle, R.A. and Henery, A. (2014) Instructed concept appropriation and L2 pragmatic development in the classroom. *Language Learning* 64, 549–578.

van Compernolle, R.A. and Henery, A. (2015) Learning to do concept-based pragmatics instruction: Teacher development and L2 pedagogical content knowledge. *Language Teaching Research* 19, 351–372.

van Compernolle, R.A., Gomez-Laich, M.P. and Weber, A. (2016) Teaching L2 Spanish sociopragmatics through concepts: A classroom-based study. *Modern Language Journal* 100 (1), 341–361.

Vygotsky, L.S. (1986) *Thought and Language*. Cambridge, MA: The MIT Press.

Appendix A: Pedagogical Diagrams Used in CBPI (Source: van Compernolle, 2014)

tu		vous
on	T-shirt-and-jeans or	nous
Ø...pas	suit-and-tie?	ne...pas

Diagram for self-presentation

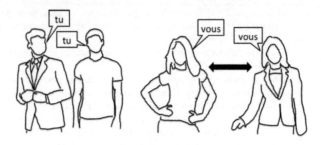

Closeness or distance?

Diagram for social distance

Relative status?

Diagram for power

Appendix B: Transcription Conventions
(from van Compernolle, 2014)

+	short pause
++	long pause
+++	very long pause
(2.0)	timed pause (2.0 seconds or more)
.	full stop marks falling intonation
,	slightly rising intonation
?	raised intonation (not necessarily a question)
↑	markedly higher pitch relative to preceding talk
↓	markedly lower pitch relative to preceding talk
(word)	single parentheses indicate uncertain hearing
(xxx)	unable to transcribe

((comment))	double parentheses contain transcriber's comments or descriptions
-	abrupt cutoff with level pitch
:	indicates elongated delivery (each colon represents one extra beat)
underline	underlining indicates stress through pitch or amplitude
=	latched utterances
[. . .]	indicates that a section of the transcript has been omitted
[	onset of overlapping speech
]	end of overlapping speech
CAPITALS	capital letters indicate markedly loud speech

Part 3

Sociocultural Perspectives on Second Language Teaching and Learning

Part 4

7 Collaborative Output: A Review of Theory and Research

Hossein Nassaji

Swain (1998, 2005) has argued that classroom activities that require second language (L2) learners to produce language forms collaboratively contribute importantly to language learning. The argument rests on the assumption that collaborative output provides learners with collective help and guided support as a result of interacting with each other in order to solve linguistic problems and produce language accurately and appropriately. The purpose of this chapter is to provide an overview of the theory and research on the role of collaborative output in L2 learning. The chapter first discusses the theoretical underpinnings of collaborative output and then examines empirical research that has explored its effectiveness. It also considers the implications of the issues discussed for classroom pedagogy and further research.

Introduction

Recent L2 theory and research strongly support the role of collaborative interaction in language learning. Theoretically, the role of interaction is informed by two main theoretical frameworks: the cognitive interactionist perspectives and sociocultural theories. The major difference between the two schools of thought is their different views on the way interaction contributes to language development.

Within the interactionist perspective, a popular framework has been Long's (1996) interaction hypothesis. From this perspective, L2 learners develop their language knowledge during interaction in which they attempt to negotiate meaning. Negotiation of meaning refers to the 'modification and restructuring of interaction that occurs when learners and their interlocutors anticipate, perceive, or experience difficulties in message comprehensibility' (Pica, 1994: 495). These processes are assumed to assist learners in communicating with their interlocutors. They also contribute to making input comprehensible, which in turn facilitates L2 acquisition (Ellis, 2008; Long, 1996; Loschky & Bley-Vroman, 1993; Pica et al., 1996).

In recent years, a growing body of research has explored the effectiveness of various types of negotiation of meaning strategies in L2 acquisition. These studies range from those investigating the effects of interactional strategies on facilitating comprehension (Gass *et al.*, 1998; Gass & Varonis, 1989; Long, 1983; Pica, 1998) to those that have examined the role of these strategies in promoting attention to form (Doughty & Varela, 1998; Fujii & Mackey, 2009; Gass, 2003; Gass & Mackey, 2006; Gass & Varonis, 1994; Iwashita, 2003; Long *et al.*, 1998; Mackey, 2007, 2012; Mackey & Philp, 1998; Oliver, 1995, 2002; Oliver & Mackey, 2003; Philp, 2003; Pica *et al.*, 1993). In general, studies of negotiation of meaning suggest that negotiated interaction facilitates language acquisition by facilitating comprehension and promoting attention to form.

Sociocultural theory also emphasizes the importance of interaction and negotiation. However, this theory places particular emphasis on the social and dialogic nature of interaction and negotiation. In this view, interaction is defined as a goal-oriented, sociocultural activity, the purpose of which is not just to transmit knowledge but to construct, reconstruct or transform knowledge (Lantolf & Appel, 1994). Thus, interaction does not simply facilitate mental processes; rather, it is an integral and inherent part of learning, without which learning cannot be achieved (Vygotsky, 1978; Wertsch, 1985). Therefore, the sociocultural perspective differs from the negotiation of meaning perspective, which simply focuses on strategies to clarify meaning such as clarification requests and confirmation checks.

Vygotskian sociocultural theory is central to the conceptualization of collaborative output (Swain, 1998, 2005) as collaboration is an important instance of social interaction. There are a number of constructs that are fundamental to Vygotsky's sociocultural theory. One of these is distinction between 'inter- and intra-psychological processes'. Vygotsky (1978) argued for a complex relationship between individual psychological development and social interaction. He believed that people's intellectual development is dependent on the interaction they have with others. To clarify this relationship, Vygotsky (1981) put forward a 'general genetic law of cultural development':

> Any function in the child's cultural development appears twice, or on two planes. First, it appears on the social plane, and then on the psychological plane. First it appears between people as an interpsychological category, and then within the child as an intrapsychological category. This is equally true with regard to voluntary attention, logical memory, the formation of concepts, and the development of volition. (Vygotsky, 1981: 163)

According to Wertsch (1985), the above law highlights two important ideas in Vygotsky's theory. First, it explains that interaction plays a crucial role in individual cognitive development. Second, it reveals the 'inherent connection' between two modes of functioning: inter-psychological (in communication) and intra-psychological (in thinking), in which social interactions act as the intermediary for individual cognitive development (Wertsch, 1985: 61).

As far as language pedagogy is concerned, the relationship between inter- and intra-psychological processes suggests that L2 teaching should incorporate student–student interaction activities because peer interaction provides students with occasions to participate in concrete social interaction, trying to solve both linguistic and communicative problems by using the target language. Language in this situation also becomes 'simultaneously a means of communication and a tool for thinking' (Swain & Lapkin, 1998: 320). When students use language to collaborate, they incorporate the L2 knowledge developed in the social interaction into their internal psychological plane, and hence they are likely to further their knowledge of the language, consciously or subconsciously (Nassaji & Tian, 2018).

In explaining the relationship between instruction and development, Vygotsky (1978) also introduced the key concept of the zone of proximal development (ZPD). The ZPD is defined as 'the distance between the actual developmental level as determined by independent problem solving and the level of potential development as determined through problem solving under adult guidance or in collaboration with more capable peers' (Vygotsky, 1978: 86). Vygotsky contends that students' developmental level is extended when they interact with peers within the ZPD. He further argues that instruction does not necessarily lead to development. Only when instruction is in students' ZPD does it become effective because it can trigger functions that are in the process of maturation (Vygotsky, 1934; cited in Wertsch, 1985). Within this perspective, the effect of interaction not only depends on the capability of the participants but also on how learners interact with one another (see e.g. Storch, 2001, 2005).

Another related notion is the concept of 'scaffolding'. The term was originally used by Bruner (1986) in his scaffolding theory. Influenced by Vygotsky's idea of an expert supporting a novice, Bruner initially used the term to show how parents interact with and aid children in their oral language development. He then used it to denote the kind of support students need from their teachers in the initial stages of their learning. In collaborative activities, scaffolding has been used to refer to the supportive environment created through the guidance and feedback that learners receive from an expert or peers during collaboration. This is what Donato (1994) referred to as 'collective scaffolding'. When learners collaborate with others, they learn to do what they have not been able to do independently. This happens particularly when learners interact with a more capable individual. In such cases, the less capable participant's language skills can be expanded and elevated to a higher level of competence. A point to note is that scaffolding is support that is not random, but rather is negotiated within the learner's ZPD. It is guided support, jointly 'constructed on the basis of the learner's need' (Nassaji & Swain, 2000: 36).

A third concept that developed from a Vygotskian framework is the idea of regulation. According to Vygotsky (1978), learning is not only a social process, but it is also a process of moving from object-regulation to other-regulation to self-regulation. Object-regulation is when the learner's behavior is controlled by objects in the environment. For example, learners may be able to respond only to the stimuli that are available in here-and-now contexts. Other-regulation occurs when the learner has gained some control over the task but still needs the help or guidance of others. Self-regulation refers to the situation in which the learner becomes skilled and able to act autonomously (Vygotsky, 1978).

The construct of regulation highlights two important themes in sociocultural theory. First, it explains that new knowledge originates in interaction and also becomes internalized through interaction. Second, it explains the transition from when someone needs assistance to when he or she begins to act independently, showing control over his or her own behavior (Donato, 1994; Lantolf & Appel, 1994). Lantolf and Appel (1994: 11) suggested that this transition 'marks the beginning of the child's control over his or her own behavior – that is, self-regulation'.

A number of studies have examined these mechanisms and have provided evidence for how collaborative interaction within the ZPD helps learners progress from lower- to higher-order mental functioning (see Lantolf, 2000; Lantolf & Poehner, 2014, for a review of these studies). When L2 learners interact in a spoken or written form during peer interaction activities, if they can successfully express their intended meanings, an internal plane of consciousness may be formed that can help their knowledge of the language to be further internalized. If they fail to express themselves independently, their interlocutor peer may assist them to clarify their points until they can consciously produce an acceptable expression and make themselves understood. This acceptable expression may become consolidated through further peer-to-peer interaction. Vygotsky emphasized internalization as a process that is only achieved when people are able to create on their internal planes what has been performed in external social reality. He defined internalization as 'an operation that initially represents an external activity is reconstructed to occur internally' (Vygotsky, 1978: 56). Thus, internalization is not a simple transfer of external social development to a higher individual mental plane. Rather, it is a transformative process that is 'the result of a long series of developmental events' that 'are culturally reconstituted and developed to form a new psychological entity' (Vygotsky, 1978: 56; see Newman & Holzman, 1993).

Implications for L2 Teaching

The concepts discussed so far have important implications for L2 teaching and particularly for how collaborative tasks can enhance L2 development. For example, the notion of the ZPD highlights the central role of collaboration in mediating learning and cognitive development. When learners collaborate within the ZPD, the act of collaboration pushes them toward higher levels of development, enabling them to learn what they are potentially able to learn (Nassaji & Swain, 2000). At every stage of the learning process, peers who negotiate within their ZPD are likely to reach a more sophisticated developmental level (Nassaji & Cumming, 2000). Collaborative learning activities also create a social context for students to interact with one another and receive feedback. This is captured in the notion of scaffolding discussed earlier. When interacting with less experienced peers, students may use their linguistic knowledge to give suggestions to other students and also consolidate their known knowledge. In interaction within the ZPD, students may also use what they already know to develop what they have not mastered independently. They may acquire new knowledge and ways of thinking with their peers' help, furthering their development and internalization. The concept of scaffolding applies to not only expert–novice interaction but also novice–novice or learner–learner interactions when L2 learners' assist each other during interaction (Lightbown & Spada, 2006).

The Importance of Output

Traditionally, the role of input (i.e. language comprehension) has been highly emphasized in L2 acquisition. Swain (1985, 1995), however, has argued that input alone is not enough and that learners need to have opportunities for output as well as input. The argument for the importance of output grew out of the findings of Swain's studies of French immersion programs in Canada, which have shown that mere exposure to meaningful content is inadequate for the acquisition of grammatical accuracy (e.g. Harley & Swain, 1984; Lapkin *et al.*, 1991; Swain, 1985, 1993). These studies have found that, although immersion students are exposed to many hours of comprehensible input, their language performance often remains inaccurate with respect to certain aspects of the L2 (such as correct gender agreement and tense marking). One reason for this, Swain has argued, is that learners in these programs do not have enough opportunities for L2 production. Thus, she has argued that, to develop language accuracy, students should have ample opportunities for output in interaction with others. She also argued that learners are not being 'pushed' in their output (Swain, 1985: 249). Thus, she has argued that learners also need to be pushed to produce output that is accurate, appropriate and coherent, what has been called 'pushed output' (Swain, 1985, 1995). Pushing learners to produce output forces them to process the language syntactically rather than semantically and hence promotes greater language accuracy.

In several of her publications (e.g. Swain, 1985, 1993, 2005), Swain has identified a number of important functions for output. One is that output promotes noticing, which is considered an essential prerequisite for language acquisition (e.g. Schmidt, 1990). When learners attempt to produce the target language, they may notice that they are not able to say what they want to say. In other words, they may notice a gap in their knowledge. Noticing a gap may prompt cognitive processes that can lead to the acquisition of new linguistic knowledge or the consolidation of existing knowledge (Swain, 1995). Output also provides a condition for formulating and testing hypotheses. It not only prompts learners to become conscious of their linguistics problems, but it also brings 'to their attention something they need to discover about their L2' (Swain & Lapkin, 1995: 373). Output also allows deeper syntactic processing. When learners produce language, they have to 'move from the semantic, open-ended, strategic processing prevalent in comprehension to the complete grammatical processing needed for accurate production' (Swain, 2000: 99). These processes assist language acquisition.

Collaborative Output

Swain (1995) has argued that L2 learners should move beyond mere talking. As noted earlier, they should be pushed to produce accurate and appropriate output and also be encouraged to collaborate and collectively solve linguistic problems. When learners engage in collaborative production of language, they negotiate meaning and also receive feedback from their peers, which improves their grammatical accuracy (Swain, 1995, 2000).

The important role of pushed output as well as collaboration provides an argument for using tasks in the classroom that promote these conditions. This can be done through using collaborative output tasks. Collaborative output tasks are classroom activities that involve learners in a joint and collaborative production of language and solving linguistics problems. Such tasks are considered beneficial for L2 learning because they facilitate both scaffolding and conscious reflection upon language use (Kowal & Swain, 1994, 1997; Swain, 1997; Swain & Lapkin, 2002). Swain (1997: 115) argued that the co-construction of language 'allows performance to outstrip competence; it's where language use and language learning can co-occur'. These processes take place when learners need to produce language in the course of interaction rather than when they are simply exposed to input.

A number of tasks can be used as collaborative output tasks. One such task is the dictogloss (Wajnryb, 1990). A dictogloss is a kind of output task that encourages learners to work together to reconstruct a text after it is presented to them orally. In this task, the teacher reads a short text more than once and then asks the students to work in groups and reproduce the text as closely as possible to the original text. The aim of a dictogloss is not only to push learners to produce output but also to promote interaction that results in both negotiation of meaning and negotiation of form. As noted earlier, negotiation of meaning refers to the use of conversational exchanges to resolve communication breakdowns. Negotiation of form refers to exchanges that trigger learners' attention to form. To complete a dictogloss, learners need to communicate with each other in order to reconstruct the original passage. Thus, the dictogloss promotes verbal interaction in a collaborative context that helps learners reach mutual understanding. Furthermore, when the participants reconstruct the text, they may discuss the lexical and grammatical forms needed for the task completion. They may do it either in the L2 or even in the first language (L1) when their L2 proficiency is low (see Haneda, 1996). Therefore, this raises learners' attention to the specific aspects of the language.

In addition to the dictogloss, other communicative tasks can also be used to promote collaborative output. Among these tasks are structure-based grammar tasks (Nassaji & Fotos, 2010). These are tasks that are designed in ways that promote learner awareness and practice of certain target forms. Ellis (2003) has described such tasks as 'focused' tasks compared with unfocused tasks, which are designed purely for communication.

However, for focused tasks to become output tasks, they should require the learner to produce a particular linguistic target that is essential for the completion of the task (Loschky & Bley-Vroman, 1993). Furthermore, to become collaborative, the task should require learners to interact with each other in order to complete the task. One way of doing so is to design the task in the form of a 'jigsaw'. Jigsaw tasks are two-way information-gap tasks in which each student holds a different portion of the information that is needed to complete the task. Learners should then share and exchange that information to complete the task. Examples of such tasks can be found in Pica *et al.* (2006). According to Pica *et al.*, for any jigsaw task to be effective, it should have the following two characteristics: (a) it should be goal-oriented and (b) it should generate negotiation of meaning.

Jigsaw tasks can be designed in the form of segmented texts that students have to put together to create the original text. An example of such tasks is provided in Pica *et al.* (2006), who described the steps in designing these tasks as follows. A text that is authentic to students or related to the content of the course is selected. Then, two versions of the text are prepared (e.g. Versions A and B), with each version containing some sentences that are exactly the same as the sentences in the original passage and some sentences that are different or inaccurate. Pairs of students can then receive the modified versions, with one student receiving Version A and the other Version B. The students then read their own version and attempt to find the similarities and the differences between their version and the original text. They also discuss and correct any errors in their version.

A third type of collaborative output task is consciousness-raising (Fotos, 1993, 1994; Fotos & Ellis, 1991). Whereas the previous two task types introduce grammar structures implicitly in communicative contexts, consciousness-raising tasks require learners to communicate with each other about the target grammar structures. Thus, the grammar forms are the task content. For example, a series of correct and incorrect sentences related to the same structure (e.g. English passive voice) can be presented to pairs of students. Students are asked to work together and identify which ones are correct and which ones are incorrect. They also try to induce the rule underlying the correct ones (see Nassaji & Fotos, 2010 for examples).

Studies of Collaborative Output Tasks

A number of studies have investigated the benefits of some of the collaborative output tasks discussed above (e.g. Fortune, 2005; Kowal & Swain, 1994, 1997; LaPierre, 1994; Lapkin & Swain, 2000; Lapkin et al., 2002; Nassaji & Tian, 2010; Swain & Lapkin, 1995, 1998, 2000, 2002, 2007; Swain et al., 2009). Kowal and Swain (1994), for example, conducted a study with Grade 8 French immersion students using a dictogloss. They found that as the students engaged in the production of the language through this task, they noticed gaps in their language knowledge that then triggered a cooperative search for a solution. They also found that the use of the task not only promoted meaningful interaction but also led to great improvement in students' knowledge of grammar. LaPierre (1994) also examined the role of the dictogloss in Grade 8 French immersion classrooms. She found a positive relationship between the linguistic forms that were correctly supplied during the dictogloss interaction and learners' subsequent production of those forms. Nabei (1996) conducted a similar study with four adult English as a second language (ESL) learners and found similar results. She found many instances where the dictogloss activity promoted opportunities for attention to form, scaffolding and corrective feedback.

Swain and Lapkin (2001) reported a study with two groups of French immersion students, and compared the effectiveness of a dictogloss with a jigsaw task, in which pairs of students worked together to create a story based on a series of pictures. The researchers did not find any significant differences between the two types of task in terms of the overall degree of form-focusedness, operationalized in terms of the number of language-related episodes. However, they found that the dictogloss task led to more accurate reproduction of the target forms than the jigsaw task.

Pica *et al.* (2006) investigated the effectiveness of collaborative jigsaw tasks. Their results from six pairs of intermediate-level English L2 learners who carried out the tasks in their classrooms showed evidence of the effectiveness of the task for drawing learners' attention to the linguistic targets (i.e. articles). Their results also showed an important relationship between learners' interactional efforts and recall of the form and functions of the target items during the tasks.

In a classroom-based study, Nassaji and Tian (2010) compared the effectiveness of two types of output tasks for learning vocabulary (English phrasal verbs): a reconstruction cloze task and a reconstruction editing task. The text editing was the kind of task that required students to correct a text in order to improve its accuracy and expression of content. The study used a pretest, post-test, delayed post-test within-subject design, in which all students performed both kinds of tasks, both collaboratively and individually. To this end, two versions of the cloze task were prepared, and students completed one collaboratively and the other individually. Similarly, two versions of the editing task were used, one collaborative and one individual. The study was conducted during a 13-week semester in two, intact, low-intermediate adult ESL classrooms with 26 students. The dyadic interactions during the task completion phase of the collaborative tasks were recorded and transcribed. The data were analyzed and compared across tasks with respect to (a) the quality and quantity of interaction generated and (b) the degree of contribution made to the learning of the target forms. The results showed that completing the tasks collaboratively (in pairs) led to greater accuracy of task completion than completing them individually. However, collaborative tasks did not lead to significantly greater gains of vocabulary knowledge than individual tasks. The results also showed an effect of task type, with the editing tasks being more effective than the cloze tasks in promoting negotiation and learning.

A number of other studies (García Mayo, 2002, 2007; Storch, 1997, 1998a, 1998b, 2001, 2005, 2007) have examined the effects of collaborative output tasks. The results of these studies have also shown the beneficial effects of such tasks in terms of opportunities for focus on form as well as for social interaction. Storch (2005), for example, examined the effectiveness of output tasks when students produced a written text either in pairs or individually. The results showed that the collaborative task led to shorter, but grammatically more accurate and more complex texts than the individual task. García Mayo (2002) examined the effectiveness of two types of collaborative output tasks: a dictogloss and a text with missing words. Participants were seven pairs of high-intermediate to advanced L2 learners. The data were analyzed both quantitatively and qualitatively. The results showed that the text reconstruction task produced a greater amount of language-related episodes than the other task. The author concluded that the text reconstruction task was more effective than the other task in drawing learners' attention to form, but stressed further research in this area.

Overall, the results of studies on collaborative output tasks have shown positive effects for such tasks on learner grammatical accuracy. Although these studies differ in terms of their degree of support for such tasks, they have all shown that such tasks can promote attention to form as learners attempt to produce output collaboratively. They have also shown that the effectiveness of such tasks may depend on the type of task, the context of study and also the learners' linguistic ability.

Conclusion and Directions for Future Research

In this chapter, I have discussed the notion of collaborative output tasks and their application to L2 learning. I began by briefly discussing their theoretical underpinning and the need for opportunities for collaborative learning, reflection and social interaction. I then discussed how such opportunities can be created in L2 classrooms. I also examined studies that have investigated the effectiveness of such tasks in L2 pedagogy.

In general, studies examining the effects of collaborative output tasks have provided support for their use and effectiveness. However, research in this area is still very limited, and many questions need further investigation. One area for further research, for example, is examining the contribution of such tasks more directly to acquisition. Previous studies have shown how collaborative output tasks promote noticing the target structure. However, noticing alone is not sufficient for language learning. Therefore, studies need to investigate more directly how these tasks contribute to acquisition. Studies should also examine the efficacy of such tasks with different groups of learners in different contexts. Such research is needed as not all language learners are the same or learn in the same way.

Although previous studies have examined the effectiveness of collaborative output tasks, there is little research on how learners perceive the usefulness of such tasks. Understanding learners' preferences and perspectives can help the teacher identify the challenges learners may have and address them to maximize the utility of such tasks. This research is also important because while some learners might prefer to work collaboratively, others might prefer to work individually. Thus, knowing learners' perspectives can prevent situations that can lead to negative effects. In this respect, we also need to know how other individual learner differences, such as learners' educational and cultural backgrounds, mediate the effectiveness of output tasks.

Finally, a collaborative task is not a unified entity and its usefulness may depend on and be influenced by not only the degree of students' interaction and reflection but also the amount and quality of both peers' and teacher's feedback. Although previous studies have examined the overall effects of collaborative output tasks, they have not explored how these effects relate to different aspects of the task. Future research thus should tease apart if possible the different components of the task and examine their unique and common contributions to task effectiveness. Within this context, the relationship between feedback and attention to form during interactional feedback exchanges that occur while learners perform the task could also be explored. Such investigations are both theoretically and pedagogically important. Theoretically, they help clarify what is in the task that contributes most to its effectiveness. Pedagogically, they can help teachers understand how to implement the task to enhance its success. Since collaborative tasks are often used in classroom or group-work contexts where not all learners participate equally, it is also worthwhile examining the relationship between the degree of learners' participation and the learning of the language forms.

References

Bruner, J.S. (1986) *Actual Minds, Possible Worlds*. London: Harvard University Press.

Donato, R. (1994) Collective scaffolding in second language learning. In J. Lantolf and G. Appel (eds) *Vygotskian Approaches to Second Language Research* (pp. 33–59). Norwood, NJ: Ablex.

Doughty, C. and Varela, E. (1998) Communicative focus on form. In C. Doughty and J. Williams (eds) *Focus on Form in Classroom Second Language Acquisition* (pp. 114–138). Cambridge: Cambridge University Press.

Ellis, R. (2003) *Task-Based Language Learning and Teaching*. Oxford: Oxford University Press.

Ellis, R. (2008) *The Study of Second Language Acquisition* (2nd edn). Oxford: Oxford University Press.

Fortune, A. (2005) Learners' use of metalanguage in collaborative form-focused L2 output tasks. *Language Awareness* 14, 21–37.

Fotos, S. (1993) Consciousness-raising and noticing through focus on form: Grammar task-performance versus formal instruction. *Applied Linguistics* 14, 385–407.

Fotos, S. (1994) Integrating grammar instruction and communicative language use through grammar consciousness-raising tasks. *TESOL Quarterly* 28, 323–351.

Fotos, S. and Ellis, R. (1991) Communicating about grammar: A task-based approach. *TESOL Quarterly* 25, 605–628.

Fujii, A. and Mackey, A. (2009) Interactional feedback in learner–learner interactions in a task-based EFL classroom. *International Review of Applied Linguistics in Language Teaching* 47, 267–301.

García Mayo, M.P. (2002) The effectiveness of two form-focused tasks in advanced EFL pedagogy. *International Journal of Applied Linguistics* 12, 156–175.

García Mayo, M.P. (ed.) (2007) *Investigating Tasks in Formal Language Learning*. Clevedon: Multilingual Matters.

Gass, S. (2003) Input and interaction. In C. Doughty and M. Long (eds) *The Handbook of Second Language Acquisition* (pp. 224–255). Oxford: Blackwell.

Gass, S. and Varonis, E. (1989) Incorporated repairs in nonnative discourse. In M. Eisenstein (ed.) *Variation and Second Language Acquisition* (pp. 71–86). New York: Plenum.

Gass, S. and Varonis, E. (1994) Input, interaction, and second language production. *Studies in Second Language Acquisition* 16, 283–302.

Gass, S. and Mackey, A. (2006) Input, interaction and output: An overview. *AILA Review* 19, 3–17.

Gass, S., Mackey, A. and Pica, T. (1998) The role of input and interaction in second language acquisition: Introduction to the special issue. *The Modern Language Journal* 82, 299–307.

Haneda, M. (1996) Peer interaction in an adult second language class: An analysis of collaboration on a form-focused task. *Japanese Language Education around the Brobe* 6, 101–123.

Harley, B. and Swain, M. (1984) The interlanguage of immersion students and its implications for second language teaching. In A. Davies, C. Criper and A.P.R. Howatt (eds) *Interlanguage* (pp. 291–311). Edinburgh: Edinburgh University Press.

Iwashita, N. (2003) Negative feedback and positive evidence in task-based interaction: Differential effects on L2 development. *Studies in Second Language Acquisition* 25, 1–36.

Kowal, M. and Swain, M. (1994) Using collaborative language production tasks to promote students' language awareness. *Language Awareness* 3, 73–93.

Kowal, M. and Swain, M. (1997) From semantic to syntactic processing: How can we promote it in the immersion classroom? In R.K. Johnson and M. Swain (eds) *Immersion Education: International Perspectives* (pp. 284–309). Cambridge: Cambridge University Press.

Lantolf, J. (2000) *Sociocultural Theory and Second Language Learning*. Oxford: Oxford University Press.

Lantolf, J. and Appel, G. (1994) *Vygotskian Approaches to Second Language Research*. Norwood, NJ: Ablex.

Lantolf, J. and Poehner, M. (2014) *Sociocultural Theory and the Pedagogical Imperative in L2 Education. Vygotskian Praxis and the Theory/Practice Divide*. New York: Routledge.

LaPierre, D. (1994) Language output in a cooperative learning setting: Determining its effects on second language learning. MA thesis, OISE, University of Toronto.

Lapkin, S. and Swain, M. (2000) Task outcomes: A focus on immersion students' use of pronominal verbs in their writing. *Canadian Journal of Applied Linguistics* 3, 7–22.

Lapkin, S., Hart, D. and Swain, M. (1991) Early and middle French immersion programs: French language outcomes. *Canadian Modern Language Review* 48, 11–40.

Lapkin, S., Swain, M. and Smith, M. (2002) Reformulation and the learning of French pronominal verbs in a Canadian French immersion context. *Modern Language Journal* 86, 485–507.

Lightbown, P. and Spada, N. (2006) *How Languages are Learned* (3rd edn). Oxford: Oxford University Press.

Long, M. (1983) Native speaker/non-native speaker conversation and the negotiation of comprehensible input. *Applied Linguistics* 4, 126–141.

Long, M. (1996) The role of the linguistic environment in second language acquisition. In W. Ritchie and T. Bhatia (eds) *Handbook of Second Language Acquisition* (pp. 413–468). San Diego, CA: Academic Press.

Long, M., Inagaki, S. and Ortega, L. (1998) The role of implicit negative feedback in SLA: Models and recasts in Japanese and Spanish. *Modern Language Journal* 82, 357–371.

Loschky, L. and Bley-Vroman, R. (1993) Grammar and task based methodology. In G. Crookes and S.M. Gass (eds) *Tasks and Language Learning: Integrating Theory and Practice* (pp. 123–167). Clevedon: Multilingual Matters.

Mackey, A. (2007) The role of conversational interaction in second language acquisition. In A. Mackey (ed.) *Conversational Interaction in Second Language Acquisition: A Collection of Empirical Studies* (pp. 1–26). Oxford: Oxford University Press.

Mackey, A. (2012) *Input, Interaction, and Corrective Feedback in L2 Learning*. Oxford: Oxford University Press.

Mackey, A. and Philp, J. (1998) Conversational interaction and second language development: Recasts, responses, and red herrings? *Modern Language Journal* 82, 338–356.

Nabei, T. (1996) Dictogloss: Is it an effective language learning task? *Working Papers in Educational Linguistics* 12, 59–74.

Nassaji, H. and Cumming, A. (2000) What's in a ZPD? A case study of a young ESL student and teacher interacting through dialogue journals. *Language Teaching Research* 4, 95–121.

Nassaji, H. and Swain, M. (2000) Vygotskian perspective on corrective feedback in L2: The effect of random versus negotiated help on the learning of English articles. *Language Awareness* 9, 34–51.

Nassaji, H. and Fotos, S. (2010) *Teaching Grammar in Second Language Classrooms: Integrating Form-Focused Instruction in Communicative Context*. London: Routledge.

Nassaji, H. and Tian, J. (2010) Collaborative and individual output tasks and their effects on learning English phrasal verbs. *Language Teaching Research* 14, 397–419.

Nassaji, H. and Tian, J. (2018) Constructivism. Issues in applying SLA theories toward creative teaching. In M. Zeraatpishe, A. Faravani, H.R. Kargozari and M. Azarnoosh (eds) *Issues in Applying SLA Theories Toward Creative Teaching* (pp. 23–36). The Netherlands: Sense Publishers.

Newman, F. and Holzman, L. (1993) *Lev Vygotsky: Revolutionary Scientist*. London: Routledge.

Oliver, R. (1995) Negative feedback in child ns-nns conversation. *Studies in Second Language Acquisition* 17, 459–481.

Oliver, R. (2002) The patterns of negotiation for meaning in child interactions. *Modern Language Journal* 86, 97–111.

Oliver, R. and Mackey, A. (2003) Interactional context and feedback in child ESL classrooms. *Modern Language Journal* 87, 519–533.

Philp, J. (2003) Constraints on 'noticing the gap': Nonnative speakers' noticing of recasts in ns-nns interaction. *Studies in Second Language Acquisition* 25, 99–126.

Pica, T. (1994) Research on negotiation: What does it reveal about second-language learning conditions, processes, and outcomes? *Language Learning* 44, 493–527.

Pica, T. (1998) Second language learning through interaction: Multiple perspectives. In V. Regan (ed.) *Contemporary Approaches to Second Language Acquisition in Social Context* (pp. 9–31). Dublin: University College Dublin Press.

Pica, T., Kanagy, R. and Falodun, J. (1993) Choosing and using communicative tasks for second language instruction. In S. Gass and G. Crookes (eds) *Tasks and Language Learning: Integrating Theory and Practice* (pp. 9–34). Clevedon: Multilingual Matters.

Pica, T., Lincoln-Porter, F., Paninos, D. and Linnell, J. (1996) Language learners' interaction: How does it address the input, output, and feedback needs of L2 learners? *TESOL Quarterly* 30, 59–84.

Pica, T., Kang, H. and Sauro, S. (2006) Information gap tasks: Their multiple roles and contributions to interaction research methodology. *Studies in Second Language Acquisition* 28, 301–338.

Schmidt, R. (1990) The role of consciousness in second language learning. *Applied Linguistics* 11, 129–158.

Storch, N. (1997) The editing talk of adult ESL learners. *Language Awareness* 6, 221–232.

Storch, N. (1998a) A classroom-based study: Insights from a collaborative text reconstruction task. *ELT Journal* 52, 291–300.

Storch, N. (1998b) Comparing second language learners' attention to form across tasks. *Language Awareness* 7, 176–191.

Storch, N. (2001) How collaborative is pair work? ESL tertiary students composing in pairs. *Language Teaching Research* 5, 29–53.

Storch, N. (2005) Collaborative writing: Product, process, and students' reflections. *Journal of Second Language Writing* 14, 153–173.

Storch, N. (2007) Investigating the merits of pair work on a text editing task in ESL classes. *Language Teaching Research* 2, 143–159.

Swain, M. (1985) Communicative competence: Some rules of comprehensible input and comprehensible output in its development. In S. Gass and C. Madden (eds) *Input in Second Language Acquisition* (pp. 235–253). Rowley, MA: Newbury House.

Swain, M. (1993) The output hypothesis: Just speaking and writing aren't enough. *Canadian Modern Language Review* 50, 158–164.

Swain, M. (1995) Three functions of output in second language learning. In G. Cook and B. Seidlhofer (eds) *Principles and Practice in Applied Linguistics* (pp. 125–144). Oxford: Oxford University Press.

Swain, M. (1997) Collaborative dialogue: Its contribution to second language learning. *Revista Canaria de Estudios Ingleses* 34, 115–132.

Swain, M. (1998) Focus on form through conscious reflection. In C. Doughty and J. Williams (eds) *Focus on Form in Classroom Second Language Acquisition* (pp. 64–81). Cambridge: Cambridge University Press.

Swain, M. (2000) The output hypothesis and beyond: Mediating acquisition through collaborative dialogue. In J.P. Lantolf (ed.) *Sociocultural Theory and Second Language Learning* (pp. 97–114). Oxford/New York: Oxford University Press.

Swain, M. (2005) The output hypothesis: Theory and research. In E. Hinkel (ed.) *Handbook on Research in Second Language Teaching and Learning* (pp. 471–483). Mahwah, NJ: Lawrence Erlbaum Associates.

Swain, M. and Lapkin, S. (1995) Problems in output and the cognitive processes they generate: A step towards 2nd language learning. *Applied Linguistics* 16, 371–391.

Swain, M. and Lapkin, S. (1998) Interaction and second language learning: Two adolescent French immersion students working together. *The Modern Language Journal* 82, 320–337.

Swain, M. and Lapkin, S. (2000) Focus on form through collaborative dialogue: Exploring task effects. In M. Bygate, P. Skehan and M. Swain (eds) *Researching Pedagogic Tasks, Second Language Learning,Teaching and Testing* (pp. 99–118). Harlow: Longman.

Swain, M. and Lapkin, S. (2001) Focus on form through collaborative dialogue: Exploring task effects. In M. Bygate, P. Skehan and M. Swain (eds) *Researching Pedagogic Tasks: Second Language Learning, Teaching and Testing* (pp. 99–118). Harlow: Pearson Education.

Swain, M. and Lapkin, S. (2002) Talking it through: Two French immersion learners' response to reformulation. *International Journal of Educational Research* 37, 285–304.

Swain, M. and Lapkin, S. (2007) The distributed nature of second language learning: Neil's perspective. In S. Fotos and H. Nassaji (eds) *Form-Focused Instruction and Teacher Education: Studies in Honour of Rod Ellis* (pp. 73–86). Oxford: Oxford University Press.

Swain, M., Lapkin, S., Knouzi, I., Suzuki, W. and Brooks, L. (2009) Languaging: Students learn the grammatical concept of voice in French. *The Modern Language Journal* 93, 5–29.

Vygotsky, L.S. (1978) *Mind in Society: The Development of Higher Psychological Processes*. Cambridge, MA: Harvard University Press.

Vygotsky, L.S. (1981) The genesis of higher mental functions. In J.V. Wertsch (ed.) *The Concept of Activity in Soviet Psychology* (pp. 144–188). Armonk, NY: M.E. Sharpe.

Wajnryb, R. (1990) *Grammar Dictation*. Oxford: Oxford University Press.

Wertsch, J.V. (1985) *Vygotsky and the Social Formation of Mind*. Cambridge, MA: Harvard University Press.

8 Promoting L2 In-Service Teachers' Emocognitive Development through Collaborative Dialogue

Próspero N. García

Introduction

Merrill Swain's influence on the fields of applied linguistics and second language acquisition (SLA) cannot be overlooked. Her innovative ideas and extensive research on language development from a sociocultural perspective in areas such as bilingual and immersion education (Swain & Lapkin, 2013), teacher development (Swain et al., 2015), cognitive change in older adults (Swain & Lapkin, 2011) and languaging as a source and facilitator of language development (Swain, 2006, 2010; Swain et al., 2010; inter alia) have influenced past and present investigators and are sure to inspire future researchers. Drawing from her notion of languaging, this chapter links Swain's work on the inseparability of emotion and cognition in language development (Poehner & Swain, 2016; Swain, 2013; Swain et al., 2015), with the emocognitive development of three experienced in-service teachers of Spanish.

Traditionally, the cognitive development of second language (L2) instructors has been linked to their internalization of pedagogical content knowledge (García, in press; van Compernolle & Henery, 2015; Williams et al., 2013), or the cognitive/emotional dissonance that emerges in the formation of novice language instructors (Johnson & Worden, 2014). However, there is a lack of research addressing the role of emotion in fostering the development of conceptual language awareness in experienced in-service L2 teachers whose first language (L1) is also the target language. This chapter addresses this gap in the literature by exploring the link between cognition and emotion in three in-service teachers of Spanish, and their transformative approaches to crisis-resolution (Vasilyuk, 1992) when their pedagogical beliefs are challenged and/or supported through collaborative dialogue, an activity wherein 'speakers are engaged in problem-solving and knowledge-building' (Swain, 2000). In this chapter, I report the results of introducing teachers to a conceptual approach to the teaching and learning of the grammatical concept of aspect through engaging with them in collaborative dialogue, which, as these data suggest, provided teachers with mediation necessary to promote their internalization of aspect.

In what follows, I explore the ways in which *perezhivanie*, the unity of emotion and cognition (Vygotsky, 1994), can shape and influence L2 in-service teachers' conceptual development through dialogic interaction with others and with the self. The chapter begins by exploring the notion of languaging and its role in language development. I continue by discussing *perezhivanie* as the unity of emotion and cognition while connecting it with current research on emocognitive L2 development. I conclude the chapter by presenting, analyzing and discussing data related to the emocognitive development of three in-service teachers of Spanish, whose L1 is also Spanish.

Dialogic Interaction as Languaging

Lantolf and Pavlenko (1995) see dialogic interaction as a social activity that arises when individuals are engaged in goal-oriented activity. As such, it may occur with others (i.e. collaborative dialogue) or with the self (i.e. private speech). Examples of dialogic interaction include, but are not limited to, a group of learners trying to solve a communicative task, a teacher providing mediation to a learner or a learner talking to himself/ herself in order to understand a complex activity. This notion is very much connected to that of languaging, whose role in the L2 classroom has been used as a tool for instruction and assessment, and has been widely researched over the last decade by Swain, Lapkin and colleagues (Brooks & Swain, 2009; Brooks *et al.*, 2010; Knouzi *et al.*, 2010; Lapkin *et al.*, 2010; Swain, 2006, 2010; Swain & Lapkin, 2002; Swain *et al.*, 2009; *inter alia*). Swain (2006: 98) originally defined languaging as 'the process of making meaning and shaping knowledge and experience through language', emphasizing the conscious use of language to mediate our performance, focus our attention and discover and connect new meanings. It is important to note that this notion encompasses much more than the mere description of oral output. According to Swain and collaborators, languaging– or talking-it-through (Swain, 2010) – refers to any type of written or spoken mediated activity with objects, other people or with the self that promotes learners' cognitive development. This perspective is especially relevant in the case of L2 learners and teachers, where instances of languaging in the form of collaborative dialogue or private speech become powerful tools to illustrate L2 learning and teaching in the foreign language classroom.

But languaging, in any one of its manifestations (i.e. written, oral, etc.), not only allows us to observe what teachers and learners know and how to offer them significant mediation aimed at their linguistic development (García, 2012); observing learners' talking-it-through also provides us with the opportunity to uncover their affective reactions and cognitive challenges (Swain, 2013) or when engaged in challenging tasks. This information allows us to pull together emotional and cognitive resources to mediate their learning (Swain, 2013: 205). In sum, languaging encourages learners and teachers to reflect on their own cognitive and emotional processes, which, in turn, may provide them with the opportunity to achieve a better understanding of their learning process as well as of themselves as language learners.

Perezhivanie and the Inseparability of Cognition and Emotion

Emotion and cognition are dialectically connected, and have a significant impact on 'what has happened in the past, what is happening now, and what will happen in the future' (Swain, 2013: 195). As such, emotions are an integral part of cognition, shaping one another and mediating our actions and the way we experience the world. Indeed, according to Swain (2013), cognition and emotion are, at the very least, interdependent and, at the very maximum, integrated with one another. Vygotsky (1994) proposes the notion of *perezhivanie* to describe the functional unity of cognition and emotion that forms the lived experiences of human beings (Swain *et al.*, 2015). In his work, Vygotsky proposes that emotions, whether interpersonal or intra-personal, are always socially constructed and culturally derived. Indeed, *perezhivanie*:

> is always related to something which is found outside the person – *and on the other hand, what is represented is how I, myself, am experiencing this,* i.e., all the personal characteristics and all the environmental characteristics are represented in an emotional experience (*perezhivanie*); everything selected from the environment and all the factors which are related to our personality and are selected from the personality, all the features of its character, its constitutional elements, which are related to the event in question. So, *in an emotional experience (perezhivanie) we are always dealing with an indivisible unity of personal characteristics and situational characteristics, which are represented in the emotional experience (perezhivanie).* (Vygotsky, 1994: 342; italics in original)

In other words, *perezhivanie* does not refer to the experience itself, but rather it signals how a person interprets and experiences something, and how it transforms his/her consciousness. In the language classroom, *perezhivanie* refers to 'how [learners] are experiencing what they are learning' (Johnson, 2015: 255). In the case of teacher development, Johnson and Golombeck (2016) indicate that it is essential for educators to understand teachers' present and past *perezhivania* (e.g. current practices and apprenticeship) in order to adequately mediate based on how teachers experience and respond to their own pedagogical endeavors. To understand development as *perezhivanie*, I propose that it is fundamental to understand (1) how emotions draw from – and foster – cognition; (2) how to effectively mediate activity in the cognitive-emotive dialectic; and (3) how teachers, as learners, make meaning and transform their consciousness through crises. Although I will talk in depth about these three issues in the next section, it is important to address the notion of crisis to understand how *perezhivanie* acts as a source and a driver of emocognitive development. *Perezhivanie* as crisis is generally characterized as 'high intensity of emotions, uncertainty and controversy between the existing understanding and new knowledge' (Dema, 2015: 41), and triggers the reconstruction of a deeply rooted emotional and cognitive experience that has been deemed insufficient (e.g. use of everyday knowledge and incomplete rules of thumb [ROTs] to orient aspectual choices in Spanish). In this sense, Vasilyuk (1992: 31) proposes that *perezhivanie* is 'a special activity that allows human beings to transform and reconstruct their psychological world, connecting consciousness and existence in terms of meaning'. This understanding of *perezhivanie* is directly linked to Vygotsky's own conception of development as 'a contradictory process characterized by longer periods of gradual growth interspersed with shorter periods of crisis and transition during which qualitative restructuring of mental functions takes place' (Mahn, 2003: 123). However short, crises and their resolution are very challenging tasks that require intensive work of consciousness through reflection on the new experience, the surrounding conditions, one's self-worth and the construction of new meanings (Dema, 2015: 41). Importantly, crises are not necessarily preceded by conflicting or negative emotions (e.g. negative feedback and being reprimanded), and may very well be motivated by positive attitudes toward new experiences (e.g. receiving a good grade or outcome, positive reinforcement). In essence, *perezhivanie* as crisis does transform our consciousness through moments of realization, which result from activities such as reflection on a new experience, re-evaluation of the surrounding conditions and self-worth, and obtaining new meanings (Dema, 2015: 41–42). As such, these moments of realization are always in motion (Swain, 2013), and experienced socially, either with the self (i.e. private speech) or with others (i.e. collaborative dialogue).

Emocognitive research on L2 development

While researchers in positive psychology have stressed the importance of the emocognitive component in promoting teacher and learner development (see MacIntyre *et al.*, 2016), SLA researchers 'rarely deal with these topics' (MacIntyre & Mercer, 2014: 156). Indeed, while interest in this topic has grown over the last few years, only a few studies address emocognitive factors in the L2 classroom from an SLA perspective (Arshavskaya, 2014; Golombek & Doran, 2014; Golombek & Johnson, 2004; Johnson & Worden, 2014; Poehner & Swain, 2016; Swain, 2013). These investigations emphasize the importance of attending to learners' emotive and cognitive needs by providing mediation that not only addresses their linguistic shortcomings (grammatical errors, lexical choices and pragmatic violations), but also their emotional needs, dealing with their doubts, feelings of frustration and/or incompetence. Poehner and Swain (2016), for example, examined the case of an English language learner who participated in a series of collaborative revision sessions that took place within the context of the university's writing program. The manifestations of the emotive reported during dialogic interactions between the mediator and the student indicated that emotion and cognition are dialectically connected, in that 'each shapes the other and how either may gain prominence during particular moments in development' (Poehner & Swain, 2016: 236).

In addition to the studies centered on L2 learners, there is also research dedicated to the analysis of the emocognitive in language teachers (Arshavskaya, 2014; Golombek & Doran, 2014; Golombek & Johnson, 2004; Johnson & Worden, 2014). Unlike the present study, however, investigations on teachers' conceptual development and *perezhivanie* only involved the participation of pre-service and novice teachers. These individuals, who were always mediated by a more expert instructor, were provided with emotional and cognitive support during dialogical interactions (i.e. mediated interviews) or written reflections (journals, blogs or reports). One of the most relevant notions raised by this body of work is that of *feeling-for-thinking*, modeled after Slobin's (1987) *thinking-for-speaking*, which embodies the need to address teachers' emotions so that conceptual development can eventually take place. This stems from the idea that teachers' emotions are particularly important in the case of expert L2 instructors, who often have a rather firm set of beliefs due to their extensive previous experience (Borg, 2011). In fact, it is by taking into account these emotional manifestations that one can document and resolve the contradictions that emerge between their standard practices and their evolving conceptual development. Drawing from Johnson and Worden (2014) and Swain (2013), the present study analyzes teachers' emocognitive manifestations in the context of dialogic interaction, and the ways in which *perezhivanie*, the unity of emotion and cognition (Vygotsky, 1994), can be both a marker and a trigger for L2 in-service (practicing) teachers' conceptual development.

The Study

Most pedagogical models dedicated to the teaching of foreign languages in the US follow a 'rules of thumb' approach (Negueruela, 2003), which tend to ignore how conceptual categories of meaning are formed in the L2. This is the case for the grammatical concept of aspect in the Spanish L2 classroom. One of the dangers of implementing this type of approach (i.e. ROTs) to teach aspect to L2 learners and in-service teachers – even those whose native language is Spanish – is that these simplified explanations eventually become part their own linguistic and pedagogical beliefs (Williams *et al.*, 2013). To confront this issue, participants in this study were exposed to a concept-based model for the teaching and learning of aspectual distinctions. In this approach, learners are actively encouraged to interact with complex grammatical notions (i.e. mood, voice, aspect) in significant, coherent and systematic ways to create new meanings in the target language. The process of materialization, manipulation and transformation of these conceptual understandings is deemed essential to promote linguistic development and critical language awareness in students as well their teachers (García, 2017, 2018; Negueruela & García, 2016). In this study, concept-based instruction was implemented as follows: Participants were first exposed to a complete and systematic aspectual explanation in the form of three concise visual representations based on García (2012), Negueruela (2003) and Yáñez-Prieto (2008) so they could manipulate those models, assign them functional value and create meaning through them in communicative activity. After that, participants engaged in dialogic interaction – with themselves or with their peers – to convey their conceptual understanding through written and/or oral verbalizations (Negueruela & García, 2016), with the goal of transforming their aspectual understanding as a first step toward internalization of this grammatical notion.

Participants and Methodology

This chapter includes the data of three experienced in-service teachers of Spanish as an L2 whose L1 was Spanish. All participants were students in a graduate teacher education program, and enrolled in an advanced Spanish grammar and linguistics course. All participants were exposed to two sessions of enrichment models to L2 instruction (i.e. concept-based instruction) that they could potentially implement in their own classes. Prior to the pedagogical implementation, participants completed a modified version of the DELE test (Diploma de español como Lengua Extranjera; Montrul & Slabakova, 2003) to measure their proficiency in the language.

As illustrated in Table 8.1, Glinda, Naomi and Michelle (all pseudonyms) had been residing in the US for more than 15 years at the time of the interview; however, they had all completed their undergraduate education in their respective countries (Puerto Rico and Nicaragua). All three instructors were bilingual in English and Spanish (their dominant language as shown by their DELE results), and had an extensive background as language teachers. While Glinda and Naomi had taught mainly at the K-12 level, Michelle had worked in her native country, Nicaragua, teaching Spanish to college students in an immersion setting for more than 20 years before moving to the US. The selection of three highly experienced and highly proficient L2 instructors in the present study was not random; it was specifically aimed at exploring the role

Table 8.1 Personal background of participating students

Name	Place of Birth	Age of onset		DELE results (proficiency)	Years teaching Spanish (level)
		Spanish	English		
Glinda	Puerto Rico	0;0	5;0	100% (50/50)	8 (K-12 and college)
Naomi	Puerto Rico	0;0	36;0	98% (49/50)	19 (K-12)
Michelle	Nicaragua	0;0	15;0	94% (47/50)	25 (K-12 and college)

of dialogic interaction in the co-construction of conceptual language awareness in a population that was likely to exhibit a rather firm set of beliefs regarding the nature and use of certain grammatical notions (for a detailed review of this topic, see Borg, 2011).

The data presented in this chapter were part of a larger project examining the development of conceptual categories of meaning (i.e. aspect) in heritage language learners (García & Perez-Cortes, ms), and pre-service and in-service teachers (García, in press) whose dominant language was Spanish. In order to explore this issue, a study was conducted over a period of 14 weeks at a public university located in the US Northeast, including multiple sets of data aimed at exploring participants development as a conceptual process (i.e. definition data, where participants explained their aspectual understanding; performance data, where participants had to write narratives in the past based on a series of comic strips; verbalization data collected during mediated interviews; and personal reflection data). These data were gathered in the context of mediated interviews, classroom observations and blog posts (for more information, see García, in press). Given the scope and the objective of this chapter, only data collected during two mediated interviews will be reported. These dialogic interactions, aimed at fostering the co-construction of conceptual meaning, took place twice: before and after being exposed to a concept-based approach to the teaching and learning of aspect (i.e. Spanish preterit and imperfect aspectual contrasts). During these sessions, participants engaged individually in mediated interviews with the researcher (me) where they were prompted to reflect on their use of preterit and imperfect in the previously written elicited narrations. Teachers were also encouraged to talk about their understanding of the concept of aspect, while they received mediation, based on their answers and observations, designed to support their developing aspectual awareness. Both mediated interviews drew from interactionist models of dynamic assessment to promote collaborative dialogue. In this form of assessment 'performance belongs neither to the mediator nor to the learner but comprises the interplay between them as they raise questions, debate ideas, brainstorm alternatives, offer explanations and jointly work out solutions to assessment tasks' (Poehner, 2008: 38). Some exchanges that occurred during the mediated interviews were also designed to promote artificial crises targeted at transforming teachers' grammatical and pedagogical beliefs through conscious manipulation (García, 2018) of the models introduced during the concept-based instruction sessions. As the next section illustrates, these cognitive-emotive episodes often surfaced as a by-product of engaging instructors in dialectical conceptualizations (Negueruela-Azarola, 2011) that either directly or indirectly challenged their knowledge and beliefs about Spanish grammar and how to teach it. Given their expertise and established mastery as language instructors, in addition to their status as L1 speakers of Spanish, some of these interactions gave way to rather emotional reactions (i.e. crises) that prompted further conceptual development. This seems to follow Poehner and Swain's (2016: 236) observations that the emotive and the cognitive are dialectically united, and that the former should be considered 'as an additional factor that might influence the cognitive process of L2 development'.

Data Analysis and Discussion

The following section examines the data obtained over the course of two mediated interviews before and after being exposed to a concept-based approach to the teaching and learning of aspect. In order to analyze these data, the dialogic interactions between three in-service teachers (Glinda, Michelle and Naomi) and a mediator were transcribed and analyzed paying particular attention to any emotive/cognitive episodes that triggered development in the instructors' conceptual awareness and understanding of the grammatical notion of aspect (see Appendix for transcription conventions).

Mediating activity and the cognitive-emotive dialectic

When examining the dialectic between the cognitive-emotive in mediated interviews, it is important to take into account what Poehner and Swain (2016) refer to as 'mediator emotionality'. That is, the analysis of the mediator's emotions that regulate learners' emotions or are affected by them (Poehner & Swain, 2016: 237). In this first example, Glinda and the mediator are discussing the use of the preterit form *llegó* ('arrived') instead of its imperfect counterpart (*llegaba*; 'arrived') in the sentence *Cuando la policía llegó* ('When the policemen arrived' [PRET]). In order to engage her in elaborating more on her answers, the mediator called forth her expertise as a language teacher:

1 MED: *Si tú vieras que tu estudiante te pregunta '¿Por qué dice llegó y no llegaba?' ¿Qué dirías?*
'If one of your students asked you, 'Why did you use arrived [PRET] and not arrived [IMP]?', what would you say?'

2 GLI: *Porque es una acción que: que tiene que terminar [...] que ocurre solamente una vez.*
'Because it's an action that: that has to end [...] that happens only once'.

By being asked about her opinion as a language professional, Glinda seemed to feel more comfortable sharing her beliefs regarding the use of these two tenses. This, in turn, revealed her dependence on simplified ROTs that might have been limiting her aspectual choices and teaching practices (Turn 2).

The role of the mediator was also the key to creating a relaxed environment in which in-service teachers were able to express their beliefs about the concept at hand (i.e. aspect) and its presentation in the language classroom. In the following episode, for example, the mediator and the teacher have been engaged in a discussion about a particularly ambiguous sentence for a rather long period time. At a certain point, the mediator senses that the teacher is starting to get frustrated, and, as a result, offers a small break in the conversation:

1 MED: *Perdón estoy haciendo un poco el abogado del diablo* ((both laughing))
'Sorry, I am playing devil's advocate'
2 GLI: *Sí: no pero si yo digo todos estuvieron felices y contentos bueno también pero no sé qué pasó donde el hospital*
'Yes: no but if I say that they were [PRET] all happy well yeah but I don't know what happened at the hospital'
3 MED: *Claro*
'Of course'
4 GLI: *Por eso yo estaba + estaba aquí y yo puse todos vivieron porque estoy imaginando qué pasó*
'That's why I was + I was here and I wrote 'lived' [PRET] because I am imagining what happened'
5 MED: *OK + Perfecto + eh vamos a pasar la página*
'OK + Perfect + eh let's turn the page'
6 GLI: Ay sí profesor ((laughing))
'Please, professor' ((laughing))

In this excerpt, the mediator appealed to humor to resolve a tense situation where Glinda is unable to provide a clear answer as to why she had used one particular verbal form over another. Despite this participant's visible frustration, she seems rather relieved when the mediator proposes to turn the page to end the current exchange (Turn 6), and, as a result, Glinda manages to elaborate on her response a bit more. This suggests that regulating teachers' emotion during interactions where manipulation of complex grammatical concepts such as aspect takes place might facilitate, rather than stall, L2 conceptual development.

Emotions as a reflection of cognition

As suggested by Johnson and Worden (2014: 145), teachers and teacher-educators collaborative dialogue 'creates multiple opportunities for teachers to externalize their thinking and, in particular, to become consciously aware of moments of cognitive/emotional dissonance'. This is precisely the case in the following example, where Glinda reacted to the mediator's request to clarify why she chose one tense (preterit) over another (imperfect) in a sentence – indirectly introducing the notion of aspectual contrasts:

1 GLI: *Dije que 'fui todas las semanas' pero ya no + ya no voy*
'I said that 'I went [PRET] every week' but I don't + I don't go there anymore'
2 MED: *Mhm ¿Y algo más?*
'And anything else?'
3 GLI: *Mhm como que la acción ya se completó*
'Like the action was already completed'
4 MED: *¿Cuándo se completó?*
'When was it completed?'
5 GLI: **Eeeeehm: +++ bueno profesor**
'**Eeeeehm: +++ bueno profesor**'
6 MED: **((laughing))**
7 GLI: **((laughing))** *para MÍ*
'**((laughing))** in MY opinion'
8 MED: **Lo siento por todas las preguntas**
'**I apologize for all the questions**'
9 GLI: **No no no [...]** *Me ayuda muchísimo*
'**No no no [...]** it helps me a lot'
10 GLI: *Porque ++ yo primera la primera vez que completé las oraciones + yo vi el año pasado y rápidamente puse fui pero cuando terminé de leer todo + que veo todas las semanas para mí es una marca una continuidad*
'Because ++ when I first completed the sentences + I saw 'last year' and I quickly wrote 'went' [PRET] but when I finished reading everything + I saw that 'every week' for me is a marker of continuity'

There are two details worth mentioning in the preceding excerpt. First, Glinda's frustration after a long period of questioning (i.e. the emotive) prompts a longer explanation regarding her cognitive process while completing the activity, which had not appeared until that moment (Turn 10). This episode is the perfect example of what Johnson and Worden (2014: 129–130) define as *growth points*, that is, 'an instantiation of a dialectic "coming into being" in specific contexts [that] can, with strategic mediation, fuel development'. In fact, it is partly due to the relaxed atmosphere created by the mediator, who apologized for his insistence, that Glinda seemed to increase her willingness to elaborate on her response.

A similar scenario occurred during Michelle's session. After being confronted about the ambiguity of one of her explanations regarding the functions of preterit and imperfect, she answers the mediator's questions with the following retort:

1 MIC: *Ya sé donde quiere llegar*
'I know where you're heading with this'
2 MED: *No, no, no*
3 MIC: ((laughs))
4 MED: *Simplemente quiero ver cómo percibes esto + no hay problema*
'I just want to see how you perceive this + no problem'

The presence of this type of humorous comment (Turn 1) suggests that Michelle is aware of the shortcomings of her own definitions of perfective and imperfective aspect. In this case, the emotion expressed by Michelle acts as a window into her developing grammatical awareness, revealing an emerging cognizance of her conflicting understanding of aspect observed in her previous incomplete explanations. Intense mediation was also the kernel of Michelle's emotive reaction featured in the next excerpt. As a result of being extensively questioned about the rationale behind her aspectual choices, Michelle felt the need to defend herself by alluding to her expertise teaching Spanish and the fact that the teaching training she received might be the cause of her shortcomings:

1 MIC: *Esto es lo que yo aprendí, ¿me comprende?*
'This is what I learned, do you understand?'
2 MED: *[Claro]*
'Of course'
3 MIC: *y en el (año) ochenta y ocho estábamos sujetos a las reglas + estas reglas*
'And in the (year) eighty eight we were subject to the rules + these rules'
4 MED: *Está bien + está bien*

'it's ok + it's ok'
5 MIC: *Pero ahora que ya estoy en el curso +*
*pues + entonces hasta yo misma y **le estoy viendo***
sentido
'but now that I am in this class + well + then
even **I am making sense of it**'
6 MIC: *[que] realmente yo sea flex + que ahora **la***
verdad que da miedo pues está siendo muy flexible
con el uso de los verbos
'that I can be truly flex + that now **the truth**
is that it's scary to be this flexible with the
use of verbs'

As illustrated in the previous excerpt, Michelle's comments made reference to her previous training and the emphasis it placed on following simplified ROTs to teach complex grammatical notions (Turn 3). Interestingly, sharing this personal experience opened up the discussion, revealing her true feelings regarding the implementation of the new pedagogical approach and the conceptual tools that she had been exposed to. As she mentions during her intervention (Turn 6), the lack of rules and increased flexibility proposed by this new way of teaching aspect *da miedo* ('is scary'), as she now has to exercise her agency instead of surrendering it to external tools that control her decisions (i.e. ROTs).

Perezhivanie: Meaning-making through crisis

The previous excerpts provided examples of how in-service teachers' emotions and cognition are clearly intertwined in the context of dialogic interactions. This section will go one step further, exploring how emotional and cognitive crises triggered moments of dissonance that culminated in the teachers' growth with respect to their developing conceptual awareness and understanding of aspect. In the following episode, for instance, Glinda argued whether both tenses (preterit and imperfect) could be pragmatically adequate in the context of the sentence *Pepito tuvo una fractura en la pierna* ('Pepito had [PRET] a leg fracture'):

1 MED: *OK. Y ¿por qué tuvo?*
'Ok. And why 'had' [PRET]?'
2 GLI: *[…] Otra vez puede ser tuvo o puede ser*
tenía porque sí puede ehm + sí puede ser tenía
por la descripción pero más bien en el momento
que estaba escribiendo la selección
'[…] Again it can be 'had' [PRET] or 'had' [IMP]
because yes it can ehm it can be 'had' [IMP]

because of the description but more because of
the moment when I was writing the selection'
3 GLI: *Pero ++ pero profesor*
'But ++ but professor'
4 GLI: *Pero yo puse tuvo una fractura porque me
estaba refiriendo a lo que pasó en el accidente
pero sí + vamos por eso digo pues **está también
tenía. Pero a mi: no sé ++ mi perspectiva + puse
tuvo pero también se puede decir tenía***
'I wrote 'had' [PRET] a fracture because I was
referring to what happened at the accident but
yes + that is why I say there is also 'had'
[IMP]. But to me: I don't know ++ my perspective + I wrote 'had' [PRET] but you could also
say 'had' [IMP]'

Although Glinda accurately acknowledged that both tenses could be
used in the context provided (Turn 2), her immediate follow-up reflection
(Turn 3) revealed that she was, in fact, not entirely sure of her previous claims, which may have been partially prompted by the mediator's
insistence on considering all grammatical possibilities (Turns 3 and 4).
Her insecurity is detected in the use of expressions such as *no sé* ('I don't
know') and the need to emphasize that her answers derive from *mi perspectiva* ('my perspective'), suggesting that further mediation and conceptual manipulation might be needed. In this example, the emergence of
the emotive is a manifestation of a potential gap in Glinda's conceptual
knowledge connected to the cognitive.

The interview between Naomi and the mediator also included an
instance of crisis that ended up revealing her struggles, eventually trigger-
ing a more elaborate explanation on the teacher's behalf:

1 MED: *[…] Imagínate que es un + que soy uno de
tus chicos y te preguntaba+ 'Profesora + ¿Por
qué estaba y no estuvo?*
'Imagine that it's one + I am one of your students and I asked you + 'Professor + why *estaba*
[IMP] and not was (PRET)?'
2 NAO: *+++ Mm+++ No sé. (laughs) Le digo a mi
estudiante + No sé*
'+++ Mm+++ I don't know (laughs) I will tell my
student that I don't know'
3 NAO: *Es tarde en el día y no puedo pensar*
'It is late in the afternoon and I can't think'
4 MED: *((laughs)) Se pierde mucho*
'It's tough'

5 NAO: *++ Yo creo que estoy lo + lo que dije en parte del informe + profesor +* **Estoy jugando con los dos tiempos**
'++ I think that I am ++ that what I said in parts of my report + professor + **I am playing with the two tenses**'
6 NAO: *Y creo que lo expliqué así + indistintamente estoy usando uno y otro*
'And I think that I explained it like this + that I am using one and the other indistinctly'
7 MED: ok
8 NAO: *Así que* **realmente lo estoy llevando + por + por la música**
'So **I am truly Like picking +what +what sounds best**'

After being engaged in the dialogical interaction for a while, Naomi reached a point where she was no longer able to respond to the requests of the mediator (Turns 2 and 3). Despite the small crisis, the relaxed atmosphere of the activity provided invaluable information about her cognitive processes when dealing with aspectual contrasts. Specifically, she confessed that she was not following any particular model or rule when choosing between preterit and imperfect, and that she was using these tenses based on auditory familiarity, a very common criterion among native speakers and heritage language learners (Liskin-Gasparro, 2000).

Crises, however, do not necessarily have to be negative or frustrating for the individual; in fact, they are defined as moments of change, emotional and enlightening experiences that are transformative in nature, where growth and development can occur (Kozulin, 2003; Vygotsky, 1994). In contrast with the previous examples, where *perezhivanie* as seen through crises were characterized as either negative events or cognitively taxing experiences, the next excerpt illustrates an example of a positive emotional episode that fostered conceptual development.

Before the start of the interview, Naomi was asked to complete a report regarding the use of preterit and imperfect and her understanding of aspect. During her conversation with the mediator, she recalled a positive development in her conceptual awareness that impacted the way she explained these tenses' uses to herself – and consequently, to her students:

1 NAO: *Ah:: de hecho una +* **una de las cosas que más me gustó del informe** *que hice fue* **entender**
'Ah:: in fact one + **one of the things that I liked the most from the report** was being able to **understand**'

2 MED: *Sí*
'Yes'

3 NAO: *Primero **me encantó** la relación de que + de que el pretérito y el imperfecto yo podía usar para decir el tiempo como quiera distintamente (e ignorar) las reglas tan + tan categóricas*
'First **I loved** that the fact that + that the preterit and the imperfect I can use to tell the time how I want indistinctly (and ignore) such categorical rules'

4 NAO: ***Pero + eh:-so me gusto + sobre todo me gustó + la libertad que tengo yo como hablante para escoger mi tiempo + para expresar mi ideas***
'**But + eh:-so I liked it + I particularly liked + the freedom I have as a speaker to choose the tense + to express my ideas**'

5 MED: *Claro*
'Of course'

6 NAO: *Sé que no es + eh yo no me voy a llevar por esas reglas + las reglas van a avisar lo que yo trato de hacer*
'I know that it is not + eh that I won't depend on those rules + but the rules will express what I am trying to convey'

7 NAO: *Usted no me está diciendo que lo que yo elegí está mal + está bien porque [...] quiero mandar un mensaje ++ fue mi decisión decirlo de esta manera*
'You are not telling me that what I chose is wrong + it's ok because [...] I want to send a message ++ it was my decision to saying it like this'

As she pointed out in the previous exchange, Naomi was inspired by the new pedagogical approach and how it explained the aspectual contrasts between preterit and imperfect. Her positive reaction to the provided conceptual tool, as reflected in Turn 3 with *me encantó* ('I loved [it]'), mediated her cognition and allowed her to transform her beliefs and develop a conceptual understanding that was not there before. This moment of enlightenment, of *perezhivanie*, enabled her to transform the concept to make it her own, and gain a much deeper understanding of a complex grammatical notion (i.e. aspect), as seen in her conceptualizations in Turns 4, 6 and 7. These moments exemplify the inseparability between emotion and cognition in the internalization of functional categories of meaning such as the concept of aspect.

Conclusion

The goal of exposing teachers to the co-construction of knowledge through dialogic interaction as well as a concept-based approach to the teaching of aspectual contrasts in Spanish was threefold: On the one hand, it was expected that this approach would allow them to transform their pedagogical beliefs in relation to the concept of aspect. It was also predicted that it would help them regain agency in their L1 in relation to the concept of aspect – which had been previously constrained by incomplete ROTs offered by the Spanish textbooks with which they taught – as they transformed their aspectual understanding through the formation of new functional meanings. Finally, exposure to these techniques and approaches was meant to change how teachers think about language teaching and their own pedagogical performance in the classroom. As observed in this chapter, these changes were not purely cognitive, but mediated by their experiences and emotions as language teachers and native speakers of Spanish. Looking at development as the unity of emotion and cognition among experienced teachers of Spanish, as has been done in the present chapter, provided necessary opportunities to observe how teachers' emotions fostered, and were impacted by, their cognition. It also allowed me to effectively mediate developmental activity in the cognitive-emotive dialectic: by creating crises through collaborative dialogue during mediated interviews, teachers were afforded the opportunity to make meaning and transform their consciousness in relation to the concept of aspect.

As suggested by Golombek and Johnson (2004) and Golombek and Doran (2014), teachers should be encouraged to exercise *feeling-for-thinking* in the type of dialogic interactions described in the present study, where the presence of a mediator can help them verbalize their emotions and address, and/or identify, any issues that might be hindering their conceptual development. As has been shown in the data, and elsewhere in the literature (Johnson & Worden, 2014; Poehner & Swain, 2016; Swain, 2013), this window into teachers' and learners' emotions and cognition can be a very effective tool for revealing how they see their own learning. In turn, this information has the potential to promote meaningful emo-cognitive development by artificially creating crisis during collaborative dialogue.

References

Arshavskaya, E. (2014) Analyzing mediation in dialogic exchanges in a pre-service second language (L2) teacher practicum blog: A sociocultural perspective. *System* 45, 129–137.

Borg, S. (2011) The impact of in-service teacher education on language teachers' beliefs. *System* 39, 370–380.

Brooks, L. and Swain, M. (2009) Languaging in collaborative writing: Creation of and response to expertise. In A. Mackey and C. Polio (eds) *Multiple Perspectives on Interaction in SLA* (pp. 58–89). Mahwah, NJ: Lawrence Erlbaum.

Brooks, L., Swain, M., Lapkin, S. and Knouzi, I. (2010) Mediating between scientific and spontaneous concepts through languaging. *Language Awareness* 19 (2), 89–110.

Dema, A. (2015) The development of language and identity: A sociocultural study of five international graduate students living in the US. Unpublished PhD thesis, University of Nevada.

García, P.N. (2012) Verbalizing in the second language classroom: The development of the grammatical concept of aspect. Unpublished doctoral dissertation, University of Massachusetts.

García, P.N. (2017) A pedagogical proposal for implementing concept-based instruction in the heritage language classroom. *Euro American Journal of Applied Linguistics and Languages (E-JournALL)* 4 (1), 1–19.

García, P.N. (2018) Concept-based instruction: Investigating the role of conscious conceptual manipulation in L2 development. In J.P. Lantolf and M.E. Poehner (eds) *The Routledge Handbook of Sociocultural Theory and Second Language Development* (pp. 181–196). New York: Routledge.

García, P.N. (in press) Dynamic assessment: Promoting in-service teachers' conceptual development and pedagogical beliefs in the L2 classroom. *Language and Sociocultural Theory*.

García, P.N. and Perez-Cortes, S. (ms) Developing grammatical categories of meaning through mediated verbalizations in the heritage language classroom.

Golombek, P.R. and Johnson, K.E. (2004) Narrative inquiry as a mediational space: Examining emotional and cognitive dissonance in second-language teachers' development. *Teachers and Teaching* 10 (3), 307–327.

Golombek, P.R. and Doran, M. (2014) Unifying cognition, emotion, and activity in language teacher professional development. *Teaching and Teacher Education* 39, 102–111.

Johnson, K. (2015) Reclaiming the relevance of L2 teacher education. *The Modern Language Journal* 99 (3), 515–528.

Johnson, K. and Worden, D. (2014) Cognitive/emotional dissonance as growth points in learning to teach. *Language and Sociocultural Theory* 1 (2), 125–150.

Johnson, K. and Golombeck, P. (2016) *Mindful Teacher Education: A Sociocultural Perspective on Cultivating Teachers' Professional Development.* New York: Routledge.

Knouzi, I., Swain, M., Lapkin, S. and Brooks, L. (2010) Self-scaffolding mediated by languaging: Microgenetic analysis of high and low performers. *International Journal of Applied Linguistics* 20, 23–49.

Kozulin, A. (2003) Psychological tools and mediated learning. In A. Kozulin, B. Gindis, V.S. Ageyev and S.M. Miller (eds) *Vygotsky's Educational Theory in Cultural Context* (pp. 15–38). Cambridge: Cambridge University Press.

Lantolf, J. and Pavlenko, A. (1998) (S)econd (L)anguage (A)ctivity: Understanding learners as people. Paper presented at the 1998 Annual Meeting of the American Association for Applied Linguistics, Seattle, Washington.

Lapkin, S., Swain, M. and Psyllakis, P. (2010) The role of languaging in creating zones of proximal development (ZPDs): A long-term care resident interacts with a researcher. *Canadian Journal on Aging* 29, 477–490.

Liskin-Gasparro, J. (2000) The use of tense-aspect morphology in Spanish oral narratives: Exploring the perceptions of advanced learners. *Hispania* 83, 830–844.

Mahn, H. (2003) Periods in child development. In A. Kozulin, B. Gindis, V.S. Ageyev and S.M. Miller (eds) *Vygotsky's Educational Theory in Cultural Context* (pp. 119–137). Cambridge: Cambridge University Press.

MacIntyre, P. and Mercer, S. (2014) Introducing positive psychology to SLA. *Studies in Second Language Learning and Teaching* 4 (2), 153–172.

MacIntyre, P., Gregersen, T. and Mercer, S. (2016) *Positive Psychology in SLA.* Bristol: Multilingual Matters.

Montrul, S. and Slabakova, R. (2003) Competence similarities between natives and near-native speakers: An investigation of the preterit/imperfect contrast in Spanish. *Studies in Second Language Acquisition* 25, 351–398.

Negueruela, E. (2003) Systemic-theoretical instruction and L2 development: A sociocultural approach to teaching-learning and researching L2 learning. Unpublished PhD thesis, Pennsylvania State University.

Negueruela, E. and García, P.N. (2016) Sociocultural theory and the language classroom. In G. Hall (ed.) *The Routledge Handbook of English Language Teaching* (pp. 295–309). New York: Routledge.

Negueruela-Azarola, E. (2011) Beliefs as conceptualizing activity: A dialectical approach for the second language classroom. *System* 39 (3), 359–369.

Poehner, M.E. (2008) *Dynamic Assessment: A Vygotskian Approach to Understanding and Promoting L2 Development*. Berlin: Springer.

Poehner, M. and Swain, M. (2016) L2 development as cognitive-emotive process. *Language and Sociocultural Theory* 3 (2), 219–241.

Slobin, D. (1987) Thinking for speaking. In L. Aske, N. Beery, L. Michaelis and H. Filip (eds) *Papers from the 13th Annual Meeting of the Berkeley Linguistics Society* (pp. 435–444). Berkeley, CA: Berkeley Linguistics Society.

Swain, M. (2000) The output hypothesis and beyond: Mediating acquisition through collaborative dialogue. In J.P. Lantolf (ed.) *Sociocultural Theory and Second Language Learning* (pp. 97–114). Oxford: Oxford University Press.

Swain, M. (2006) Languaging, agency and collaboration in advanced second language proficiency. In H. Byrnes (ed.) *Advanced Language Learning: The Contribution of Halliday and Vygotsky* (pp. 95–108). London: Continuum.

Swain, M. (2010) Talking-it-through: Languaging as a source of learning. In R. Batestone (ed.) *Sociocognitive Perspectives on Language Use and Language Learning* (pp. 112–130). Oxford: Oxford University Press.

Swain, M. (2013) The inseparability of cognition and emotion in second language learning. *Language Teaching* 46, 195–207.

Swain, M. and Lapkin, S. (1998) Interaction and second language learning: Two adolescent French immersion students working together. *The Modern Language Journal* 82, 320–337.

Swain, M. and Lapkin, S. (2002) Talking it through: Two French immersion learners' response to reformulation. *International Journal of Educational Research* 37 (3–4), 285–304.

Swain, M. and Lapkin, S. (2011) Languaging as agent and constituent of cognitive change in an older adult: An example. *Canadian Journal of Applied Linguistics* 14 (1), 104–117.

Swain, M. and Lapkin, S. (2013) A Vygotskian sociocultural perspective on immersion education. *Journal of Immersion and Content-Based Language Education* 1 (1), 101–129.

Swain, M., Lapkin, S., Knouzi, I., Suzuki, W. and Brooks, L. (2009) Languaging: University students learn the grammatical concept of voice in French. *The Modern Language Journal* 93, 5–29.

Swain, M., Kinnear, P. and Steinman, L. (2015) *Sociocultural Theory in Second Language Education: An Introduction through Narratives* (2nd edn). Bristol: Multilingual Matters.

van Compernolle, R.A. and Henery, A. (2015) Learning to do concept-based pragmatic instruction: Teacher development and L2 pedagogical content knowledge. *Language Teaching Research* 9 (3), 351–372.

Vasilyuk, F.E. (1992) *The Psychology of Experiencing*. New York: New York University Press.

Vygotsky, L.S. (1994) The problem of the environment. In. R. van der Veer and J. Valsiner (eds) *The Vygotsky Reader* (pp. 338–354). Oxford: Blackwell.

Williams, L., Abraham, L.B. and Negueruela-Azarola, E. (2013) Using concept-based instruction in the L2 classroom: Perspectives from current and future language teachers. *Language Teaching Research* 17 (3), 363–381.

Yáñez-Prieto, M. (2008) On literature and the secret art of the invisible words: Teaching literature through language. Unpublished doctoral dissertation, The Pennsylvania State University.

Appendix: Transcription Conventions

+	Short pause
++	Long pause
+++	Very long pause
( )	Single parentheses indicates uncertain hearing
(xxx)	Unable to transcribe
(( ))	Double parentheses contain transcriber comments or descriptions
:	Indicates elongated delivery. Each colon represents one extra beat
underline	Indicate stress through pitch or amplitude
[...]	Indicates that a section of the transcript has been omitted
[	Begin of overlapping speech
]	End of overlapping speech
CAPITALS	Capital letters indicate markedly loud speech
ITALICS	Indicates that the speaker is using the target language (Spanish)
'	Beginning of translation
'	End of translation
BOLD	Added emphasis on relevant emocognitive episodes

9 Languaging in a Gerontological Context: From Conception to Realization

Sharon Lapkin

Context

In 2004, Merrill and I received funding from Canada's Social Sciences and Humanities Research Council (SSHRC) for a project entitled 'Sociocultural Perspectives on the Output Hypothesis: Three Contexts'. This chapter is related to the third of those contexts, a gerontological one, and tells the story of how insights gained from Merrill's research on second language learning in a French immersion setting informed a subsequent multiple case study in a long-term care facility. This shift in focus can be attributed to Merrill's developing the construct of languaging (Swain, 2006), to her life experiences and to her immense creativity.

Why did Merrill make the transition from a second language learning context to a gerontological one? Our research on the second language learning of French immersion students had been fueled by theoretical constructs developed by Merrill. The theoretical milestones in her thinking included comprehensible output, collaborative dialogue and finally languaging (see Lapkin, 2013). The second part of our funding proposal outlined a study that would examine the talk of immersion students (and other French second language students) who had reached the post-secondary level as they worked through cognitively complex language-related problems; we studied the students' learning in progress, documenting how the learners' languaging mediated their learning of a grammatical concept (Brooks *et al.*, 2010; Knouzi *et al.*, 2010; Swain *et al.*, 2009).

Building on the Vygotskian idea that social activity is a source of higher mental processes, and because of her personal experiences with her parents' cognitive decline, Merrill suggested that the impact of cognitively demanding talk (languaging) could usefully be explored in a new (for us) gerontological context. We wrote up these ideas as the third part of our funding application. At first, I thought that Merrill had taken leave of her senses, as we had never worked together outside the world of second language teaching and learning. I let myself be persuaded to do some relevant reading and to venture into the unknown with her. The adventure turned into a decade of research with many unforeseen and perhaps unforeseeable challenges and rewards!

Theoretical Basis

During the life of the project, Merrill refined and built upon the concepts of output and collaborative dialogue to develop the construct of languaging, the 'act of using language to mediate cognition – to bring thinking into existence' (Swain, 2010: 115). Unlike social chit-chat or superficial exchanges of information (e.g. 'what time does the train arrive from Montreal?' 'in half an hour'), languaging is effortful; languaging mediates our thinking, whether in speaking or in writing. In Merrill's words:

> In my view, the concept of languaging opens up how we might see the role of language in cognition: as an agent in the creation of higher mental processes and as a mediator of them. If it were not for language, how would we focus attention, consider the past, plan, and imagine the future? A person is also languaging when reasoning, problem-solving, and so forth. When language is used for these functions, the individual is languaging. My hypothesis is that if an older adult is *not* given opportunities to language, then the power to create meaning, to plan, to attend, to organize, and to problem solve will dissipate. Thus, one possible reason for mild cognitive loss among older adults may lie in the lack of opportunities they have to language. If opportunities are limited, then cognitive loss rather than cognitive maintenance or development might occur. If this is the case, then providing opportunities to language may be one route to cognitive maintenance and development, and positive affective change. (Swain, 2013: 5–6)

For this 'older adult' project, we hypothesized that one-on-one languaging between a research assistant and a long-term care resident with mild cognitive impairment would restore some aspects of memory and engender an enhanced sense of well-being in the older adult. While initially we focused on the idea of improvements in cognition, as we continued to work through the case studies comprising our project, we began to subscribe fully to Vygotsky's claim that: 'The separation of the intellectual side of our consciousness from its affective, volitional side is one of the fundamental flaws of all of traditional psychology...' (as cited in Wertsch, 1985: 189).

Steps Taken to Conceptualize and Design the Study

Once the project was funded, we organized a think-tank of about a dozen people, among them the project team and some of the researchers whose work we had cited to support our funding request. We also contacted a long-term care facility, Magnolia Place (MP, pseudonym), located within a reasonable distance of the university. When approached, the facility administration was sufficiently interested to send a representative to the meeting. During the meeting, we exchanged ideas to obtain a deeper understanding of relevant research findings and identify further reading that might be helpful. Among the topics that were discussed in some depth were the following:

- Types of activities that might successfully lead to languaging opportunities.
- The extent to which our intervention could vary from participant to participant.
- The necessity of 'training' the research team and the nature of that training.
- The measures/tests we should use for research credibility and to maximize the chance of documenting changes from pre- to post-test.

The long-term care facility expressed keen interest to be involved in our proposed research project; it would be their first venture into research and they wanted to build a research profile. Their relative inexperience with research would prove to be a significant challenge in getting the study off the ground.

Participant Selection

The proposal went through the university and MP ethics processes; individual permissions had to wait until the MP administrative staff had selected our participants. They did so based on the selection criteria that we had settled on after much discussion with the team and the think-tank consultants. These were:

- The presence of mild cognitive impairment.
- Social isolation.

The selection of participants was complex. We depended entirely on the MP staff to pull files of appropriate persons, based on the information in those files and their own knowledge of the individuals. Included in the files were the scores each resident had obtained upon admission to the facility on the Mini-Mental State Exam (MMSE; Folstein *et al.*, 1975), a measure used to assess cognitive ability (see Barkaoui *et al.*, 2011 for details) and capable of 'separating patients with and without cognitive impairment' (Barkaoui *et al.*, 2011: 64). With respect to the social isolation criterion, we were entirely in the hands of the staff to make that judgement; we had specified that target residents would be those who had few visitors and little meaningful contact with other residents or staff. I will say more about how the characteristics of the people chosen to participate matched up with our criteria below.

MP staff made a selection of five potential participants from whom they then obtained consent; in most cases it was necessary to send a letter of consent to the person holding power of attorney for the resident. Although the staff proceeded with good will, they failed in a few cases to think through their choices. A case in point: one participant had Parkinson's disease; his contributions to the languaging sessions were monosyllabic, such that the data we collected were too limited to be analyzed. We matched up the remaining four with two graduate students, along with Merrill and myself, in one-on-one pairings.

Volunteer/Researcher Training

We all attended a seminar given by MP staff to orient ourselves to the physical layout of the facility and to the routines in place. We became familiar with the residents' bill of rights, and we obtained police checks and TB tests as required of all volunteers. As a research team, we also gathered ideas for interactive activities that would elicit languaging from the participants; examples include reading newspaper/magazine articles together and discussing them, writing poetry, telling autobiographical narratives and so on. These ideas and others are summarized in a handbook we prepared (Swain & Lapkin, 2016) long after the termination of the project. The handbook is intended for volunteers in long-term care facilities and others interacting with older adults with mild memory loss.[1]

Instrument Selection

Barkaoui *et al.* (2011) describe in detail the measures we used in our research, including a critique of those instruments that developed as we became more familiar with them. Intended to measure cognition and affect in a pre-/post-test design, the measures were appropriate and respected in the gerontology field, although their use in our study presented unforeseen challenges. After the fact, we realized that staff in the facility were relatively inexperienced in research procedures, and many of the test data were rendered unusable. For example, we assumed that individual measures would be administered by the *same* staff member at both the pretest and post-test stages; but we failed to specify this procedure to the staff.

We ultimately chose three measures for our study and decided on a pretest/post-test design. These were:

(1) The MMSE (mentioned earlier), which is an objective measure of mental status; it measures orientation to time and place, attention and calculation, immediate and delayed recall and some language functions (Barkaoui *et al.*, 2011; Folstein *et al.*, 1975).

(2) The Geriatric Evaluation by Relatives Rating Instrument (GERRI), measuring perceptions of cognitive functioning, social functioning and mood (Schwartz, 1983). The latter instrument was to be completed by a relative or someone very familiar with the resident. In fact, it was a staff person who administered the GERRI (and not always the same staff person for pre- and post-tests). In at least one case (that of Mike, discussed below), it would have been possible to have the GERRI administered by a relative, resulting in more reliable and valid findings; unfortunately, we failed to specify that wherever possible, the person closest to the resident should complete the questionnaire. If that person were to be a staff member, he/she should administer both the pre- and post-tests.

(3) The Multifactorial Memory Questionnaire (MMQ) (Troyer & Rich, 2002); it is self-administered and therefore non-problematic.

In an article that followed data collection, Barkaoui *et al.* (2011) examined two of the older adult case studies in depth (Lapkin *et al.*, 2010; Swain *et al.*, 2013). The authors analyzed the pretest and post-test scores, comparing them to interview data from the two researchers who had been paired with the two residents in question. These interviews focused on the perceptions and assessments of the two researchers with respect to the items of all three of the measures used in the multiple case study. The interview data (and our data analyses) documented the process of cognitive and affective change. The fact that there were discrepancies between the 'objective' measures and the researcher perceptions led the research team to conclude: 'A pre-test/post-test design is limited in that it only answers the yes/no question of whether a change happened, but it does not capture the process of change and the nature and causes of change (or no change)' (Barkaoui *et al.*, 2011: 71).

Procedures

Each researcher made 10–12 visits to her participant. Each visit lasted approximately one hour and took place in the resident's room.[2] The visits spanned a 6–10 week period over the summer/fall of 2006. Each session was audio-recorded (our ethical clearance did not include permission to videotape in the facility) and transcribed in full. Qualitative data analyses ensued, including discourse analysis (Swain *et al.*, 2013) and microgenetic analysis (Lapkin *et al.*, 2010; Lenchuk & Swain, 2010; Motobayashi *et al.*, 2014). Microgenetic analysis, 'the study of the dynamic process of developmental change' (Wertsch & Hickman, 1987) is illustrated in the sections that follow; both Merrill and I used it to analyze selected excerpts of the transcripts of our interactions with the participants with whom we had been paired.

Introducing Mike

When I first met Mike,[3] he was 71 and had been living in MP for two years. Although he had daily visits from his wife, Anna, their interactions were reported to be routine and did not involve languaging. Mike had been a social activist during his life, and had participated in the resident's council at MP (an advisory committee of residents who represent the interests of all residents to the administration). At the time of our visits, however, Mike had discontinued his involvement. Some of the staff referred to him as depressed, although we do not know whether he had been diagnosed as such. At the pretest, Mike scored 26 on the MMSE, on the border between the lower end of normal cognitive function and mild dementia.

Mike self-identified as a musician; he was knowledgeable about individual composers and classical music and had played wind instruments as a young person. The radio in his room was always tuned to the publicly funded national station that played classical music for most of the day. He had five children with his first wife; one of those children visited once or twice a year.

A Languaging Activity

During our ninth session together, we discussed poetry (see Lapkin *et al.* [2010] for an extended example). In this case, we worked on interpreting a short poem by Edna St. Vincent Millay. Our interaction below constitutes languaging that instantiates cognitive effort and affective engagement. By this time, Mike and I had had eight visits (of just under an hour each), we had 'connected'; we respected each other's intellectual and personal qualities, and Mike was willing to 'buy into' each new activity that I suggested. Here is part of our discussion:

Turn number	Researcher (Sharon)	Turn number	Participant (Mike)
1	(hands Mike a sheet of paper with a poem in large print) Here…	2	What are we going to do with this [poem]?
3	Well we're going to read it and see if we know what it means; it's called the *First Fig*.	4	No, it's not helping (Sharon has turned on the light to try to help Mike see the enlarged poem better)
5	How about if I read it cause it's really short?	6	OK
7	It's only four lines long, and it says *My candle burns at both ends; It will not last the night; But ah, my foes, and oh, my friends-- It gives a lovely light!* Should I read it again?	8	That's uhh the same kind of poem that Blake wrote.
9	How is it the same?	10	It's allegorical.

11	Yes, so can we figure out what the allegory is? Should I read it again?	12	Yeah, please.
13	(reads poem again)	14	[long pause] I uh I think that means...[long pause] Uhh...No.
15	Well, let's see. *My candle burns at both ends* ... when we talk about burning the candle at both ends, we're talking about what?	16	Living life to the fullest.
17	Yes, I think that's it. OK, and then, *it will not last the night,* the candle will not last the night.	18	No. That means that life is short.
19	Uh huh. *But ah my foes and oh my friends* *It gives a lovely light.* So it's burning at both ends, it's going to be short and brilliant.	20	Yeah. [long pause] And...
21	And although *it will not last the night* *It gives a lovely light.*	22	Means life is good.
23	Yeah. While it's burning it's wonderful.	24	Yeah!
25	Yeah, I think that's what it is.	26	Yeah!

In Turn 2, Mike takes some initiative by asking what we will do with the poem I have handed him (in large print, because of his failing eyesight). When he has difficulty reading it, I read it aloud to him and he offers a comparison with William Blake (Turn 8); we had looked at one of Blake's poems together in a previous session. I inquire about the nature of the similarity, and Mike specifies that both poems are allegorical. I pursue this assertion, asking if he can explain, and reread the poem. Mike makes a heroic effort, marked by two long pauses in his response (Turn 14), and a final 'No', indicating that he is giving up. (I had seen him react this way in the past.) So, in Turn 15, I take the first line of the poem and ask Mike what it might mean, and he comes up with an interpretation in Turn 16, 'living life to the fullest'. I continue with the next line of the poem (Turn 17) and then repeat it, specifying that 'the candle will not last the night', and Mike acknowledges it, saying 'No'. He goes on to interpret the line as meaning that life is short. I agree (Turn 19) and read the remaining lines of the poem. Mike hesitates (Turn 20), so I rephrase/reread in Turn 21, and this triggers Mike's interpretation that 'life is good' in Turn 22. I echo that interpretation in the following turn 'while it's burning it's [life is] wonderful' and Mike agrees with an enthusiastic 'yeah!' (Turn 24).[4] The final two turns confirm the interpretation, with both of us expressing satisfaction and affection in our respective responses. Our delight is clear in the tone of these exclamations (Yeah!) in the audiotapes of our languaging session. Cognitive effort and affective engagement are both present and inextricable as we talk through (as we language) the Edna St. Vincent Millay poem.

In fact, after the above segment draws to a close, Mike offers more information about Edna St. Vincent Millay, saying that she had written love poems. When I offered to locate some of those, we laugh together as he rejects my offer, saying that I 'have too much on my plate'. He is recognizing that I usually leave each session with 'homework', and wants to spare me!

Introducing Alise

Aged 75 when we began data collection at MP, Alise had been a resident there for three years. She had had multiple sclerosis for about 20 years and used a wheelchair. She was always surrounded by books, cherished possessions in her world. Alise stated that she had no friends among the other residents (Lenchuk & Swain, 2010) and staff found Alise anti-social. Alise felt that the staff found her 'nuts', and Merrill also reported (in the journal she kept throughout her visits with Alise) that the staff treated her with condescension.

Alise had four children but was in contact on rare occasions with only one of them. Her MMSE score of 24 indicated that she had mild dementia. In view of her social isolation, she was enthusiastic about her visits with Merrill, who expressed great interest in Alise's life history. The varied topics Alise and Merrill talked about included religion, Richard Burton's life and performances, world history, immigration and racial discrimination, among others. In the segment of transcript reproduced below, Alise and Merrill are focusing on Alise's living through the Second World War in Latvia; she then spent a short time in Germany, before emigrating to the US and then Canada.

A Languaging Activity

The following excerpt occurs during Merrill's second visit to Alise, and illustrates how Merrill extracts the story of a key episode in Alise's life: 'leaving my country' (Turn 4). Poignantly, in their first meeting together, Alise indicated that there was 'nothing' interesting to say about her life. This remark stands in sharp contrast to excerpts such as the following one, in which Alise recounts dramatic events in her youth. In response to Merrill's question about her most unforgettable experience, Alise talks about the final period of the Second World War when Germany was retreating from Latvia (Turn 4). She clearly feels an affiliation with the Germans, in contrast to the Russians, who at the outset of the Second World War, were occupying Latvia, Estonia and Lithuania.

Turn number	Researcher (Merrill)	Turn number	Participant (Alise)
1	In your life, what's the most unforgettable experience you have had?	2	There were so many.
3	So many. Tell me about one.	4	...leaving my country. The Germans were there, they were losing the war, and they were going back to Germany, and for some crazy reason, they had asked anybody who wants to come, from Latvia to Germany...
5	One soldier...? Asked?	6	I don't know if it was one or if it was a group.
7	Uh huh.	8	But for some reason, I had said...or, I think my parents had said I could go.
9	Uh huh.	10	And, so I went with these Germans.
11	You, just by yourself	12	Yeah. And... there wasn't anything wrong; it was all sort of army like.[5]
13	Uh huh. So you were the only Latvian that went back to Germany with them?	14	No, not the only one, but in that group.
15	In that group? Uh huh.	16	But I wasn't there that long -- the war was over. Then ...uh, I got back to my own family, my brother found me.
17	In Germany?!	18	In Germany. I don't know how that came about.
19	Hmm.	20	But he found me and took me home.
21	So you went back to Latvia?	22	Yeah.
23	So, you went back to Latvia and you rejoined your family?	24	Yeah, but it wasn't under Germany any more – Germany lost the war.
25	Right.	26	And they simply left these countries that they had occupied...the Baltic states, and ... I don't know what else... Uh, that means we got freedom!

Merrill requests clarification about who invited Latvians to leave with the Germans (Turn 5) and Alise expresses uncertainty (Turn 6), but specifies in Turn 8 that probably her parents had given her permission to leave. Merrill keeps up the momentum of the story as Alise retrieves more information from her memory; notice Merrill's prompts and short questions in Turns 7, 9 and 11 as examples. Asking whether Alise was the only Latvian to go with the Germans (Turn 13) elicits from Alise that she was one of a group who left (Turn 14). Merrill's repeating 'in that group?' (Turn 15) keeps Alise languaging: we learn that shortly after arriving in Germany, the war ended and that somehow her brother found her there (Turn 16).

What an emotional impact those events must have had! We hear the feeling of surprise expressed in Merrill's clarification request cum exclamation 'In Germany?!' in Turn 17, echoed by Alise in the following turn. As we imagine a scenario where Alise's brother (who was in the German army) would actually reconnect with his sister so far from home, Alise sounds bewildered by how that reunion happened: 'I don't know how that came about'.

From Turns 7 through 20, then, we have evidence of the impact of languaging on both cognition (as Alise retrieves more details from her memory) about Alise's leaving Germany toward the end of the war) and affect (surprise, bewilderment) mingling together in the dramatic narrative.

The story continues with the siblings' return to Latvia to rejoin their family (Turns 20–23). Alise offers additional information in Turn 24, specifying that Latvia was no longer 'under Germany' because Germany had lost the war, and when prompted by Merrill (Turn 25), explains further that Germany abandoned the Baltic states that they had taken from Russia near the beginning of the war (Turn 26). The two long pauses during Turn 26 reflect the effort Alise is expending to reconstruct details of that period of wartime history; for example, she talks first about 'these countries that they had occupied' and then specifies 'the Baltic states'. Her languaging in that turn reflects both the cognitive effort Alise is making to access her memories and recount a coherent story, and a feeling of exhilaration in the exclamation: 'that means we got freedom!'

Shortly after the excerpt of transcript analyzed above, Alise declares: 'I hate war and everything about wars!' She explains: 'there were people who were worse off… who lost their countries and families' and concludes that she 'was lucky'. Recreating and recalling this part of her life history reminds Alise that she has been fortunate; this activity makes substantive demands on Alise's cognitive resources and is emotionally charged throughout. As Poehner and Swain (2016: 227) explain, Vygotsky teaches us that one cannot separate the cognitive from the emotive without 'separating the thinking of human beings from the fullness of their real lives'.

Summary and Concluding Thoughts

As veteran researchers in applied linguistics, Merrill and I submitted a funding proposal that included well-defined goals and a robust design. Once funded, we consulted experts in gerontology and studied instruments that would, in principle, enable us to measure change. We encountered unexpected obstacles, in part because we had to rely on MP staff to select participants who did not always conform to our selection criteria.

We made erroneous assumptions about how and by whom the instruments we used in the study would be administered. We trusted that quantitative measures in a pretest/post-test design would yield evidence of change over time. Initially, we underestimated the key role of researcher perceptions of change, and the power of our qualitative data analyses to document changes in cognition and affect in our participants.

In this chapter, I selected excerpts from the transcripts that have not previously (in our published work) been the focus of our microgenetic analyses to illustrate the positive impact that languaging can have on both cognition and well-being. We witnessed languaging enable Mike to interpret a poem and Alise to reconstruct a narrative of part of her life history. Merrill and I shared their emotions – Mike's elation as he succeeded in interpreting a poem and Alise's 'feeling lucky' that she and her family successfully survived the war – emotions that unfolded during our discussions with these residents. In our publications on the older adult project, we have documented cognitive change and enhanced self-esteem among our participants. We have realized that, as Vygotsky suggested, one cannot untangle cognition from affect as they go hand in hand.

I hope that this chapter illustrates the power of an overarching construct (languaging) within a Vygotskian sociocultural theory of mind to facilitate a transition from one academic field to another. In 'crossing over' to gerontology from educational linguistics, the integrity of the theory was respected and shown to be useful in a new context. As Vygotsky (1987) claimed, the source of the development of higher mental processes is social activity, and using language mediates that development.

The personal rewards that accrued from my own participation in the older adult project cannot be underestimated. I would not have chosen to work in a long-term care facility with people experiencing cognitive decline, but as I explained, Merrill and our funding proposal led me there. The connection I made with Mike and his wife persists to this day. After the data collection was complete, I continued to visit Mike regularly until about four months before his death (around the time that he was diagnosed with Alzheimer's Disease). I also continued to meet occasionally with Mike's wife who had given permission for Mike to participate in our research and who appreciated the progress Mike had made during the study; she too perceived improvement in his cognition and sense of well-being.

Similarly, Merrill too continued to visit Alise and sent her regular postcards from her travels away from Toronto. The visits ceased when Alise became too ill to sustain them. Through Mike and Alise, Merrill and I were exposed to intellectual topics that we had only superficially explored in the past, and we gained a wonderful sense of satisfaction as our relationships developed through languaging. It was a win-win situation for researcher and resident alike!

The last word goes to Merrill: [Languaging provides] 'one route to improving that cognitive/affective bundle which is at the heart of quality of life issues' (Swain, 2013: 17).

Acknowledgments

First and foremost, my thanks to Merrill for career-long colleagueship, mentorship and friendship; Merrill provided important feedback during the writing of this chapter. I would also like to thank Birgit Harley, Iryna Lenchuk, Paula Psyllakis and Linda Steinman for comments on an earlier draft of this chapter.

Notes

(1) A copy of the handbook can be obtained by writing to merrill.swain@utoronto.ca or sharon.lapkin@utoronto.ca, or at https://www.kensingtonhealth.org/KH/media/Ken singtonHealth/Gardens/Useful-Conversations-For-Residents-With-Mild-Memory-L oss-Handbook.pdf.
(2) There are no shared rooms in MP, so that relative privacy and quiet were ensured.
(3) The names of the residents are pseudonyms.
(4) A reviewer made the point that scaffolding occurs in the excerpt shown here. Swain *et al.* (2015: 150) point out that: 'Although Vygotsky did not use this term, scaffolding is often linked to the emergence of the zone of proximal development. This concept is aligned with SCT if the scaffold is removed gradually and is contingent upon the responsiveness of the learner to it'. Indeed, scaffolding occurs in many places in the two excerpts included in this chapter. For a fuller account of how scaffolding has come to be viewed in social cognitive theory (SCT), see Swain *et al.* (2015: 25–26).
(5) I interpret this utterance to mean that Alise did not feel threatened in the company of the German retreating forces.

References

Barkaoui, K., Swain, M. and Lapkin, S. (2011) Examining the quality of measures of change in cognition and affect for older adults: Two case studies. *Journal of Aging Studies* 25, 62–72.

Brooks, L., Swain, M., Lapkin, S. and Knouzi, I. (2010) Mediating between scientific and spontaneous concepts through languaging. *Language Awareness* 19, 89–110.

Folstein, M.F., Folstein, S. and McHugh, P.R. (1975) Mini-mental state: A practical method for grading the cognitive state of patients for the clinician. *Journal of Psychiatric Research* 12, 189–198.

Knouzi, I., Swain, M., Lapkin, S. and Brooks, L. (2010) Self-scaffolding mediated by languaging: Microgenetic analysis of high and low performers. *International Journal of Applied Linguistics* 20, 23–49.

Lapkin, S. (2013) 'Merrill Swain'. In C. Chapelle (ed.) *The Encyclopedia of Applied Linguistics* (pp. 1–4). Oxford: Wiley Blackwell.

Lapkin, S., Swain, M. and Psyllakis, P. (2010) The role of languaging in creating zones of proximal development (ZPDs): A long-term care resident interacts with a researcher. *Canadian Journal on Aging* 29, 477–490.

Lenchuk, I. and Swain, M. (2010) Alise's small stories: Indices of identity construction and of resistance to the discourse of cognitive impairment. *Language Policy* 9, 9–28.

Motobayashi, K., Swain, M. and Lapkin, S. (2014) Autobiographic episodes as languaging: Affective and cognitive changes in an older adult. *Language and Sociocultural Theory* 1, 75–99.

Poehner, M.E. and Swain, M. (2016) L2 development as cognitive-emotive process. *Language and Sociocultural Theory* 3, 219–241.

Schwartz, G.E. (1983) Development and validation of the Geriatric Evaluation by Relatives Rating Instrument (GERRI). *Psychological Reports* 53, 478–488.

Swain, M. (2006) Languaging, agency and collaboration in advanced second language learning. In H. Byrnes (ed.) *Advanced Language Learning: The Contribution of Halliday and Vygotsky* (pp. 95–108). London: Continuum.

Swain, M. (2010) Talking-it-through: Languaging as a source of learning. In R. Batstone (ed.) *Sociocognitive Perspectives on Language Use and Language Learning* (pp. 112–130). Oxford: Oxford University Press.

Swain, M. (2013) Cognitive and affective enhancement among older adults: The role of languaging. *The Australian Review of Applied Linguistics* 36, 4–19.

Swain, M. and Lapkin, S. (2016) *Useful Conversations for Residents with Mild Memory Loss: Suggestions for Volunteers in Long-Term Care Facilities*. Toronto, ON: Kensington Research Institute.

Swain, M., Lapkin, S., Knouzi, I., Suzuki, W. and Brooks, L. (2009) Languaging: University students learn the grammatical concept of voice in French. *Modern Language Journal* 93, 5–29.

Swain, M., Kinnear, P. and Steinman, L. (2011; 2nd edn 2015) *Sociocultural Theory in Second Language Acquisition: An Introduction through Narratives*. Bristol: Multilingual Matters.

Swain, M., Lapkin, S. and Deters, P. (2013) Exploring the effect of languaging activities on cognitive functioning: The case of an older adult in a long-term care facility. *Activities, Adaptation and Aging* 37, 1–18.

Troyer, A.K. and Rich, J.B. (2002) Psychometric properties of a new metamemory questionnaire for older adults. *Journal of Gerontology* 57B, 19–27.

Vygotsky, L.S. (1987) *The Collected Works of L.S. Vygotsky, i. Problems of General Psychology. Including the Volume Thinking and Speech* (eds. R.W. Reiber and A.S. Carton). New York: Plenum.

Wertsch, J.V. (1985) *Vygotsky and the Social Formation of Mind*. Cambridge, MA: Harvard University Press.

Wertsch, J.V. and Hickman, M. (1987) Problem-solving in social interaction. In M. Hickman (ed.) *Social and Functional Approaches to Language and Thought* (pp. 251–266). Orlando, FL: Academic Press.

10 Mentorship as Mediation: Appreciating Merrill Swain

Linda Steinman

Clark (2010: viii) referred to mentoring as a 'delicate dance'. This analogy resonates with me as both mentoring and dancing are rigorous endeavors fraught with opportunities for missteps and pain, but when performed well, they are acts of beauty.

How does one 'train' to become a doctoral supervisor? There are no sophisticated courses or programs. In considering my own development as a graduate supervisor, I have come to realize the subtle yet profound influence of my own supervisor – Dr Merrill Swain. As my contribution to this edited volume, I present a case of a singular supervisor/supervisee relationship. I employ Orland-Barak's (2010) three-point framework for mentorship: appreciation, participation and improvisation, and illustrate how Merrill Swain embodied those characteristics during my three years as a graduate student at the Ontario Institute of Education (OISE) at the University of Toronto (UT).

Vygotskian sociocultural theory (SCT), acknowledged by Orland-Barak, is central to this case study as mentorship is a particular form of mediation. Other key aspects of SCT relevant to my experience as a mentee are imitation (on my part; modeling on my supervisor's part); agency; and the bidirectional movement between scientific and spontaneous concepts.

Not only SCT, but also two memes come to my mind when I think about Merrill and me. One is 'digging deep' (Merrill) and the other is 'paying it forward' (me). I will elaborate later in this chapter.

A case study is bounded and contextualized (Duff, 2014; Yin, 2009). That is, a case study vividly describes a specific slice of time and experience that has some significance. So, although my relationship with Merrill has developed to the present day in ways that are gratifying and unexpected and she continues to be a source of inspiration to me, this case record mainly addresses the formal mentorship period.

It is not an easy task to offer appreciation for a long, industrious and illustrious career. There are many ways to design a tribute text and this one is organized into theoretical perspectives that have absorbed Merrill Swain over the past 40+ years (and more to come).

As Merrill moved through the areas of research captured in the 14 chapters of this book, she was not alone. Accompanying her, considering the paradigms and bridging them were hundreds of researchers and students whom she inspired at a distance and many with whom she worked intimately as a professor and supervisor. I was fortunate to be one of the latter group.

It is to this special role of supervisor that I devote this chapter. Although supervisor and supervisee was our documented relationship appearing on forms and curricula vitae, I have reconsidered our roles as mentor and mentee. First, I will touch on some literature that focuses on academic mentorship. In particular, I will draw generously and appreciatively on the work of Orland-Barak (2010), which seems to theorize and capture what Merrill brings to the mentor role. Equally compelling to me is the work of Gallimore *et al.* (1992).

I will follow with a brief narrative of the development of the mentor/mentee relationship between Merrill and me and how I benefitted not only as a doctoral student at OISE UT at the turn of the millennium (2000–2003), but also how I continue to draw on many lessons learned from Merrill – lessons explicit and implicit, intended and unintended, conscious and subconscious. I realize that I 'wear' Merrill in my own role of graduate supervisor (and, I hope, *mentor*) to the many graduate students I have worked with since leaving OISE.

I will draw connections between Vygotskian SCT concepts and the Swain-style mentorship as I experienced it.

Literature on mentoring: Orland-Barak

In the table of contents of Orland-Barak's 2010 text, key words point to the many facets of mentorship: *praxis*; *dialectic*; *apprenticeship*; *common sense*; *growth*; *discursive*; *confronting gaps*; *accountability*; *rigid views*; *moral stances*; *modes of support*; *positioning*; *commitment*; *ethics of care*; *negotiating*; *loyalty*; *reciprocity*; *appropriation*; *authenticity*; *imposing*; *interventions*; *cultural values*. All of these elements are organized into three main behaviors: *appreciation*; *participation*; and *improvisation*. I recognize Merrill in each of these dimensions.

Appreciation

Orland-Barak nicely carves *Appreciation* into three stages. *Construal* refers to taking in the situation enacted/interacted through dialogue. *Appraisal* indexes finding out the nature and realities of the individual and determining what is familiar/acceptable and what is not. Appraisal seems like the data-gathering part of the relationship. (Had this chapter been a research study, an activity theory analysis would prove enlightening.) *Evaluation* is the third dimension of appreciation and involves taking stock of if and how the construal and appraisal are serving the mentor/mentee ship. Is the mentee prepared to and capable of carrying out the intended work? Is the mentor appropriate for the task? Shot through all of these dimensions are dialogue and self-reflection. That is, the mentor looks inward as well as outward. Occasionally, Orland-Barak refers to the relationship and to the individual as *text* and to me, this seems to drive home the point that these three phases of appreciation do correspond to how we approach traditional texts and other novel situations. We skim a text looking for signs of familiarity, of relevance, of connection, of energy and then determine whether to engage in a close reading.

Participation

How does the mentor bring the mentee into the community of practice? It was a welcome discovery that Orland-Barak draws on Vygotsky as she describes this dimension, which entails the appropriation and mastery of physical and psychological tools as part of participation in collective and individual activities (Vygotsky, 1978: 61, as cited in Orland-Barak) '...the appropriation of mediational means across time and interaction'. What are the rights, duties and obligations of both mentor and mentee? Mentors are 'activists who act as agents and models who maximize opportunities' and practice an 'ethics of care' (Orland-Barak citing Noddings, 1988). Orland-Barak writes of co-participation to describe the process that for Vygotsky was the zone of proximal development (ZPD), Rogoff (1990) termed 'guided participation', Heath (1989) referred to as 'the learner as cultural member' and Lave and Wenger (1991) called 'legitimate peripheral participation' (as cited in Rogoff *et al.*, 1993).

Improvisation

Improvisation is 'synthetic and compositional and directed towards the establishment and maintenance of a relationship between actor and material, actor and instrument (tool), and other participants' (Orland-Barak, 2010: 90 citing Yinger, 1990: 86). These are on-the-spot construals but Orland-Barak and those she cites emphasize that these are not automatic reflexes; rather, they are a result of past patterns and modes of reasoning that come to bear on the seemingly spontaneous acts. There is a focus on interpretation of the here and now rather than on prediction and systematic inquiry. To my mind, this dimension of improvisation speaks to the state of *connoisseurship* of Eisner (1998), in the sense that a novice supervisor would have little to draw on whereas someone with a good deal of experience has 'past patterns' to recollect.

When first encountering Orland-Barak's mentorship framework, I kept thinking that *Imagination w*as the component that began with

'I', rather than *Improvisation*. Imagination might well be included here. While one improvises in response to current stimuli, one also needs to envision, to gaze beyond at yet-to-happen possibilities.

Meeting Merrill Swain

I first encountered Merrill in 2000 when I began a late-career PhD at OISE/UT. I was 50 years of age and had been teaching English as a second language (ESL) and training ESL teachers for decades at a community college. While this did not make me unique, I did not have the typical profile of a graduate student. (At least, this is what I thought and felt at the time. I now see more and more advanced-career graduate students.)

All graduate students, MA and PhD, in the (then) second language education (SLE) program in the Department of Curriculum, Teaching and Learning, passed through Merrill Swain and Sharon Lapkin's (gentle, expert) hands as they co-taught a required year-long colloquium course. I had not had much contact with second language acquisition (SLA) theory nor with SLA researchers despite having completed an MEd in Curriculum at another university in southern Ontario several years earlier. Only when I was in the OISE program did I discover that many faculty in the SLE program at the time had impressive national and international reputations.

It quickly became clear to me that Merrill was an A-lister in the field. I should have been, could have been, intimidated, but somehow I was not. An experienced teacher myself, I watched closely how all my professors managed their classes, interacted with their students and seized (or not) opportunities for service. Overarching descriptors that come to mind about Merrill were, and still are, *alert*, *open* and *committed*.

One of the assignments in the colloquium course was the creation of a poster representing an intended research project. In my poster and accompanying text, I pointed out that some learners resist producing certain phrases and types of discourse even if they know the correct way to do so because they dislike it for one reason or another. I called this circumstance, for reasons that made sense at the time, '*stomach interference*'. I fully expected Merrill to say something along the lines of: 'Well, too bad. They need to produce correct forms'. Instead, she fixed her eyes on me steadily (those who know her will easily recognize the gaze to which I refer) and said simply 'Then they shouldn't use those words'. I was surprised. She had passed a test that I had not realized I was administering. Gallimore *et al.* (1992: 27) opened (and ended) their commissioned article on mentorship with the intriguing question: 'To what extent is the novice first bonded to the domain of competence to be acquired and then to the mentor?'. In other words, is it personal chemistry or scholarly reputation that first attracts someone to a potential mentor? Domain of competence was by then, undeniable, and I felt a spark of chemistry.

So, not fully understanding how supervisors and supervisees come to be a team, I determined that Merrill would become my supervisor. Gallimore *et al.* (1992) posed yet another question: 'Does the [*mentoring*] relationship arise from existing arrangements, or is it deliberately created?' I was pretty deliberate. I presented Merrill with a proposal that I doubt resembled anything she had either worked on or worked with in her own research. She had every right (and maybe did once or twice) to try to point me elsewhere for supervision, but I wanted what I sensed to be her openness and her interest in all things both traditional and novel. I intuited, and soon this was confirmed, that Merrill welcomes not only different ideas but also a wide range of people into her life.

I observed Merrill mentoring others. A feature of the OISE program during the time I was there was a lunchtime seminar series where students' works-in-progress (often at the conceptual stage) were presented for feedback from professors and other students. Merrill and Sharon always attended. They were attentive. They listened critically not only in an appreciative way but also in a participatory way and invariably helped the student to improve their work. The presenter and other hungry students (not hungry for food despite the lunch hour; rather, we sought connection and interaction with those more knowledgeable than us) hung on to their wise words. They/we learned how something might be reimagined to be more doable or more worthwhile. This was a special time for socialization into scientific concepts and language. All present were attuned (stepping in and out of the conversation) as the novice presenter and the two professors negotiated toward the development of the presenter and other graduate students at the table. Even then, when I was not particularly fluent in the language of SCT, I referred to that 10th-floor room as the ZPD as so much of my (our) learning happened there. Kozulin and Presseisen (1995: 74) emphasize the 'centrality of the human mediator', which outpaced, for me, other symbolic and psychological tools in my development. What was offered to us was 'apprenticeship in thinking' (Rogoff, 1990). During my time at OISE, I watched as Merrill took a leadership role in the program when necessary, and shared her expertise not only with her supervisees and students in her own classes but also bore some responsibility for *all* students on the tenth floor. I hope I exhibit the same responsibility.

Needing to return to my professional life (and salary), I quickly moved through the program. Soon after receiving my PhD, I was fortunate to be offered a tenure-track position at the university where I was (and still am) and called upon to mentor a great many students. I think of Merrill often as I move through my professional life. In terms of appreciation, I know that I listen to unfamiliar and sometimes outlandish ideas for research projects with an open mind, as Merrill listened to mine. I try hard to 'suspend disbelief' (Husserl, 1970) as long as I can.

I value the importance of helping students to form networks to enter the scholarly space and although I am not nearly as adept and well connected in this space as Merrill is, I encourage students to talk to other students, to form independent relationships with other professors as potential committee members and to take opportunities to make their work visible and audible. Merrill, I know, has benefitted greatly from a wide and committed network, so I understand the value of making the effort and taking the time to connect.

A Post-OISE Vignette (the ZPD extends past graduation. I am still learning.)

Merrill, Penny Kinnear and I are at Georgetown University at a conference on narratives as we prepare to co-author a textbook. The narrative academic field is somewhat novel to Merrill. There was probably not a single individual who Merrill had interacted with before. Here, I sensed, she felt somewhat novice like, as I often do at conferences. Yet, Merrill remained open and alert to new ideas. She was well able to enter into new spaces without discarding the familiar. This speaks to me of all three of Orland-Barak's dimensions: appreciating a new subject, participating in the activities of this new group and improvising as to how (and if) she would incorporate this new information into her schema and future work.

Evidence of Merrill's openness to new ideas and change is her work on chapter three of the co-authored textbook that followed this Georgetown trip (Swain *et al.*, 2015), where Merrill relooks at earlier data through a new lens and comes to new and deeper understanding. In this chapter featuring two French immersion students, Sophie and Rachel, Merrill is explicit about her own ongoing development as a researcher and an appreciator of new trends.

Sociocultural Theory

In her introduction to Orland-Barak's text, Clark (2010: viii) writes of mentoring as a 'theory of action and interaction... professional and personal transformation'. This clearly speaks to SCT insofar as it emphasizes the centrality of interaction and transformation as the intended site of and the consequence of learning. Mentorship as conceived and explained by Orland-Barak (not so much by the many websites, both academic and corporate, that offer a fairly technical and prescribed view of mentoring) can be understood using an SCT gaze. Called to mind are 'scaffolds', a term not coined by Vygotsky but often used as a verb in the service of the ZPD; the roles, often shifting, of novice and expert (co-thinkers); transformation of spontaneous knowledge into scientific knowledge and back again when necessary; transformation of both mentor and mentee; and the connection between cognition and affect (mentoring cannot succeed on a purely cognitive level). There must be an ethic of care (Noddings, 1988) and an intersubjectivity between mentor and mentee that lead to trust and commitment.

A mentor carries the signs, symbols and meanings of a doctoral program, the scholarly milieu, the culture of the community of researchers. The right mentor, often unconsciously, explicates the meanings, the practices, the conventions of the scholarly community and makes evident the spaces for agency. Mentoring is an opportunity for enacting a ZPD (many of them), and for adaptive imitation leading to appropriation to whatever extent possible. Merrill uses the term 'languaging' to distinguish effortful talk that creates meaning from ordinary transactional talk (see Swain, 2006). Though we never used the word at the time, languaging ensued during those hours in Merrill's office as she and I attempted to bridge our divides and make sense of what each of us was familiar with as we moved forward. Our background differences remained a strength in our collaboration post-OISE. This was highlighted for me by an interaction during our book writing. Something unexpected had come up which puzzled us. At the same moment, both with furrowed brows, Merrill mused 'I wonder who has written about this' and I said 'I wonder if I've ever experienced this in a class'. I use this example when explaining the term 'epistemology' to students. For Merrill the heuristic was research; for me it was practice. This was a dialectic that contributed to our collaboration.

My engagement through close proximity with a more experienced thinker revealed the processes as well as the products of Merrill's thinking. 'By internalizing the consequences of joint activity, the novice [me] acquired some very crucial knowledge about the domain and also started to recognize his or her [my] own strengths and weaknesses' (Gallimore *et al.*, 1992: 23). I learned to ask different types of questions and where to search for answers. Our interaction supported what students in one of my SCT courses and I dubbed 'imitation plus' to describe adaptive imitation that points to potential for innovation. This term seems applicable to my experience as a mentee. Merrill did not expect me to be a clone, nor, as I reflect, did she expect others to be slavish to her ideas. There was not really, during the time I was at OISE, a quintessential *Swain style* of study. Everyone who was working with her then was engaged in something unique; we were bound by the conventions of good research but there was plenty of room for innovation. Merrill's hands held the reins but they did so gently so that there was plenty of give.

Merrill is a respecter of the practice of teaching. My experience was quite classroom based and I sensed her interest in this experience rather than a devaluing of it. We danced for a while, Merrill moving out of the research texts into practice, while I moved out of the classroom into the research material. I learned much about the scientific concepts and she seemed to be intrigued by some of the everyday experiences. We shared the novice–expert roles. I felt gently guided into new discourses, and I remember this gentleness as I work with experienced teachers who have come to my graduate courses at much the same stage as I was when I studied at OISE. So Merrill's mentoring has transcended the place in which it unfolded as I now channel much of what I experienced myself as a mentee.

Memes

Merrill's influence can be described not only in academic discourse, but also in the language of popular culture. Moving away from mentoring frameworks and SCT, I would like to offer two memes that are brought to (my) mind when I consider mentorship, Merrill Swain and me: digging deep and paying it forward.

Digging deep

Originally I was going to describe Merrill's orientation to her work as *leaning in*. This phrase was given a new connotation by Sharon Sandberg (2013), a wonder woman in the corporate world. *Leaning in* was a call to women to fully commit to their profession. Recent literature, though, has critiqued the notion leaning in as being uncritical and shallow for exhorting women to follow trodden paths. That is, it calls for women to strive to be equal to men in power in what seems to be direct imitation fashion. Instead, bell hooks (2013) coined the subsequent meme of *digging deep*. This action entails a search for substance, for transformation, for new ways of seeing and being in a just world. I like this image and this seems to me to be what Merrill does, in her relationships, in her scholarship and in her thinking.

Paying it forward

'Paying it forward' comes from a feel-good, non-reflexive practice of taking care of someone with whom you have no relationship because someone has done this for you. It makes you feel good and it is hoped that they will follow suit (i.e. pay the favor forward). Unbeknown to Merrill, there is a paying it forward cycle here that began perhaps before Merrill (only Merrill can speak to how she carries the practices of those who mentored her), continued with Merrill, carried on (I hope) by me and perhaps passed along after me. It is similar to 'the elevator being sent back down' with the mentor in it to bring a novice along for the ride. Actor Kevin Spacey, in an address at the University of Virginia, recalled his own mentor, the late actor Jack Lemmon about whom Spacey said:

> As one of America's most legendary actors, Jack certainly did not need to be running a workshop, but he believed in the philosophy that if you've

been successful in your chosen path, then you should help those who are just starting out. He coined the phrase 'sending the elevator back down'. (Rhodes, 2014)

Mentoring, as addressed in multiple university and corporate websites and brochures, takes mainly a technical approach, clarifying distinctions between advising and mentoring, and listing the personal qualities of a good mentor (in isolation from any particular mentee). The complexity and the humanity of mentoring seem not to be truly appreciated at university. Jacobs (1997) referred to mentoring as 'the forgotten fourth leg of the academic stool'. Universities valorize the trio of professional contribution, teaching and service while the category of mentorship is sidelined.

Gallimore *et al.* (1992) trenchantly pointed out that it is in the everyday not only in the intellectual encounters, on task, that socialization and appropriation occur. More is learned than is taught. So, it was when my mentor was not focused on me, but instead on someone else's work or talking about her own work that her thinking and her way of asking questions and probing and decision-making became evident to me. In other words, mentoring happens unintentionally in the everyday, not only in the specialized tasks. This makes me think about the value of on-site education whenever possible instead of distance where the everyday, the off-task, seemingly unremarkable is not visible. Merrill, a natural collaborator, made *her* thinking visible and audible on many occasions both when I was central and when I was on the periphery.

I realize that this chapter is characterized perhaps by genre-disorder, and not only because I have just cited a Hollywood actor. This present chapter is not a study although Merrill is a text from which I have learned much. It is not really a case since it is not bounded by precise timelines and does not really present a problem. As a narrative, it is disrupted too often by references to theory and other sources. Perhaps it can be read as an essay of the left hand (Bruner, 1979) and evidence of the importance Bruner placed on teaching and on the relationship of both the left hand and the right hand. On teaching, Bruner (1979: 2) challenged teachers to 'lead the learner to construct a reality on his own terms'. In his text *On Knowing: Essays for the Left Hand*, Bruner suggests that the right hand represents scientific knowledge, fact, accuracy, while the left hand is involved in the artistic, creative and abstract and less comfortable. The mentor/mentee relationship often considered one of passing knowledge and fact is, according to some literature and to my own experience as a mentee, one of creativity and insight. The right hand and the left hand should be foregrounded and backgrounded as needed.

I wrote this essay to illustrate that Merrill Swain's contributions to the field are not only her wide and deep knowledge of SLA but also her excellence as a mentor, who appreciates, who participates and who improvises in imaginative ways.

References

Bruner, J. (1979) *On Knowing: Essays for the Left Hand* (2nd edn). Cambridge, MA: Harvard University Press.

Clark, C. (2010) Foreword. In L. Orland-Barak (ed.) *Learning to Mentor-as-Praxis* (p. viii). New York: Springer.

Duff, P. (2014) Case study research on language learning and use. *Annual Review of Applied Linguistics* 34, 233–255. doi: 10.1017/S0267190514000051.

Eisner, E.W. (1998) *The Enlightened Eye: Qualitative Inquiry and the Enhancement of Educational Practice*. Upper Saddle River, NJ: Merrill.

Gallimore, R., John-Steiner, V.P. and Tharp, R.G. (1992) *The Developmental and Psychological Foundations of Mentoring*. New York: Institute for Urban and Minority Education, Teachers College, Columbia University.

hooks, bell (October 28, 2013) 'Dig Deep: Beyond Lean In'. *The Feminist Wire*.

Husserl, E. (1970) *The Idea of Phenomenology*. The Hague: Nijhoff.

Jacobs, H. (1997) Mentoring: The forgotten fourth leg of the academic stool. *Translational Research* 129 (5), 489. doi: http://dx.doi.org/10.1016/S0022-2143(97)90001-9

Kozulin, A. and Presseisen, B.Z. (1995) Mediated learning experience and psychological tools: Vygotsky's and Feuerstein's perspectives in a study of student learning. *Educational Psychologist* 30 (2), 67–75.

Noddings, N. (1988) An ethic of caring and its implications for instructional arrangements. *American Journal of Education* 96 (2), 215–230.

Orland-Barak, L. (2010) *Learning to Mentor-as-Praxis*. New York: Springer. doi: 10.1007/978-1-4419-0582-6

Rhodes, J. (2014) Why Kevin Spacey thinks we should send the elevator back down. *The Chronicle of Evidence-Based Mentoring*, October 21. See https://www.poynter.org/news/send-elevator-back-down (accessed 4 February 2017).

Rogoff, B. (1990) *Apprenticeship in Thinking. Cognitive Development in Social Context*. New York: Oxford University Press.

Rogoff, B., Mistry, J., Göncü, A., Mosier, C., Chavajay, P. and Heath, S. (1993) Guided participation in cultural activity by toddlers and caregivers. *Monographs of the Society for Research in Child Development* 58 (8), 1–179. doi: 10.2307/1166109

Sandberg, S. (2013) *Lean In: Women, Work, and the Will to Lead*. New York: Knopf.

Swain, M. (2006) Languaging, agency and collaboration in advanced second language proficiency. In H. Byrnes (ed.) *Advanced Language Learning: The Contribution of Halliday and Vygotsky* (pp. 95–108). London/New York: Continuum.

Swain, M., Kinnear, P. and Steinman, L. (2015) *Sociocultural Theory and Second Language Education: An Introduction through Narratives* (2nd edn). Bristol: Multilingual Matters.

Yin, R.K. (2009) *Case Study Research Design and Methods*. Thousand Oaks, CA: SAGE.

Part 4

Issues and Developments in Language as Social Action

11 Language Play and Double Voicing in Second Language Acquisition and Use

Elaine Tarone

Introduction

An admirable characteristic of Merrill Swain's contribution to the field of second language acquisition (SLA) has been her openness to using different theoretical lenses to better understand how learner language is acquired and used by second language (L2) learners in the process of making meaning. For example, Swain (2013) reviews four different theoretical lenses through which she has, over time, understood the same bit of oral dialogue (initially reported in Kowal & Swain, 1997). The lens she concludes with focuses on the inseparability of emotion from cognition in SLA. As a member of a group of researchers called the Douglas Fir Group (2016), Swain has proposed the use of a transdisciplinary framework that also encourages the use of multiple lenses to study SLA in an increasingly multilingual world.

The present chapter builds on Swain's work by using different lenses to highlight the bilingual's imaginative appropriation and use of emotion-infused target language (TL) 'voices' in two domains: interactional narratives and presentational discourse. It reviews recent research exploring the way L2 learners and bilinguals (1) playfully enact others' 'voices' in unrehearsed interactional L2 narratives and (2) learn to mirror the 'voices' of exemplary others to improve their intelligibility in L2 presentational discourse.

Variation, Language Play and Heteroglossia in SLA

Many SLA researchers (e.g. Douglas Fir Group, 2016) are shifting away from a decontextualized cognitivist approach to the study of SLA and toward more transdisciplinary research on SLA and use, one that uses multiple theoretical lenses to study the impact of social context on the development of interlanguage systems. The developmental process of SLA is conceived of as '...emergent, dynamic, unpredictable, open-ended and intersubjectively negotiated' (Douglas Fir Group, 2016: 19), an integrated, multimodal, embodied process in which social contextual factors such as interlocutor, meaning-making, style and identity formation centrally shape L2 learning outcomes.

Variationist sociolinguistic research on SLA has assembled substantial evidence that social context, and interlocutor in particular, systematically affects the L2 variants that L2 learners acquire and produce (see Bayley & Preston, 1996; Bayley & Tarone, 2011; Beebe, 1980; Beebe & Giles, 1984; Preston, 1989; Tarone, 1988, 2000a; Tarone & Liu, 1995). These studies show that learner language, particularly when it is produced outside the foreign language classroom, is variable; interlanguage variation is systematically influenced by social context, particularly by the interlocutor and broader audience of the learner's speech. Bell (1984) argues that the language styles produced by any speaker are complex products of interactive 'audience design' in that all speakers agentively adjust their speech styles to produce desired impacts on their interlocutors (their audience) in the context of speaking. Rampton (2014) shows what happens when that desired impact is to distance oneself from the audience. In audience design there is a complex interplay of the speaker's expression of identity (or sense of self) in relation to alterity (the awareness of other selves) (Forman, 2014).

When a learner studies a TL inside a classroom, he or she is largely cut off from exposure to the varied non-classroom communities of fluent speakers who engage in audience design as they use the TL. Whether it is a traditional or immersion classroom, such TL learners have very little contact with a range of TL registers, dialects and other language varieties. As a result, they don't know how people like and unlike them actually use the language in non-classroom settings. Tarone and Swain (1995: 167) showed the serious consequences of this fact for young language immersion learners: 'students increasingly avoid using their L2 in peer–peer interactions in immersion classrooms as they move into higher primary grade levels'. Tarone and Swain argued that this was because they were not exposed to the TL register they needed to express a pre-teen identity. Suzannah, an immersion program graduate in their study, says:

> ... when we get older ... we start speaking in a way that they don't teach us in French, how to speak. So I don't know if it's slang or just the way kids speak ... I speak differently to my friends than I do to my parents. It's almost a whole different language, and ... they don't teach us how to speak [French] that way. (Tarone & Swain, 1995: 172)

When she finally studied abroad, Suzannah was excited to learn such 'cool' expressions as 'Je crise mon camp' (I'm clearing off) and 'etre pas mal tannée' (to be fed up). Tarone and Swain concluded that fifth-grade immersion learners' need to express their pre-teen identities was so much stronger than the school pressure to speak only French that they switched to English for the only teen vernacular they knew. One might say that their willingness to communicate in the French L2 (cf. Clement *et al.*, 2003) was affected by whether they had access to varieties of French they needed to form their identities.

Sociocultural theory provides an alternative lens for understanding interlanguage variation, one that includes the dimension of emotion. Bakhtin (1981, 1984) coined the term 'heteroglossia' to refer to the range of styles and language varieties a speaker appropriates from others. Because these varieties retain, in the mind of the speaker, core elements of the personalities and emotional stances of persons, Bakhtin called them 'voices':

> Repertoires ... are assembled out of a social heteroglossia that consists of a number of distinct 'voices' of others that have been appropriated into a single speaker's repertoire or into the 'dialogized heteroglossia' of a system of stylistic registers. The anchoring points of a stylistic continuum along which speakers position themselves sociocentrically with respect to their conversational partners are often the voices of *exemplary others*; stereotyped, essentialized voices of exemplary others are crucial to anchoring the linguistic system by which speakers index their own situational and social positions. (Hastings & Manning, 2004: 300–301)

Hastings and Manning (2004: 291) focus on the dialogue between the speaker's identity ('self') and what they call 'alterity:' the identities of those exemplary others who influence 'the acts of speakers expressing or voicing some self'.

Bakhtin was interested in the way speakers play around with these 'voices' for their own emotional amusement and pleasure, ironically exploiting an interplay among their multiple voices. Cook (1997: 228) classifies ludic language play into two types: play with language form (sounds, rhymes, rhythms, puns) and semantic language play, which is 'play with units of meaning, combining them in ways which create worlds which do not exist: fictions'. Bakhtin views a speaker's heteroglossia as a fertile space for the exercise of what he called 'double voicing', a kind of imaginative play that draws on a multiplicity of 'voices'. As Bakhtin (1981: 60–61) says, 'The creating consciousness stands, as it were, on the boundary line between languages and styles ... Only polyglossia fully frees consciousness from the tyranny of its own language and its own myth of language'.

Double voicing crucially relies on heteroglossic speakers' mastery, at a single point in time, of many different genres, registers, dialects and other varieties of language, and as such should be of great interest to researchers studying bilinguals and L2 learners (Tarone, 2000b: 34).

Cook (1997, 2000) identified the Bakhtinian notion of language play[1] as central to research on SLA and use. It is, as Cook (1997: 230) points out, 'ludic' discourse, and as such, a form of authentic discourse that had been left out of previous SLA research. Unlike the discourses studied by SLA researchers, he argued, ludic discourses are '... not used to solve a practical problem; they are not "task based". They are language for enjoyment, for the self, for its own sake'.

Several SLA studies, beginning with Broner and Tarone (2001), show that ludic language play definitely occurs in the discourse of L2 learners and bilinguals (see Belz, 2002; Forman, 2011, 2014). Broner and Tarone (2001: 372) provide multiple examples of semantic language play and double voicing by bilingual children in a fifth-grade Spanish immersion program, as they 'took on different roles and spoke with different voices, both in English and Spanish ... Sometimes the children acted out parts in a drama, taking the part of someone else: a villain, a radio announcer, a rock star'. Leonard, for example, spoke with the voice of a fellow student when narrating an event that had occurred earlier in the classroom:

Example (1)

(1) I was like, 'Brandon?' and he's, '*no es mi culpa que uso mi dedo medio para mi*'.
    (It's not my fault I use my middle finger for myself).

Broner and Tarone (2001) argue that Leonard's words are not intended to be a verbatim replay of Brandon's words. Rather, Leonard presents them as 'a dramatization for effect, with the speaker's point of view clearly attached', in a way that resembles 'the sort of parody that Bakhtin (1981) discusses at length, in which one speaks with the voice of another while maintaining his or her own voice as commentary' (Broner & Tarone, 2001: 372).

Documenting TL 'Voices' in Presentational[2] and Interactional Speech

Many SLA studies have documented the occurrence of ludic language play and double voicing in the speech of L2 learners and bilinguals, and speculate about its possible role in SLA. 'Performed other' and 'self' voices have been shown to occur in both the interactional and presentational modes of speech. In the former, L2 learners dramatize the voices of others in constructed dialogue in casual narration and in the latter, they 'mirror' the voices of selected model speakers in rehearsed monologues.

Constructed Dialogue in Unrehearsed, Unscripted Oral Narratives

Leonard's bit of language play in Example (1) can be viewed as a form of dramatization that discourse analysts have called 'constructed dialogue'. Tannen (2007) coined the term to refer to a narrator's created 'performance' of imagined dialogue by a character in a story, a performance that is typically delivered with some emotion, and which can contain elements of irony and even mockery. Clark and Gerrig (1990), Mathis and Yule (1994) and Yule (1995) have studied monolingual English speakers' use of constructed dialogue in casual oral discourse to dramatically enact the imagined voices of characters in oral narratives, often introducing these performances with new 'quotatives', phrases such as 'He goes…' or 'I'm like…' or even 'zero quotatives'. In Example (2), a speaker dramatizes two lines of dialogue, the first preceded by the quotative 'I'm like' and the second by a zero quotative:

Example (2)

… I'm like, 'LOOK don't you'
(falsetto) 0: 'No no no—I don't mean it—I don't mean it'

(Mathis & Yule, 1994: 68)

Interestingly, the voices of others in constructed dialogue, infused with emotion as they typically are, are often marked by the use of altered voice quality, as in the falsetto reported in Example (2), as well as by non-verbal shifts in body position.

Although it has been established (cf. Broner & Tarone, 2001; Forman, 2011, 2014) that constructed dialogue occurs as a form of language play in bilinguals' oral discourse, there has been little attempt until recently to compare the linguistic forms a bilingual uses in performing TL voices in constructed dialogue with the linguistic forms used in the bilingual's own L2 voice. If those voices are linguistically different, what does that tell us about the linguistic and social nature of the bilingual's second acquired language?

Two case studies document and compare the linguistic structure of the TL voices performed in constructed dialogue with the linguistic structure of the bilingual's L2 voice. The first study analyzes the suprasegmental features of pitch, volume and voice quality used by a bilingual in constructed dialogue to mark the voice of speakers of his L2, English. Moreno (2016) examines the way 28-year-old 'Heriberto', a bilingual Spanish–English speaker from Chile living in the US, uses English, his second-acquired language, in his oral narratives as he performs the voices of English-speaking co-workers, former roommates and a student at the school where he works. Moreno's quantitative Praat[3] analysis (Boersma, 2001; Boersma & Weenink, 2017) of his suprasegmentals when producing the English voices of others shows clear differences between the intonation and stress patterns in his performance of Heriberto's voice versus his own. Heriberto uses a more typically Hispanic syllable-timed pattern of intonation and intensity in quoting himself or providing background narrative, and a more stereotypically American stress-timed pattern in performing the voices of English speakers in constructed dialogue. In Example (3), Heriberto's rhythm and pitch patterns shift when he moves from performing the voice of Charlie, his former roommate, to performing his own voice.

Example (3)

(c) And then he goes like (.) 'BRO (.) what the HECK are you DOin?'
(d) And then I just told him tell I TOLD him
(e) 'oh I'm just goin on a date with Leah @virtual @ world' (Moreno, 2016: 24–25)

In Line (c), Heriberto's performance of the voice of Matt sounds like stereotypical California 'surfer talk'; he slows his rate of speaking, pauses dramatically and highlights the words 'bro' and 'heck' with a shift in voice quality and 'bro' and 'doin' with extra-high level 4 pitch. Moreno (2016: 25) views this as 'a prime example of stylization', which Bakhtin (1981: 362) defines as 'an artistic representation of another's style, an artistic image of another's language'. Figure 11.1 shows Moreno's figure 1.3, a Praat analysis of pitch and amplitude comparing Heriberto's stylization in Line (c) with his representation of his own voice in Line (e). In this figure, rhythmic changes in amplitude over time are shown at the top and changes in pitch are shown at the bottom of each example.

There is a clear difference between the stereotypically American English suprasegmentals using a wider pitch range and stress-timed rhythm in Line (c), and the stereotypically Hispanic suprasegmentals with a much narrower pitch range and a more regular syllable-timed rhythm in Line (e). These examples of constructed dialogue provide clear evidence that Heriberto can alter his suprasegmental phonology at will to perform a more American-sounding accented voice in a narrative otherwise delivered in a more Hispanic-accented voice. This fact raises interesting questions for language educators, of course; if Heriberto can use a wider pitch range and stress-timed rhythm to speak English, why doesn't he do that when speaking in his own voice? Issues of identity and alterity seem relevant.

LaScotte (2016, in press) examines shifts in lexical and syntactic complexity, accuracy and fluency (CAF) that occur when two French–English bilingual speakers produce constructed dialogue in English, their later-learned language. The two speakers, 'Sylvie' and 'Marine', are first-year teachers in a French immersion school in the US, both in their early twenties. Marine appears to be the more proficient of the two English speakers. Their oral interaction on a wide range of topics, carried out

Figure 1.3: PRAAT Display, 'Matt' voice (Example 2, line c) v. 'self' voice (Example 2, line e)

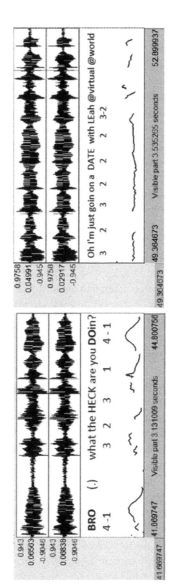

Figure 11.1 Moreno's Praat analysis of Heriberto's voices

Note: With thanks to Leah Moreno, the copyright holder, for permission to reprint this figure.

in English in a casual setting, was recorded, and the narratives[4] that they produced were isolated for analysis comparing the linguistic CAF of their English-enacted voices in constructed dialogue, with the CAF patterns of their own L2 voices in their narrative discourse.

The study found clear differences in accuracy between the speakers' enacted English voices and narrative discourse. Sylvie's enacted voices, most of them those of native speakers of English, either parents or children at her school, are more than 20% more accurate than the rest of her narrative discourse in her own voice. In addition, certain kinds of errors (e.g. subject-verb agreement) that occur in her own voice do not appear at all in her enacted voices. In comparison, while the more-proficient Marine, like Sylvie, also shifts in accuracy between enacted voices and narrative discourse, these shifts are statistically less dramatic and sometimes in the opposite direction. A telling example occurs with English question formation. In her own voice in narrative discourse, Marine does not produce any errors in WH questions; however, when she enacts the English voice of Sylvie, her interlocutor and a less-proficient speaker, she does produce such an error; she constructs Sylvie's question as, 'Why did you do?'. Such shifts in accuracy between enacted voices and one's own voice in narrative discourse are complex, and appear to be conditioned in part by whether the voices being enacted are those of more- or less-proficient speakers of English. There are clear cases where it appears that the narrator's English accuracy improves when enacting the voice of a more-proficient speaker of English, and decreases when enacting a less-proficient speaker (LaScotte, 2016).

There are also differences in measured fluency between the speakers' enacted voices and their own in narrative discourse. Sylvie's enacted voices are consistently and clearly more fluent than her own voice in her narrative discourse; a much less dramatic difference in fluency also occurs between Marine's own voice and her enacted voices.

Finally, both speakers shift in level of complexity when moving between enacted voices and their own voices in narrative discourse; however, again there are clear individual differences, as these shifts occur in opposite directions. Sylvie's syntax is more complex in her own voice than in her enacted voices, while the opposite is the case for Marine. LaScotte attributes these distinctive outcomes to different narrative styles rather than different proficiency levels or differences in who is being quoted. Sylvie takes more time setting up her stories and usually offers a complex interpretation of events and their outcomes, with the result that her grammatical complexity in her own voice in the narrative discourse is greater than that of her enacted voices. Marine, on the other hand, gives very brief segments of narrative discourse before jumping into the enactment of her characters' voices; the outcome is more complexity in her enacted voices than in her own voice. LaScotte and Tarone (2019) replicate this study with 10 lower-proficiency L2 learners, showing they also agentively shift accuracy and fluency in narrative performances as they move from one internalized voice and social identity to another.

Such findings suggest a different theoretical lens for viewing the development of interlanguage.

Both studies raise very intriguing questions for language educators. For example, how does an L2 learner acquire the ability to display more native-like patterns of phonology and syntax in instances of constructed dialogue than in his or her own voice? Is the fact that constructed dialogue is typically delivered with more emotion relevant? And to what extent can a fluent bilingual incorporate constructed dialogue patterns into his or her own voice when desired and needed? In the next section, we examine a longitudinal pedagogical study that explicitly taught English L2 speakers to appropriate, or 'mirror', the voices of more intelligible English speakers that they themselves had selected as models. This study demonstrates how the mirroring process changed a graduate student's use of English suprasegmentals and non-verbal patterns.

'Mirroring' Model Target Language Voices in Presentations

US international teaching assistants (ITAs) who are not native speakers of English often need to improve their intelligibility in their roles as university lecturers. For their purposes, intelligibility is far more important than 'nativeness' (Derwing & Munro, 2015: 1), and researchers (e.g. Anderson-Hsieh, 1992; Anderson-Hsieh et al., 1992; Kang, 2010) have established that intelligibility in English is most improved by modifications in suprasegmental features of English such as intonation (pitch range and movement) and prominence (emphasis of linguistic units within thought groups). While suprasegmentals have been stubbornly difficult to teach using methods relying on linguistic analysis alone, some ITA educators (e.g. Lindgren et al., 2003; McGregor et al., 2016) have been successful in using a more holistic top-down pedagogical approach called the 'Mirroring Project'. Meyers (2013, 2014) and Tarone and Meyers (2018) use video and Praat software (Boersma & Weenink, 2017) to document the way a Mirroring Project successfully helped one ITA adopt the 'voice' of a selected model speaker, and improve the intelligibility of her English discourse in a formal, presentational mode of speaking.

During spring semester 2012, 'Mary' (a pseudonym), a PhD student in business from mainland China, tested into a 15-week upper-level ITA training class at the University of Minnesota. In her mid-twenties, Mary had studied English in China since elementary school, and had been living in the US for two years. She selected a non-native speaker of English as a speaking model for her ITA class project: Yang Lan, a very dynamic speaker sometimes known as 'the Oprah of China'. Mary chose to mirror a short part of Yang Lan's (2011) Ted Talk.

The ITA course began with 11 weeks of explicit instruction and video-recorded practice focused on suprasegmentals needed to improve intelligibility and highlight information structure in English presentations, such as intonation, pausing and placement of phrase-level stress to assign prominence to linguistic units in thought groups. Praat software (Boersma & Weenink, 2017) was used to provide electronic visual feedback to the learners on their own use of these suprasegmentals, and the instructor used the video-recorded practices to also provide feedback on accompanying non-verbals. This explicit instruction was followed in the last three to four weeks of the course by a holistic, top-down 'Mirroring Project' (Lindgren *et al.*, 2003; Meyers, 2013, 2014; Tarone & Meyers, 2018).

The goal of the Mirroring Project was to help ITAs integrate and apply their explicit knowledge about improving intelligibility by appropriating the 'voice' of a self-selected speech model. Each ITA chose to 'mirror' a video-recorded segment of English presentational speech by a speaker they wanted to emulate. They were instructed not just to memorize and repeat decontextualized phrases, but to communicate the same level of emotion that their model speaker did in establishing rapport with their audience (Gorsuch, 2003). They were taught to try to express through their intonation, rhythm and non-verbal communication the same level of emotion as that of their video-recorded model.

Mary videoed three rehearsed, presentational talks during the semester.[5] At the end of Week 3 (Recording 1), Mary presented a simulated but not scripted self-introduction as part of a first-day overview of an imagined accounting class to a physical audience consisting of an undergraduate student, another ITA and the ITA course instructor. Recording 2 in Week 13 was Mary's first attempt to mirror a segment of Yang Lan's Ted Talk. The instructor operated the camera while Mary spoke; there was no other physical audience. Recording 3 in Week 14 was Mary's final rehearsed and scripted mirroring presentation. During the week between Recordings 2 and 3, Mary viewed Recording 2, compared it to Yang Lan's Ted Talk and identified her own strengths and weaknesses in her use of segmentals, volume, suprasegmentals, body language and expression of emotion, as compared to Yang Lan. The instructor also gave specific feedback on these areas. Before creating Recording 3, Mary revised and practiced her script in private several times so she knew it by heart.

The initial short segments of each of Mary's Recordings 1, 2 and 3 were analyzed acoustically using Praat pronunciation software (Boersma & Weenink, 2017), focusing specifically on patterns of pitch and intensity. Initial segments were selected for analysis to ensure consistency in terms of pitch variation as related to key choice for intonational paragraphs (Pickering, 2004). Based on Praat analyses, tables were created showing the pitch and intensity levels displayed in the three recording samples. Because acoustic analysis cannot capture all the important differences between Mary's intelligibility and effectiveness in Recordings 1, 2 and 3, the researchers also did a perceptual analysis of each recording, identifying thought groups, prominent words and syllables, and patterns of intonation in relation to her intelligibility, as well as Mary's use of gesture, facial expression, eye contact and changes in body position in relation to her suprasegmentals.

The results of these analyses demonstrated impressive changes in Mary's suprasegmental and non-verbal patterns before and after incorporating Yang Lan's presentational voice into her recorded speech. Table 11.1 compares the Praat results of the specific pitch (in Hz) and intensity (in dB) levels that Mary used in her video-recordings at Times 1, 2 and 3.

At Time 1, Mary's maximum pitch (307.68 Hz) is much lower than that at Times 2 (414.55) and 3 (396.77 Hz), and her pitch range (135.22) is very restricted, like that of non-native speakers of English in Pickering (2001, 2004). However, her pitch range widens progressively over time, moving from 135.22 to 257.25 at Time 2 and 314.7 at Time 3. This increase in pitch range enables Mary to use intonation more clearly and intelligibly to mark information structure as she mirrors Yang Lan. Acoustic analysis also shows an improvement in Mary's assignment and signaling of primary stress to make words prominent (Hahn [2004] shows that such signaling is related to listeners' ability to recall information in lectures). For example, although at Time 1 Mary does assign correct primary stress to make key words prominent, her narrow pitch range makes it extremely difficult for listeners to hear which words she is making prominent. By contrast, at Times 2 and 3, Mary's use of a higher Fo/pitch for the prominent words in each thought group makes them much more salient.

Perceptual analysis of the three recordings focuses on intelligibility and expression of emotion in Mary's speech as well as her use of synchronous non-verbal expression. In Recording 1, Mary does not clearly signal thought groups or convey prominence. Her speech patterns in Recording 1 are monotonous, and so low in overall volume that she is hard to hear at times. The resulting overall perception of Mary is that she lacks confidence and feeling; she appears distant and disengaged from her audience, and does not use effective non-verbal communication patterns (e.g. gestures, facial expressions and body movement) that might not only help signal prominence, but better communicate rapport, such as gestures, facial expressions and body movement.

Table 11.1 Comparison of pitch and intensity Mary produced at Times 1, 2 and 3

	Time 1	Time 2	Time 3
Mean pitch (Hz)	231.15	270.65	267.71
Max pitch (Hz)	307.68	414.55	396.77
Min pitch	172.46	157.30	82.05
Pitch range	135.22	257.25	314.72
Mean intensity (dB)	60.10	59.34	59.57
Max intensity	73.53	74.31	75.58
Min intensity	24.94	45.15	44.96
Intensity range	48.59	29.16	30.62

Source: Tarone & Meyers (2018: 213).

In Recording 2, her first attempt to mirror Yang Lan, Mary's speech is much more audible than in Recording 1 and we see the impact on intelligibility of the wider pitch range we saw in Table 11.1. For example, the clause 'The night before I was heading for Scotland' shows quite noticeable variation in pitch levels, with the characteristic 'jump up step down' intonation pattern of North American English (Bolinger, 1964).

In Recording 3, Mary has improved her overall volume, pausing, pitch range and use of prominence, and her emotional expressiveness is much more noticeable. For instance, when Mary says, 'Guess who was the performing guest? Susan Boyle', her pitch range is more varied than it was in Recording 2, and there is clear lengthening to make the words 'who', 'guest' and 'Boyle' more prominent. The photographs in the Appendix show us something the acoustic analysis cannot: the way Mary uses non-verbals in synchrony with the prominent syllables highlighted by suprasegmentals. In contrast with her performance in Recording 1, Mary uses very expressive and expansive gestures, her arms moving more widely and in time with prominent syllables. We also see her move her gaze, looking back and forth at different members of her imagined audience just like Yang Lan. By adopting and mirroring the voice of the 'exemplary other', Mary has dramatically improved the intelligibility and emotional impact of her English speech in performing this scripted, rehearsed presentation.

Meyers is presently taking the next step in this line of research, asking: To what extent are English L2 learners like Mary able to transfer the voice of the 'exemplary other' from memorized scripts to their unscripted production of disciplinary content in presentational discourse? For example, can Mary creatively embody the way Yang Lan might teach an introduction to an accounting class? Moreno's and LaScotte's studies of bilinguals who spontaneously create constructed dialogue using the voices of different TL speakers encourage us to believe that such transfers are not only possible, but may commonly occur in the world outside the classroom.

Conclusion

We have seen that L2 learners and bilinguals appropriate and use different TL voices in both presentational and interactional modes of speech, and that the linguistic characteristics of these different voices can be surprisingly distinctive. This phenomenon deserves more study. It suggests that interlanguage can be viewed as including a set of voices internalized from, and still imbued with, the emotions, personalities, and social stances of their original speakers. Second-language learners' appropriation and use of emotion-infused voices of others, expressing 'self' by enacting 'alterity', offer interesting possibilities for their development of heteroglossic voices to express their own complex emotions and identities. Future study applying alternative theoretical lenses is needed to further our understanding of voice and emotion in SLA, and use this understanding to improve the effectiveness of L2 pedagogy.

Notes

(1) Bakhtin's definition of language play contrasts sharply with that of Vygotsky. Vygotsky uses the same term to refer to the serious process of rehearsal for the purpose of internalizing new information or language, as in private speech (for discussion, see Broner & Tarone, 2001; Lantolf, 1997).

(2) For the purposes of the American Council on the Teaching of Foreign Languages (ACTFL) language proficiency assessment, Swender and Duncan (1998) identify the three modes of communication in L2 use as presentational, interpersonal and interpretive. Most SLA research has focused on the interpersonal mode.

(3) Praat is a software program for phonetic analysis developed by Boersma and Weenink at the University of Amsterdam; the word 'Praat' is the imperative form of the verb 'to speak' in Dutch.

(4) 'Narratives' are defined as oral episodes recapitulating personal experience as an event or a sequence of events including one or more characters and a central 'plot' (Kvernbekk, 2003).

(5) Links to these videos, as well as Yang Lan's Ted Talk, are available in Meyers (2013) and Tarone and Meyers (2018).

References

Anderson-Hsieh, J. (1992) Using electronic visual feedback to teach suprasegmentals. *System* 20 (1), 51–62.

Anderson-Hsieh, J., Johnson, R. and Koehler, K. (1992) The relationship between native speaker judgments of nonnative pronunciation and deviance in segmentals, prosody and syllable structure. *Language Learning* 42, 529–555.

Bakhtin, M. (1981) *The Dialogic Imagination: Four Essays by M.M. Bakhtin* (M. Holquist, ed. and C. Emerson and M. Holquist, trans). Austin, TX: University of Texas Press.

Bakhtin, M. ([1929]1984) *Problems in Dostoevsky's Poetics* (C. Emerson, ed. and trans). Minneapolis, MN: University of Minnesota Press.

Bayley, R. and Preston, D. (eds) (1996) *Second Language Acquisition and Linguistic Variation*. Amsterdam: John Benjamins.

Bayley, R. and Tarone, E. (2011) Variationist perspectives. In S. Gass and A. Mackey (eds) *Routledge Handbook of Second Language Acquisition* (pp. 41–56). New York: Routledge.

Beebe, L. (1980) Sociolinguistic variation and style shifting in second language acquisition. *Language Learning* 30, 433–447.

Beebe, L. and Giles, H. (1984) Speech accommodation theories: A discussion in terms of second language acquisition. *International Journal of the Sociology of Language* 46, 5–32.

Bell, A. (1984) Language style as audience design. *Language in Society* 13, 145–204.

Belz, J. (2002) Second language play as a representation of the multicompetent. *Self in Foreign Language Study* 1 (1), 13–39.

Boersma, P. (2001) Praat, a system for doing phonetics by computer. *Glot International* 5 (9/10), 341–345.

Boersma, P. and Weenink, D. (2017) Praat: Doing phonetics by computer [computer program]. See http://www.praat.org/ (accessed 26 January 2017).

Bolinger, D. (1964) Around the edge of language: Intonation. *Harvard Educational Review* 34, 282–296.

Broner, M. and Tarone, E. (2001) Is it fun? Language play in a fifth grade Spanish immersion classroom. *Modern Language Journal* 85, 363–379.

Clement, R., Baker, S.C. and MacIntyre, P.D. (2003) Willingness to communicate in a second language: The effects of context, norms, and vitality. *Journal of Language and Social Psychology* 22 (2), 190–209.

Clark, H. and Gerrig, R. (1990) Quotations as demonstrations. *Language* 66 (4), 764–805.

Cook, G. (1997) Language play, language learning. *ELT Journal* 51 (3), 224–231.

Cook, G. (2000) *Language Play, Language Learning.* Oxford: Oxford University Press.

Derwing, T.M. and Munro, M.J. (2015) Pronunciation Fundamentals: Evidence-Based Perspectives for L2 Teaching and Research. Amsterdam: John Benjamins.

Douglas Fir Group (Atkinson, D., Byrnes, H., Doran, M., Duff, P., Hall, J.K., Johnson, K., Lantolf, J., Larsen-Freeman, D., Norton, B., Schumann, J., Swain, M. and Tarone, E.) (2016) A transdisciplinary framework for SLA in a multilingual world. *Modern Language Journal* 100 (Supplement 2016), 19–47.

Forman, R. (2011) Humorous language play in a Thai EFL classroom. *Applied Linguistics* 32, 541–565.

Forman, R. (2014) Speaking L2 in EFL classes: Performance, identity and alterity. *Innovation in Language Learning and Teaching* 8 (2), 99–115.

Gorsuch, G.J. (2003) The educational cultures of international teaching assistants and U.S. universities. *TESL-EJ* 7 (3), 1–17.

Hahn, L. (2004) Primary stress and intelligibility: Research to motivate the teaching of suprasegmentals. *TESOL Quarterly* 38 (2), 201–223.

Hastings, A. and Manning, P. (2004) Introduction: Acts of alterity. *Language & Communication* 24, 291–311.

Kang, O. (2010) Relative salience of suprasegmental features on judgments of L2 comprehensibility and accentedness. *System* 38 (2), 301–315.

Kowal, M. and Swain, M. (1997) From semantic to syntactic processing: How can we promote it in the immersion classroom? In R.K. Johnson and M. Swain (eds) *Immersion Education: International Perspectives* (pp. 284–309). Cambridge: Cambridge University Press.

Kvernbekk, T. (2003) On identifying narratives. *Studies in Philosophy and Education* 22, 267–279.

Lan, Y. (2011) The generation that's remaking China. *Ted Talks.* See http://www.ted.com/talks/lang/en/yang_lan.html (accessed 5 January 2017).

Lantolf, J. (1997) The function of language play in the acquisition of L2 Spanish. In W.R. Glass and A.T. Perez-Leroux (eds) *Contemporary Perspectives on the Acquisition of Spanish* (pp. 3–24). Somerville, MA: Cascadilla Press.

LaScotte, D.K. (2016) 'So please be nice in class!': An analysis of the complexity, accuracy, and fluency of two English learners' language through a heteroglossic lens. MA Qualifying Paper, University of Minnesota, Twin Cities. See http://conservancy.umn.edu/handle/11299/179951 (accessed 24 February 2018).

LaScotte, D.K. (in press) Enacting voices: An analysis on the complexity, accuracy, and fluency of heterogrlossic speech. *Journal of Second Language Studies.*

LaScotte, D.K. and Tarone, E.E. (2019) Heteroglossia and constructed dialogue in SLA. *Modern Language Journal*, 103.

Lindgren, J., Meyers, C.M. and Monk, M. (2003) Approaches to Accent: The Mirroring Project. Paper presented at the Annual Conference of Teachers of English to Speakers of Other Languages (TESOL), Baltimore, Maryland.

Mathis, T. and Yule, G. (1994) Zero quotatives. *Discourse Processes* 18, 63–76.

McGregor, A., Zielinski, B., Meyers, C. and Reed, M. (2016) An exploration of teaching intonation using a TED Talk. In J. Levis, H. Le., I. Lucic, E. Simpson and S. Vo (eds) *Proceedings of the 7th Pronunciation in Second Language Learning and Teaching Conference* (pp. 143–159). Ames, IA: Iowa State University.

Meyers, C. (2013) Mirroring project update: Intelligible accented speakers as pronunciation models. *TESOL Video News.* See http://newsmanager.commpartners.com/tesolvdmis/issues/2013-07-27/6.html (accessed 9 September 2016).

Meyers, C. (2014) Intelligible accented speakers as pronunciation models. In J. Levis and S. McCrocklin (eds) *Proceedings of the 5th Pronunciation in Second Language Learning and Teaching Conference* (pp. 172–176). Ames, IA: Iowa State University.

Moreno, L. (2016) Channeling Charlie: Suprasegmental pronunciation in a second language learner's performance of others' voices. MA Qualifying Paper, University of Minnesota, Twin Cities. See http://conservancy.umn.edu/handle/11299/183052 (accessed 24 February 2018).

Pickering, L. (2004) The structure and function of intonational paragraphs in native and nonnative speaker instructional discourse. *English for Specific Purposes* 23, 19–43.

Preston, D. (1989) *Sociolinguistics and Second Language Acquisition*. Cambridge: Blackwell.

Rampton, B. (2014) *Crossing: Language and Ethnicity Among Aolescents*. New York: Routledge.

Swain, M. (2013) The inseparability of cognition and emotion in second language learning. *Language Teaching* 46 (2), 195–207.

Swender, E. and Duncan, G. (1998) ACTFL performance guidelines for K-12 learners. *Foreign Language Annals* 31 (4), 479–491.

Tannen, D. (2007) 'Oh talking voice that is so sweet': Constructing dialogue in conversation. In D. Tannen (ed.) *Talking Voices* (2nd edn; pp. 102–132). New York: Cambridge University Press.

Tarone, E. (1988) *Variation in Interlanguage*. London: Edward Arnold Publishers.

Tarone, E. (2000a) Still wrestling with 'context' in interlanguage theory. *Annual Review of Applied Linguistics* 20, 182–198.

Tarone, E. (2000b) Getting serious about language play: Language play, interlanguage variation and second language acquisition. In B. Swierzbin, F. Morris, M. Anderson, C. Klee and E. Tarone (eds) *Social and Cognitive Factors in SLA: Proceedings of the 1999 Second Language Research Forum* (pp. 31–54). Somerville, MA: Cascadilla Press.

Tarone, E. and Liu, G.-Q. (1995) Situational context, variation, and second language acquisition theory. In G. Cook and B. Seidlhofer (eds) *Principle and Practice in Applied Linguistics: Studies in Honour of H.G. Widdowson* (pp. 107–124). Oxford: Oxford University Press.

Tarone, E. and Swain, M. (1995) A sociolinguistic perspective on second-language use in immersion classrooms. *Modern Language Journal* 79, 166–178.

Tarone, E. and Meyers, C. (2018) The Mirroring Project: Improving suprasegmentals and intelligibility in ESL presentations. In R. Alonso (ed.) *Speaking in a Second Language* (pp. 197–223). Amsterdam: John Benjamins.

Yule, G. (1995) The paralinguistics of reference: Representation in reported discourse. In G. Cook and B. Seidlhofer (eds) *Principle and Practice in Applied Linguistics: Studies in Honour of H.G. Widdowson* (pp. 185–197). Oxford: Oxford University Press.

Appendix: Mary's Body Movements Signaling Prominence at Times 1 and 3

Time 1: 'ToDAY we're going to cover...'

Time 3: 'Guess WHO was the performing guest?'

Time 3: 'I told her I'M going to SCOTland'

12 Monolingual Versus Multilingual Language Use in Language Classrooms: Contested and Mediated Social and Linguistic Practice

Patricia A. Duff

Introduction

Language policies related to the status and use of (multiple) languages in classrooms have attracted considerable interest throughout the modern history of language education (see reviews in Hall & Cook, 2012 and Turnbull & Dailey-O'Cain, 2009). Communicative language teaching, for example, in contrast with earlier approaches such as grammar-translation, emphasized the benefits of *maximal exposure* to meaningful target language (TL) input and interaction in language classrooms. However, in addition to recommending ample use of the TL, some current theoretical and pedagogical trends promote the deliberate, judicious use of teachers' and learners' languages and their (multilingual) metalinguistic knowledge in classrooms. This multilingual practice is described variously as translanguaging or as heteroglossic pedagogy and social practice.

A growing body of research addresses both broad theoretical positions (essentially monolingual-TL use primarily, versus strategic use of multiple languages). Merrill Swain has been a prolific, inspiring contributor to such discussions, based on her cutting-edge theoretical and empirical work, some of which is cited in this chapter. The widespread phenomenon of English-medium instruction in many parts of the non-Anglophone world has given rise to a renewed appreciation of the complexities of delivering curriculum and instruction primarily in a language that is not typically the dominant language of either teachers or students, especially when teachers have not had instruction in applied linguistics or content-based language pedagogy (Coleman, 2006; Fenton-Smith *et al.*, 2017). A focus on multilingual repertoires in instructional settings (whether for English or other languages) is claimed to foreground teachers' and students' agency and identities, their multicompetencies, their background knowledge or schemata, and the dynamic, contingent social practices that take place in actual classroom discourse and activity (Creese & Blackledge, 2015). This approach is possible, it is argued, because learners (and teachers) are able to draw on their interests and knowledge (linguistic, cultural and other) in ways that are considered legitimate and valued in class. This multilingual orientation to education also underscores the notion that students' first languages (L1s) can play important social and cognitive roles in second language (L2) education. In this chapter, I describe some of the debates and perspectives regarding maximal use of L2 in classrooms versus more flexible and, indeed, intentional multilingual practice. I then explain how and why perspectives on this topic have changed, and how a more nuanced approach might be taken.

Background

Based on input and interaction hypotheses and principles underlying communicative and task-based language teaching approaches, research on language use in foreign language (FL) classrooms in the early 1990s (e.g. Duff & Polio, 1990; Polio & Duff, 1994) suggested that, in addition to other optimized curricular features (e.g. focusing on tasks based on students' genuine communicative needs and interests), students required (and deserved) maximal, consistent, high-quality in-class exposure to and use of the TL. This principle entailed providing meaningful linguistic input, interaction and output (or production) in order to fulfill a range of linguistic, interpersonal and task-oriented functions.

My early research with Charlene Polio aimed to quantify the amount of TL use by teachers in language classrooms and examine the functions of learners' L1 when used (Duff & Polio, 1990; Polio & Duff, 1994). The research grew out of our own experiences and disappointments in a Mandarin Chinese course at a university in the US. From our perspective, the course lacked sufficient TL use by the instructor. Students, including us, were learning *about* the language but had limited exposure to it or reason to use Mandarin during class time. Yet, the classroom was FL learners' primary way of accessing Mandarin language input outside of Sinophone contexts such as Greater China, since the internet, with all its ample affordances for language learning, was still nascent at the time.

This research on instruction in a number of distinct languages ($n = 13$) at one US university (Duff & Polio, 1990) revealed that teachers' TL use in the classes observed ranged from just a small fraction of the time (10%) to most or all of the time, depending primarily on the type of FL involved; that is, classes in Romance languages such as French and Spanish displayed the most TL use and African languages the least, with

Asian languages somewhere in between. Most of the ensuing research on teachers' L1/L2 use (described below) has focused on European languages (French, German, Spanish) taught in Anglophone institutions, or English taught in non-Anglophone contexts. These many years later, I still believe that careful attention needs to be paid to the kinds and amount of target input students receive and produce in both FL and L2 contexts and across a wide range of languages. We need to ascertain what students are expected to do with – and in – the L2, as well as what kinds of support they are given (in L1, L2 or other languages or via other semiotic resources) to achieve those goals. Importantly, we must also take into account the many factors that influence L1 use by teachers and students and also consider both its potential benefits and detriments.

At about the time of our publications on L1-L2 use in the early 1990s, concern was expressed by English as a second language (ESL) professionals that such policies (TL-only/mostly) favoring maximal TL use, especially by students with limited L2 proficiency, could seriously disadvantage immigrant children or adults (in L2 English) in their adjustment to mainstream education and life in North America (e.g. Auerbach, 1993). Note that this context and demographic of learners was completely different from those we had been investigating (see response by Polio, 1994) Critiques of 'English-only' policies in English L2 classrooms in a wide variety of settings nationally and internationally have ensued since then, based on the needs and trajectories of lower-proficiency immigrant learners, on the one hand, and 'foreign language' teachers and students, on the other, both of which groups may be ill-served by such stringent policies. Concerns were expressed that learners' mother tongues were becoming a 'neglected resource' (Atkinson, 1987) or, to put it more starkly, were forbidden or taboo, or worse, were the 'enemy' in L2 education (Swain et al., 2011). The view was that policies proscribing any use of learners' L1s might not be conducive to the development of bilingualism, biculturalism and the affirmation of learners' lives, knowledge and identities and, furthermore, reduced opportunities for explicit cross-linguistic metalinguistic awareness-raising.

Research over the past two decades has primarily (as in our earlier work) explored the functions served by students'/teachers' L1 and L2 use in FL classrooms – or in particular proxy sites, such as in computer-mediated classroom-related virtual communication spaces. The goal has been to better understand the language alternation from a functional view as well as ascertain teachers' beliefs and interpretations of what transpires or should transpire, according to policies or conventions, in those sites (e.g. de la Campa & Nassaji, 2009; Edstrom, 2006; Gaebler, 2013–2014; Kim & Elder, 2005; Rolin-Ianziti & Brownlie, 2002; Rolin-Ianziti & Varshney, 2008). Some of the studies also consider how and why such (maximal-L2) language policies – official or unofficial – are implemented and enforced (if at all), and to what effect. Some scholars (e.g. Mökkönen, 2013) have documented how students themselves may begin to enforce L2-only norms established by teachers by policing one another's use of L1/L2 (i.e. through peer socialization: 'Use English!'), in parallel with how their teachers correct students for using other languages (and especially their L1), rather than the L2. Alternatively, students may knowingly subvert L2-only classroom policies for various peer-affiliative reasons, as in Mökkönen's research in elementary school English immersion classrooms in Finland.

Since the early 1990s, therefore, a vast amount of research and writing has been produced on the larger issues surrounding multilingual language use (also called codeswitching, alternation, L1+L2 use or translanguaging, though the terms are not necessarily synonymous) in classrooms with language learners. It is not possible in this chapter to provide a comprehensive account of the entire body of research (refer to Hall & Cook, 2012 for a wider range of studies on what they call 'own-language' [L1] vs. TL use in many classroom settings around the world). However, a number of factors have given rise to new perspectives on multilingual educational practice and also new ways of thinking about old topics such as L1 versus L2 use in language education; these factors include increasing transnationalism and transmigration, the affordances of the internet, electronic translation tools and new (and social) media, greater ethnolinguistic diversity of language learners, more opportunities for study abroad, flexible and distance learning, combined with new theoretical perspectives related to multilingualism and mediated language learning (see e.g. Douglas Fir Group, 2016), and 'post-Method' thinking.

In the remainder of this chapter, I discuss the research according to arguments either in favor of (1) more extensive L2 or monolingual (L2 only) language use, or (2) greater multilingual social practice. I conclude with a set of overarching principles and factors derived from this body of work and suggestions for future work that reflects a more situated, agentive and nuanced view of mediated language learning.

Arguments and Research in Favor of (Mostly) Monolingual L2 Classrooms

The core principle in the early research was that L2 learners need extensive exposure to oral (and written) language, pitched at an appropriate level and in alignment with their interests and goals, and part of a well-designed curriculum. In addition to the work by Duff and Polio referred to earlier, many others doing research with learners with a strong foundation in their L1 (e.g. Anglophone FL learners in US universities; Anglophone students in French immersion or Core French classes) have supported or documented this 'L2-mostly' instructional approach and also some of the factors that can facilitate, complicate or mitigate its implementation. For example, in French instruction in Canada (both in Core French – also known as French as a Second Language – and French immersion), there has been significant scholarship supporting the view that teachers and students should optimize their use of French in such courses, conceding, however, that learners' L1 can play an important role when used by teachers and students in particular ways (Turnbull, 2001; Turnbull & Arnett, 2002; Turnbull & Dailey-O'Cain, 2009).

Many public and private English language school programs have 'English-only' language policies (and 'pledges' by clients/students to uphold those policies) both in and out of class (e.g. in corridors, dormitories), whether for adults or children. Similar policies with language pledges in other L2 settings also exist (e.g. Chinese-L2 programs in Beijing for American students). For example, the long-established Princeton University in Beijing Program has the following pledge, which is even provided on the program website (https://pib.princeton.edu/academics/language-pledge): 'I hereby pledge to use, in all my contacts, no language other than Mandarin Chinese for the duration of the program. I understand that failure to abide by the pledge will result in my dismissal from the program and forfeiture of tuition'. The explanation given is that this policy is designed to help students (with exceptions allowed, such as communication with family members back in the US or when dealing with emergencies) so they will not 'ruin the learning atmosphere for other students'. Many summer intensive language programs for other languages have similar pledge requirements (e.g. Middlebury Language Schools; http://www.middlebury.edu/ls/academics/language-pledge).

One rationale for this kind of policy is that it gives same-L1 peers license and opportunities to practice using their L2 together when it would otherwise be sociolinguistically unnatural to do so and when they might be shunned by same-L1 peers for trying to practice their L2 instead of using their shared L1. Some study abroad language programs have even considered (L1) 'media pledges' and not just L2-only use among participants, with the goal of restricting students' access to Facebook, streamed L1 media, etc., for similar reasons (Godwin-Jones, 2016). Indeed, for some schools, these policies may actually be part of a powerful marketing strategy. Such L2-only policies are currently quite contentious though. The cognitive and linguistic burdens of immersion in an L2 and the inability to express oneself freely in one's L1 can be challenging for some learners in such programs (and non-native-speaker teachers) and can be inefficient for certain kinds of explanations. For example, in a study involving classroom observation and interviews by Duff and Li (2004)[11] in a first-year Mandarin university course, the teacher who was the focus of the study reported:

> I agree it is better to immerse the students in the target language as much as possible. However, forbidding any use of native language in a [foreign language] FL classroom is unnecessary. The native language can facilitate FL learning if used appropriately and in a timely way, especially at the beginning stage when students could be overwhelmed or even

intimidated by unreasonable target language use that far exceeds their level. ... However, I do believe as time goes along, we need to maximize target language use to the extent possible.

The students in the study concurred. Half said it was 'effective' or 'highly effective' to have some explanations pertaining to Chinese characters, grammar and other topics given in English. One stated a fairly commonly held view among the students:

I guess it would be very effective [for the teacher to speak only Mandarin all of the time] but 80% of the people would probably defect and then the ones would stay, it would probably be very effective for them. Cause it takes a while too. Even now [we] have problems understanding things. Maybe you [=we] wouldn't have as many problems if it was always in Chinese. But there's many things that you cannot explain until you have a certain level... I think it's [best] to combine both [languages] and then at an intermediate level or whatever go all Chinese.

Another student who was asked about the L1–L2 balance in the course stated:

I think [the mix of Chinese and English in class] is great. I do. I think that it's too soon to be speaking constantly in Chinese. I think she [instructor] needs to speak English for us to understand completely. At least for me to understand completely. But when she talks in Chinese and says phrases in Chinese and repeats things using our vocabulary, of course I would expect she would be saying it in Mandarin. But I think especially at the first year... you need to mix a little bit of the English, otherwise I think it becomes too difficult and too frustrating if it's constantly in that language.

These comments concerned the *teacher's* L2 use primarily in an FL course. Limited research (to my knowledge) has examined issues that arise when L2-only policies are enforced in out-of-class interactions with FL instructors, such as during office hour consultations when lower-proficiency students are required to use their L2 but struggle to do so. Some research has looked at *students'* L1/L2 in-class use with their classmates, however. Expecting students to use the L2-only among peers can be enabling – in the sense that they are encouraged to produce the L2, as noted above – but it can also have a silencing or stultifying effect on communication for some students in certain contexts. Tarone and Swain (1995) observed that children in L2 immersion programs (e.g. Spanish-L2 in Minnesota or French-L2 in Ontario) often switched to their L1 for interpersonal peer–peer communication even after several years in elementary school L2 immersion during which they had primarily used their L2. This shift to L1 in the later grades seemed to occur precisely because the students could not be as playful or colloquial in their L2 (Spanish or French) as in English. That is, they lacked suitable vernacular speech forms (such as slang) to fully display their identities and roles or to employ a wider variety of speech acts with their peers. The more formal – and sanitized – academic register used by their teachers, their primary source of oral L2 input, simply did not prepare them for (or allow) this wider variety of non-academic but highly valued sociolinguistic forms. Such classrooms, over time, become increasingly diglossic in that respect, particularly in 'off-task' interactions excluding the teacher.

The challenge, then, is for teachers to provide *sufficient optimized exposure* to a range of high-value registers, genres and so on, in the L2 so that students can comprehend, cultivate and mobilize larger L2 linguistic and sociolinguistic repertoires (depending, of course, on their purposes for L2 learning) and develop L2 identities in the process. They must also develop sufficient *accuracy*, *fluency*, and *complexity* in their L2 (Housen & Kuiken, 2009), which requires considerable amounts of practice (particularly *fluency*). Swain's (1985) important constructs of *comprehensible output* and *pushed output* support the view that students should have meaningful opportunities to both hear (or read) and *produce* the L2 in order to develop.

Arguments and Research in Favor of More Openly Multilingual Classrooms

Pedagogy in K-12 bilingual/immersion instructional programs in Canada typically requires a complete separation of languages, with only the L2 (e.g. French) used during class time in the early years of immersion programs, except in English language arts, and other ways of compartmentalizing L1 and L2 in bilingual programs (e.g. alternating days of instruction in one or the other language). This ideology of language separation or compartmentalization, in principle, has teachers and students use only the TL (French) in their French immersion programs and proscribes English (L1) use. Teachers may even pretend to be monolingual L2 (French) speakers to simulate a totally L2 immersive learning environment and to create a context where children must communicate in French. Some years later in the elementary curriculum, additional subject-matter courses may be taught in English but the main principle is that there should not be a combination of languages used within a given course: English courses are taught in English and those designated as French-medium (mathematics, etc.) are taught in French.

However, as Cummins (2007) has argued, not integrating students' languages, in the case of French immersion programs in Canada or other bilingual educational contexts, is highly unnatural and perpetuates what he calls a 'dual solitudes' approach and ideology. Furthermore, in most cases, students are emerging bilinguals (or trilinguals) and teachers are (at least in French immersion programs) multicompetent in two or more languages – not monolingual francophones, as they may appear to be. Yet, the policies and traditions in those contexts do not permit teachers to draw on the other languages they and students know in order to facilitate cross-linguistic learning, consciousness-raising and transfer (Cook, 2001; Cummins, 2007). Thus, rather than openly socializing students into such multilingual practices and the identities associated with them, using themselves as models, the multilingual teachers are required to adopt and perpetuate monolingual ideologies or norms (even if inconsistent in enacting them; Mökkönen, 2013). Cook (2001) insists that we should be aiming for (linguistic) multicompetence in language education, not 'dual monolingualism' (English-only in English-medium classes and French-only in French ones, for example) (see Fortune & Tedick's chapter in this volume for an alternative perspective on this issue).

Scholars critical of the earlier or traditional approach to L2-mostly (i.e. more monolingual) classrooms, especially the most dogmatic version, note that such policies unnaturally deny students (and teachers) opportunities to perform their multilingual competencies and identities in class time in the way they would in many bilingual situations outside of class. Further, in a monolingual L2 classroom students and teachers are unable to use the L1 explicitly to scaffold the L2 and other content-matter learning and use (Swain et al., 2011). Arguments and instructional materials supporting a more bi- or multilingual and multiliterate approach are plentiful nowadays (e.g. Cummins, 2007; Levine, 2011) not just in Canada and the US (García et al., 2017) but in many other countries as well (e.g. Cenoz & Gorter, 2015). In addition, although most of the early research on this topic focused on oral classroom discourse, a growing body of research is looking at other modalities, such as reading and writing, or providing input in one modality and language, with the expectation that students will produce discourse through a different modality in a different language. For example, they will read a text in their L1 and produce oral or written responses in the L2, and vice versa (Canagarajah, 2013a, 2013b; Cenoz & Gorter, 2015; García et al., 2017). Or they will interview members of their communities in their shared (e.g. heritage) L1 and then produce dual-language books, stories or 'identity texts' in the L2 (and often the L1 as well; see Cummins, 2007; Cummins & Early, 2011).

Concerns, even in FL contexts, have been expressed in terms of teachers' preparedness to enact communicative language teaching maximizing TL use, given their own proficiency levels, their contexts, the nature of the curriculum and high-stakes assessment that does not in fact reward communicative competence but focuses more on lexico-grammatical knowledge and reading comprehension (Liu et al., 2004). Forcing maximal use of TL use in English as a foreign language (EFL) contexts, it is felt, undermines local language teachers' expertise as bilinguals with knowledge of both languages (and the national curriculum and assessment system) that might help scaffold their learners' TL development through metalinguistic explanations, translation and so on (Li, 1998). For example, in FL contexts like English in Korea and other parts of Asia that have tried to implement monolingual policies in elementary schools such as 'Teaching English through English' (TETE), it is often noted that such policies are less effective than they should be in providing students with high-quality English education experiences; what is more, they foster a culture of expensive, after-school, prep school ('shadow education') coursework with native or more proficient English speakers, or encourage participation in early study abroad programs to Anglophone countries to complement or compensate for what is perceived to be inadequate instruction at school (Li, 1998; Liu *et al.*, 2004). Also, when these countries enact such policies, they often allocate substantial government budgets to recruit native English speakers, who typically have no knowledge of students' L1s or the local national curriculum, to serve as monolingual English-speaking language models or assistants in classrooms. All of these factors serve to undermine the confidence, legitimacy and professional identities of local non-native English teachers (or other non-native TL teachers in different contexts, such as Anglophone teachers of Mandarin in British Columbia; e.g. Lecki, 2011).

Wang and Kirkpatrick (2012) critiqued monolingual-L2 policies adopted over the past decade in China for the teaching of Mandarin to foreign learners coming from many different L1 backgrounds. The authors argued that, since English is typically a lingua franca for learners in China, more could be done *in English* (in a 'judicious' manner – a frequent qualifier in the literature generally) to support Chinese teaching. (On the other hand, the demographic diversity could also present a strong argument for focusing on students' shared L2, Chinese, rather than seeking recourse to another lingua franca that teachers and students might not all be equally proficient in – though that was not the researchers' own view.) And, since many trained Chinese teachers of L2 Chinese have opportunities to travel overseas to teach Chinese, they increasingly require high proficiency in English as well as in Chinese, because English may be the L1 or lingua franca of students not only in China but also abroad. English is therefore increasingly used in their teacher education programs even in China and for Chinese language education. However, more than half the university Chinese-L2 teachers in Wang and Kirkpatrick's study of 24 university-level Chinese teachers subscribed to a Chinese (L2)-only approach (also called a 'virtual' approach) and the remainder believed in a 'maximal' or 'optimal' L2 approach; 'optimal' refers to strategic and possibly liberal use of the L1, if desired. The teachers also reported feeling inadequate when using English with more proficient English-speaking students (again, in my view, a good argument for focusing on the effective use of Chinese instead). 'Chinese-only' signs were posted in some of their program corridors, similar to the 'English-only' ones described in many Anglophone education contexts. In fact, some teachers even made connections between Chinese use and patriotism. One quoted a Chinese Nobel Prize winner who said: 'We should defend ourselves against the invasion of English' as the rationale for upholding the Chinese-only policy. Codeswitching, according to several of the teachers, was a 'stain on their Sinophone identity', 'pretentious' and 'fake' (Wang & Kirkpatrick, 2012: 8). Thus, political and linguistic ideologies of cultural and linguistic purity (and superiority) were very evident and implicit in the language-use policy.

The benefits of strategic L1 use in L2 classrooms have been well documented over the past two decades. For example, Swain's constructs of *languaging* and *collaborative dialogue* (e.g. Swain & Lapkin, 2000) emphasize the value of having students engage in dialogue with one another to solve particular language problems in their L2 by using their metalinguistic and other knowledge (from L1, L2, etc.). Much of this reported collaborative dialogue involved students' L1 (typically English in Canadian French immersion or French as a second language [FSL] contexts), even when discussing French lexical, grammatical and other issues. The L1 and the talk about language serve as a scaffold to mediate students' cognition about the L2. (The students also apparently had ample exposure to L2 French in their programs, which is a critical consideration.)

Other related research adopting a Vygotskian sociocultural perspective, like Swain and Lapkin's (2000), concurs that the L1 can serve an important scaffolding or mediating role in L2 classrooms (e.g. Antón & DiCamilla, 1998; Storch & Wigglesworth, 2003; Swain & Lapkin, 2013; Swain *et al.*, 2011). More recently, scholars drawing on the principle of *translanguaging* and *heteroglossia* (e.g. Canagarajah, 2013a; Creese & Blackledge, 2010) argue that disallowing students' on-task use of their various languages in class denies them their linguistic, cognitive and social resources and capital, and, therefore, aspects of their identities and voice as well. Levine (2011, and elsewhere) summarizes and illustrates sociocultural and ecological approaches to multi-code use in language classrooms, citing examples from German as an FL in the US.

These researchers, collectively, have thus argued that trying to socialize students into strict L2-only use in classrooms is unnatural, unrealistic and unhelpful to particular types of learners and to learning in general. Furthermore, it may impede fruitful and efficient discussion of particular topics for which students may lack the requisite L2 resources (e.g. culture, grammar, metalanguage) and for which reference to their L1 or other languages would also enhance their metalinguistic awareness. Concept-based instruction, for example, according to Negueruela and Lantolf (2006: 82), 'supports explicit teaching in grammar [e.g.

tense-aspect systems] to promote the learner's awareness and control over specific conceptual categories as they are linked to formal properties of the language'. Both the L1 and L2 are used (according to students' preferences) to assist with the learning of concepts such as grammatical mood and aspect and in their verbalizations about their cognition about the concepts and related linguistic choices.

In addition, translation is a sophisticated skill that seems to be coming back into vogue, particularly in advanced language classes (Cook, 2010; Cummins, 2007; Hall & Cook, 2012). For many bi- or multilinguals, moving seamlessly across languages is perhaps second nature, but for classroom-based L2 learners it is a skill that must also be learned and cultivated. However, given the fraught and often maligned history of grammar-translation teaching and assessment approaches from the 20th century, and critiques of it not preparing students well to communicate in everyday contexts, especially in oral communication, there has been less applied linguistic research on *translation* than other aspects of instruction, at least within recent work dealing with L1-L2 classroom language.

Table 12.1 summarizes some of the points made so far. Although I have presented the two main positions in the text and in the table as a binary, that is an oversimplification for heuristic reasons primarily.

Ways Forward: Mediating Policies, Pedagogies and Practices

Teachers and policy-makers must understand the local contexts and demographics of L2 instruction, the socio-cognitive processes of L2 learning and bilingualism (and additive vs. subtractive language education) and the pedagogical possibilities as well as concerns regarding the use of students' languages in classrooms. Understanding these issues well will allow them to make reasoned, contextualized accommodations regarding multilingual language use in their classrooms both by teachers and students. Being punitive or dogmatic about L1/L2 use is likely to be counterproductive in many contemporary language learning situations. Indeed, communicative language teaching is now much more flexible in this regard (Duff, 2014). Codeswitching or translanguaging strategically can be a resource and a form of social practice not just in the service of learning and 'doing' languaging, but also for identity enactment, creativity, analysis and play. In some contexts, students' languages are also being strategically incorporated into high-stakes assessment (e.g. high school matriculation exams) so they can demonstrate their knowledge of concepts (e.g. in mathematics) in the languages they feel most competent in and not in official languages only (Shohamy, 2017). Such developments reflect the growing recognition that forcing immigrant students to perform in their L2 only in various curricular areas may disadvantage them because they may underperform due to language, not key conceptual or disciplinary knowledge.

Table 12.1 Monolingual vs. multilingual language classrooms

Factors	Monolingual (L2/TL primarily)	Multilingual (L1, L2, L3...)
Cognitive load, processing	• L2-heavy use may place a higher cognitive load on particular tasks than would occasional recourse to the L1	• Leveraging students' knowledge and understandings in L1 may reduce cognitive load of language/content processing in L2 • Teaching students how to move across language systems in strategic ways may make them metalinguistically more aware and more fluent in translanguaging
Teachers' proficiency, agency, confidence and experience	• These aspects may impact implementation of the maximal-L2 approach, thereby undermining pedagogy and teachers' agency and identities	• The teacher (if bilingual, and not a native speaker of L2) models multicompetence and can provide L1 explanations and correspondences, if needed
Affective considerations: Students' and teachers' anxiety and guilt	• Student anxiety may increase when fully surrounded by L2 • Teachers and students may feel guilty when resorting to L1 counter to policy • Teachers may feel anxious when not able to fully implement an L2-mostly/only curriculum	• Anxiety and guilt are likely not an issue unless worried about insufficient immersion into or development of L2
Intersubjectivity among learners (or between teachers and learners)	• Intersubjectivity can be fostered but may not be as attainable for lower-level learners than for those who are more proficient	• L1 use helps create greater intersubjectivity, but other factors are also at play
Parental pressures (and program marketing)	• May support greater L2 use, especially when children have limited exposure to L2 outside of class	• Immigrant/minority-language parents may prefer more multilingual approaches to validate home languages and permit greater parental involvement • However, some parents may want to maximize L2 development through immersion, especially when large numbers of same-L1 peers study together
Intensity of L2 exposure and frequency of encounters with particular grammatical, lexical, pragmatic and other forms	• Likely greater with more L2 use, and still thought to be very important in L2 learning	• Likely somewhat reduced, or mediated by other languages; however, salience of particular forms may be increased through L1 metalanguage and awareness-raising activities
Quality of L2 exposure and instruction	• Depends on instruction, teachers' proficiency and training	• Depends on instruction, teachers' proficiency and training • Lowering expectations regarding L2 use may lower L2 standards and communicative practices

Factors	Monolingual (L2/TL primarily)	Multilingual (L1, L2, L3...)
Role and recognition of students' 'funds of knowledge'/communicative repertoires	• Limited formal inclusion of prior learning based on L1	• More possibility to tap into students' prior linguistic (L1 or other language) knowledge
Opportunities for languaging/translanguaging	• Restricted, depending on students' L2 proficiency	• Possible at all proficiency levels
Opportunities to foster metalinguistic or concept-based knowledge about L2	• This may depend on proficiency level, teaching approach and age of learners	• Opportunities across proficiency levels for deep concept-based learning

Negotiating such matters within programs and classrooms, providing sufficient linguistic – and, where relevant, multilingual – scaffolds for students and supporting decisions with research-based evidence are all necessary elements of well-informed pedagogy and policy. Having teachers examine their own L1/L2 use and beliefs or ideologies and those of students may help them develop reflexivity and awareness about their decision-making (e.g. Macaro, 2001, 2009) and their pedagogical practices as well. They could perhaps consider alternatives, including the strategic use of translation, L1–L2 contrasts or movement from one linguistic mode to another in different phases of an activity. Planning ahead of time how to use the L1 to scaffold the L2 in particular situations in a principled manner is recommended (Swain *et al.*, 2011). Fortunately, many new resources discuss translanguaging and multilingualism in L2 education and provide valuable examples and insights, particularly for K-12 teachers (e.g. Cummins & Early, 2011; García *et al.*, 2017).

There is no single best way to teach languages or to teach academic content through languages when considering the many kinds of languages involved in language education worldwide – indigenous, classical, foreign, heritage, second, global lingua francas such as English and 'less-commonly taught' languages such as Vietnamese or Ukrainian. Instructional contexts and learner characteristics also vary considerably. Clear, context-appropriate, attainable educational objectives are key. As the Douglas Fir Group (2016) suggested, we need to critically examine current local/global trends, resources, ethnolinguistic ecologies and demographics, as well as prevailing linguistic and educational ideologies when considering L2 learning and teaching.

In addition, research on learner agency, autonomy and motivation stresses the provision of *choice* for learners – based on their comfort levels, preferred learning styles and strategies, needs and interests, and resources (Duff & Doherty, 2015). Understanding important differences among L2 learners/users in terms of desire for more versus less L2 use (and, conversely less vs. more L1) and in relation to particular pedagogical functions is therefore essential. Learners who have previously had extensive naturalistic exposure to the L2 may find limited access to L2 speech in classrooms at odds with their goals and expectations and their preferred learning 'habitus'. On the other hand, students with only formal, structured prior exposure to the L2 through instruction, possibly with limited L2 use, may be intimidated by large amounts of L2, particularly if they don't understand it or classroom instructions and explanations. In the Duff and Polio (1990) study, when students and teachers were interviewed about their respective perceptions and preferences regarding L1/L2 use and functions, students often reported very modest expectations about the amount of L2 that could or should be provided by teachers, particularly in non-European languages. As for teachers, there appeared to be varying degrees of alignment between their actual practice and their perceptions of their behaviors (English vs. L2 use, specifically) – often leading to inflated estimates of their actual L2 use based on recorded classroom observations of teacher talk. Furthermore, teachers who wished to start with more L1 use in lower levels or phases of L2 teaching with the goal of increasing their L2 use over time sometimes found themselves still using relatively little L2 even with more advanced students, despite their good intentions. Their L1 dependence became entrenched as they focused primarily on grammatical or metalinguistic explanation in class, even though all four skills were to be taught.

Future research could aim to ascertain teachers' and learners' views and experiences by means of first-person teaching/learning narratives or journals, interviews, classroom observations, stimulated recall and researchers' functional analyses of classroom language use. As in Kobayashi's research (Duff & Kobayashi, 2010; Kobayashi, 2003), researchers can also document students' in-class and out-of-class language use during assigned activities, noting how students might codeswitch heavily or use significant amounts of L1 (Japanese) in the early stages of an activity or project when first planning the activity together, then switch to greater L2 use over the course of the project while preparing for, and delivering, in-class group presentations, for example. Kobayashi's research revealed how university students strategically used their L1 to help define and manage the phases of their project and negotiate the meanings and structures of particular language forms (e.g. adjectives or speech acts) that appeared on or accompanied their English PowerPoint slides. Moore (2013) conducted similar research in a Japanese-L1/English-L2 activity-based context involving oral presentations.

Studies can also compare L2 learning outcomes (e.g. in terms of accuracy, fluency and complexity) and levels of satisfaction under conditions of different classroom language policies and practices. Many descriptive studies, as noted earlier, have undertaken functional analyses of teachers' codeswitching or L1/L2 use in many kinds of programs and at different proficiency and age levels. Some sociolinguistic and discourse/conversation analytic studies (e.g. Üstünel & Seedhouse, 2005) have been conducted on the organization and management of interactions that draw on learners' multiple languages and modalities to better understand communication processes, creativity, resourcefulness, participation, identity performance and learning.

Longitudinal case studies, furthermore, might enhance work in this area by examining if, how and when teachers' and students' linguistic practices change over time as they gain additional experience, mentoring and L2 proficiency – and how students' L1/L2 use and L2 learning develop accordingly. Relatedly, longitudinal research should be conducted on student teachers' or new teachers' experiences and how, if at all, their beliefs and practices related to L1/L2 evolve over time (e.g. as Bateman, 2008 did with 10 student teachers of L2 Spanish in the US and as others have done with fewer participants or for a shorter time; e.g. Macaro, 2001). The relationship between sponsor teachers' L1–L2 practices and policies in teaching practicum contexts and those of student teachers could also be examined as part of professional socialization.

Conclusion

In conclusion, L1/L2 or monolingual/multilingual debates continue to be of considerable theoretical interest in our field. The research has moved well beyond (K-16) FL/L2 classrooms in North America to content-based, L2-medium-of-instruction and EFL (or other L2) programs in many other parts of the world and involving a wider constellation of languages and teaching cultures. The associated policies and practices can be very consequential for teachers and learners, sometimes leading to attrition: teachers leaving the profession because of frustration, guilt, difficulty or insecurity, on the one hand, or unmet (or possibly unreachable) expectations about L2 use or pedagogies, on the other. Students, too, may quit if they feel their linguistic expectations and needs are not being met. It is therefore necessary, albeit complex, to try to accommodate teachers and learners with varying backgrounds, abilities and desires with respect to classroom language policies and practices, and to conduct innovative research on both the learning processes and outcomes.

Acknowledgment

Professor Merrill Swain, whose stellar contributions to applied linguistics scholarship are honored in this book, generated important theoretical insights, constructs and empirical data relevant to the debates represented in this chapter (and others), as did many of her former colleagues and doctoral students at the Ontario Institute for Studies in Education at the University of Toronto. I dedicate this chapter to her, with my profound gratitude and admiration.

Note

(1) The original draft of the chapter had a section on L1 versus L2 use that was removed from the published paper due to space limitations. This is therefore previously unpublished data.

References

Antón, M. and DiCamilla, F. (1998) Socio-cognitive functions of L1 collaborative interactions in the L2 classroom. *Canadian Modern Language Review* 54 (3), 314–342.

Atkinson, D. (1987) The mother tongue in the classroom: A neglected resource? *ELT Journal* 41 (4), 241–247.

Auerbach, E.R. (1993) Reexamining English only in the ESL classroom. *TESOL Quarterly* 27 (1), 9–32.

Bateman, B.E. (2008) Student teachers' attitudes and beliefs about using the target language in the classroom. *Foreign Language Annals* 41 (1), 11–28.

Canagarajah, A.S. (ed.) (2013a) *Literacy as Translingual Practice: Between Communities and Classrooms*. New York: Routledge.

Canagarajah, A.S. (2013b) *Translingual Practice: Global Englishes and Cosmopolitan Relations*. New York: Routledge.

Cenoz, J. and Gorter, D. (eds) (2015) *Multilingual Education: Between Language Learning and Translanguaging*. Cambridge: Cambridge University Press.

Coleman, J. (2006) English-medium teaching in European higher education. *Language Teaching* 39, 1–14.

Cook, G. (2010) *Translation in Language Teaching: An Argument for Reassessment*. Oxford: Oxford University Press.

Cook, V. (2001) Using the first language in the classroom. *Canadian Modern Language Review* 57, 399–423.

Creese, A. and Blackledge, A. (2010) Translanguaging in the bilingual classroom: A pedagogy for learning and teaching? *Modern Language Journal* 94 (1), 103–115.

Creese, A. and Blackledge, A. (2015) Translanguaging and identity in educational settings. *Annual Review of Applied Linguistics* 35, 20–35.

Cummins, J. (2007) Rethinking monolingual instructional strategies in multilingual classrooms. *Canadian Journal of Applied Linguistics* 10 (2), 221–240.

Cummins, J. and Early, M. (2011) *Identity Texts: The Collaborative Creation of Power in Multilingual Schools*. Stoke on Trent: Trentham Books.

de la Campa, J. and Nassaji, H. (2009) The amount, purpose, and reasons for using L1 in L2 classrooms. *Foreign Language Annals* 42 (4), 742–759.

Douglas Fir Group (2016) A transdisciplinary framework for SLA in a multilingual world. *Modern Language Journal* 100 (Supplement 2016), 19–47.

Duff, P. (2014) Communicative language teaching. In M. Celce-Murcia, D. Brinton and M.A. Snow (eds) *Teaching English as a Second or Foreign Language* (4th edn; pp. 15–30). Boston, MA: Heinle Cengage.

Duff, P. and Polio, C. (1990) How much foreign language is there in the foreign language classroom? *The Modern Language Journal* 74, 154–166.

Duff, P. and Li, D. (2004) Issues in Mandarin language instruction: Theory, research, and practice. *System* 32 (3), 443–456.

Duff, P. and Kobayashi, M. (2010) The intersection of social, cognitive, and cultural processes in language learning. In R. Batstone (ed.) *Sociocognitive Perspectives on Language Use and Language Learning* (pp. 75–93). Oxford: Oxford University Press.

Duff, P. and Doherty, L. (2015) Examining agency in (second) language socialization research. In P. Deters, X. Gao, E. Miller and G. Vitanova (eds) *Interdisciplinary Approaches to Theorizing and Analyzing Agency and Second Language Learning* (pp. 54–72). Bristol: Multilingual Matters.

Edstrom, A. (2006) L1 use in the L2 classroom: One teacher's self-evaluation. *Canadian Modern Language Review* 63 (2), 275–292.

Fenton-Smith, B., Humphreys, P. and Walkinshaw, I. (eds) (2017) *English Medium Instruction in Higher Education in Asia-Pacific: From Policy to Pedagogy*. Cham: Springer International.

Gaebler, P. (2013–2014) L1 use in FL classrooms: Graduate students' and professors' perceptions of English use in foreign language courses. *The CATESOL Journal* 25 (1), 66–94.

García, O., Johnson, S.I. and Seltzer, K. (2017) *The Translanguaging Classroom: Leveraging Student Bilingualism for Learning*. Philadelphia, PA: Caslon.

Godwin-Jones, R. (2016) Emerging technologies integrating technology into study abroad. *Language Learning & Technology* 20, 1–20.

Hall, G. and Cook, G. (2012) Own-language use in language teaching and learning. *Language Teaching* 45 (3), 271–308.

Housen, A. and Kuiken, F. (2009) Complexity, accuracy, and fluency in second language acquisition. *Applied Linguistics* 30 (4), 461–473.

Kim, S. and Elder, C. (2005) Language choices and pedagogic functions in the foreign language classroom: A cross-linguistic functional analysis of teacher talk. *Language Teaching Research* 9 (4), 355–380.

Kobayashi, M. (2003) The role of peer support in ESL students' accomplishment of oral academic tasks. *Canadian Modern Language Review* 59 (3), 337–368.

Lecki, S.E. (2011) The non-native modern language teacher: Language practices, choices, and challenges. MA thesis, The University of British Columbia, Vancouver. See https://open.library.ubc.ca/cIRcle/collections/ubctheses/24/items/1.0071760 (accessed 3 November 2018).

Levine, G.S. (2011) *Code Choice in the Language Classroom*. Bristol: Multilingual Matters.

Li, D. (1998) 'It's always more difficult than you plan and imagine': Teachers' perceived difficulties in introducing the communicative approach in South Korea. *TESOL Quarterly* 32 (4), 677–703.

Liu, D., Ahn, G-S., Baek, K-S. and Han, N-O. (2004) South Korean high school English teachers' code switching: Questions and challenges in the drive for maximal use of English in teaching. *TESOL Quarterly* 38 (4), 605–638.

Macaro, E. (2001) Analysing student teachers' codeswitching in foreign language classrooms: Theories and decision making. *Modern Language Journal* 85 (4), 531–548.

Macaro, E. (2009) Teacher use of codeswitching in the second language classroom: Exploring 'optimal' use. In M. Turnbull and J. Dailey-O'Cain (eds) *First Language Use in Second and Foreign Language Learning* (pp. 35–49). Bristol: Multilingual Matters.

Mökkönen, A.C. (2013) Newcomers navigating language choice and seeking voice: Peer talk in a multilingual primary school classroom in Finland. *Anthropology and Education Quarterly* 44 (2), 124–141.

Moore, P.J. (2013) An emergent perspective on the use of the first language in the English-as-a-foreign-language classroom. *The Modern Language Journal* 97 (1), 239–253.

Negueruela, E. and Lantolf, J.P. (2006) Concept-based instruction and the acquisition of L2 Spanish. In R. Salaberry and B.A. Lafford (eds) *The Art of Teaching Spanish: Second Language Acquisition from Research to Praxis* (pp. 79–102). Washington, DC: Georgetown University Press.

Polio, C. (1994) Comments on Elsa Roberts Auerbach's 'Reexamining English only in the ESL classroom': A reader reacts... *TESOL Quarterly* 28 (1), 153–157.

Polio, C.G. and Duff, P.A. (1994) Teachers' language use in university foreign language classrooms: A qualitative analysis of English and target language alternation. *Modern Language Journal* 78 (3), 313–326.

Rolin-Ianziti, J. and Brownlie, S. (2002) Teacher use of the learners' native language in the foreign language classroom. *The Canadian Modern Language Review* 58 (3), 402–426.

Rolin-Ianziti, J. and Varshney, R. (2008) Students' views regarding the use of the first language: An exploratory study in tertiary context maximizing target language use. *The Canadian Modern Language Review* 65 (2), 249–273.

Shohamy, E. (2017, July) The socio-political-economic ideologies of English: What is the cost? Plenary talk at the Korean Association of Teachers of English, Hankuk University, Seoul, Korea.

Storch, N. and Wigglesworth, G. (2003) Is there a role for the use of the L1 in an L2 setting? *TESOL Quarterly* 37 (4), 760–770.

Swain, M. (1985) Communicative competence: Some roles of comprehensible input and comprehensible output in its development. In S. Gass and C. Madden (eds) *Input in Second Language Acquisition* (pp. 235–253). Rowley, MA: Newbury House.

Swain, M. and Lapkin, S. (2000) Task-based second language learning: The uses of the first language. *Language Teaching Research* 4 (3), 251–274.

Swain, M. and Lapkin, S. (2013) A Vygotskian sociocultural perspective on immersion education: The L1/L2 debate. *Journal of Immersion and Content-Based Language Education* 1 (1), 101–129.

Swain, M., Kirkpatrick, A. and Cummins, J. (2011) *How to have a Guilt-Free Life Using Cantonese in the English Class: A Handbook for the English Language Teacher in Hong Kong.* Hong Kong, China: Research Centre into Language Acquisition and Education in Multilingual Societies, Hong Kong Institute of Education.

Tarone, E. and Swain, M. (1995) A sociolinguistic perspective on second language use in immersion classrooms. *Modern Language Journal* 79 (2), 166–178.

Turnbull, M. (2001) There is a role for the L1 in second and foreign language teaching, but ... *Canadian Modern Language Review* 57, 531–540.

Turnbull, M. and Arnett, K. (2002) Teachers' uses of the target and first languages in second and foreign language classrooms. *Annual Review of Applied Linguistics* 22, 204–218.

Turnbull, M. and Dailey-O'Cain, J. (eds) (2009) *First Language Use in Second and Foreign Language Learning.* Bristol: Multilingual Matters.

Üstünel, E. and Seedhouse, P. (2005) Why that, in that language, right now? Code-switching and pedagogical focus. *International Journal of Applied Linguistics* 15 (3), 302–324.

Wang, D. and Kirkpatrick, A. (2012) Code choice in the Chinese as a foreign language classroom. *Multilingual Education* 2 (3), 1–18. See https://link.springer.com/content/pdf/10.1186%2F2191-5059-2-3.pdf (accessed 3 November 2018).

13 Assisted Performance through Instructional Coaching: A Critical Sociocultural Perspective

Mari Haneda[1], Brandon Sherman and Annela Teemant

Instructional coaching. I would describe it as having a partner to help me think. And it has stretched me. I mean, [the coach] coming in and saying 'where do you want to go? How do you want to get there? And why do you want to get there?' has made me really think about what I'm doing in my classroom. I mean before, it was pretty automatic, you know? Let's just get through this skill in the basal and we're done for the day. And now it's like I don't want to do that anymore. I want to make them [kindergarteners] think and I want to make them be responsible and I want to bring back the fun. (Lisa, exit interview)

Lisa (pseudonym) is a veteran kindergarten teacher with 19 years of teaching experience. She works in a US Midwestern inner-city elementary school located in a low socioeconomic neighborhood. Her kindergartners include a large number of Spanish-speaking English learner (EL) students. Her exit interview was the endpoint of her participation in a longitudinal professional development (PD) project, of which instructional coaching was a key component. As revealed in Lisa' comments, she felt that having a coach as a thinking partner made her more mindful of her instructional goals, how to achieve them and why she wanted her kindergartners to achieve them. At the time of her participation in the PD, Lisa's school district was focused on high-stakes testing and prescriptive use of a prepackaged curriculum series. As Milner (2013: i) argues, 'Scripted and narrowed curriculum moves teaching away from professionalization by not allowing teachers to rely on their professional judgment to make curricula decisions for student learning'. The teachers in Lisa's school reported feelings of being generally demoralized. This included Lisa, who had felt she had lost her autonomy as a teacher.

It was against this background that Lisa participated in a PD project that adopted a critical sociocultural perspective on learning and teaching and used instructional coaching to support teacher pedagogical growth. While instructional coaching can manifest in different forms, taking a critical sociocultural perspective has specific implications for the goal(s) of coaching and its methods. Rather than merely supporting teachers to more effectively enact prescribed curricular standards, the goal of this form of coaching is to help teachers reflect on the nature of learning and to develop practices that encourage students to take ownership of their own learning. Grounded in the framework of critical sociocultural theory (e.g. Lewis *et al.*, 2006; Stetsenko, 2014; Vossoughi & Gutiérrez, 2016), this coaching approach conceptualizes the relationship between the coach and the teacher to be dialogic.

In this chapter, our aim is to illustrate how Lisa experienced 'assisted performance' (Tharp & Gallimore, 1988) through critical sociocultural instructional coaching (Teemant *et al.*, 2014) and how the coach participated in the process of Lisa's learning. It draws on data from seven cycles of video-recorded coaching meetings spread over one academic year between Sabrina (pseudonym), a veteran coach, and Lisa, an experienced kindergarten teacher. We focus on 'teacher growth' (Blase & Blase, 1998; Young *et al.*, 2005) where Lisa was observed to have difficulty but succeeded in growing professionally as she enacted practices that she had originally thought to be impossible with her emergent bilingual students. We also focus on how the coach assisted the teacher in overcoming the challenges she faced.

Assisted Performance and Critical Sociocultural Instructional Coaching

Fundamental to Vygotsky's theory of learning and development is that people learn through their joint participation in purposive shared activities, particularly when a more capable participant provides deliberate assistance. This concept was further developed by Swain as 'collaborative dialogue' (e.g. Swain, 2000; Swain & Lapkin, 2001) to signal the importance of peers in providing assistance to one another. In Vygotskian terms, teaching is effective only when it '*awakens and rouses to life those functions which are in a stage of maturing which lie in the zone of proximal development*' (ZPD) (Vygotsky, as cited in Tharp & Gallimore, 1988: 31, italics in the original). Viewed in this light, teaching can be seen as assisting students to do what they cannot yet do alone, without assistance. However, like students, teachers also have their own ZPDs; they, too, benefit from contingently responsive assistance, which enables them to grow as professionals. Instructional coaching is one of the means through which such assistance can be provided to pre- or in-service teachers (see the case of Merrill Swain as an academic mentor in Steinman's chapter in this volume). Furthermore, when well imple-mented, the dialogic dynamic that is created between coach and teacher can subsequently be enacted in the teacher–student relationship in the classroom.

In the literature on coaching, however, dialogue and the dialogic rela-tionship has received very little attention. Instead, the focus has tended to be on topics such as the efficacy of instructional coaching (e.g. Neuman & Wright, 2010; Teemant et al., 2011), coach roles and practices (e.g. Bean et al., 2010; Walpole & Blamey, 2008) and coaching as educational reform within schools (Coburn & Woulfin, 2012). Moreover, the empha-sis has tended to be on coaching approaches that are predicated on 'best practices' – those that are designed to support federally initiated reform initiatives in the US, such as 'Reading First' (Bean et al., 2010).

By contrast, the coaching experienced by Lisa was independent of state mandates. Instead, it built on Vygotskian sociocultural theory of the relationship between teaching and learning, while simultaneously taking a critical equity orientation inspired by Freire's (1970/2002) work.

The critical sociocultural teaching model, toward which this coach-ing is aimed, is based in part on 'Standards for Effective Pedagogy' pro-posed by Tharp et al. (2000). Tharp's pedagogical model is anchored in five sociocultural theory-informed pedagogical principles (i.e. standards), which represent a consensus in educational research on recommended teaching practices for language-minority students. In the teaching model with which Lisa was grappling, these are augmented by a sixth principle, Critical Stance (CS), developed by Teemant et al. (2014). CS represents a critical equity orientation and a transformative conceptual shift that has fundamental implications for the original five. Through this form of instructional coaching, teachers are encouraged to anchor their practice in the following six principles:

- Joint Productive Activity (teacher and students producing together).
- Language and Literacy Development (developing language and lit-eracy across the curriculum).
- Contextualization (connecting school to students' lives).
- Challenging Activities (teaching complex thinking).
- Instructional Conversation (IC; teaching through conversation in a small group).
- CS (teaching to transform inequities).

Infusing the first five principles, CS introduces the Freirean idea that teachers should engage students in dialogue so that they can develop 'the critical capacity to make choices and transform' reality (Freire, 1970/2002: 4). While CS introduces critical thinking, it goes beyond this with the ultimate aim of students' naming, reflecting upon and taking action to remedy societal inequities that they encounter in their lives and communities. The idea of CS is also central to the coach–teacher relationship in that the coach helps the teacher to assess her/his pedagogical practices from the critical sociocultural perspective and to consider alternative practices that allow students to take more ownership of their own learning. In pedagogical terms, a distinctive feature of critical sociocultural teaching is its emphasis on small group activity centers – a teacher center (IC) and multiple independent student centers. Small group configurations, especially ICs, create the necessary conditions for teachers to regularly assess, assist and advance students' learning within their ZPDs (Vygotsky, 1997).

In coaching sessions, the coach–teacher conversation is designed to model the IC configuration. At any given time, in their lessons, teachers are encouraged to design learning activities that incorporate at least three of the six principles identified above. By engaging with instructional coaching, teachers experiment with and learn to enact these pedagogical principles in the context of their own classrooms, working with existing curricula and modifying or extending them. The critical sociocultural instructional coaching model (Teemant et al., 2014), like other coaching models, involves multiple cycles of individualized instructional coaching, spread over one academic year. Each coaching cycle includes a 30-minute pre-conference (co-planning a lesson), a 45-minute classroom observation and a 30-minute post-conference (reflection and setting next goals). These coaching conversations are conducted one-on-one, allowing the coach to work within the teacher's ZPD.

Research on Teacher–Coach Interactions

In this chapter, we define teacher growth as uptake of practices, changes in general pedagogical approach or changes in expressed pedagogical beliefs, values and/or principles. However, within research on instructional coaching, where teacher growth has been the focus, it has been considered primarily in terms of self-reporting or pre/post-efficacy measures in quasi-experimental studies. This has resulted in much less attention being paid to the qualitative changes that teachers experience through teacher–coach interactions over time. A small body of research exists that has examined coach–teacher conversations. For example, Heineke (2013) analyzed the interactions of four coach–teacher dyads over one school year, using structural discourse analysis. Although this analysis generated insights concerning the balance in coach–teacher talk, the extent of coaches' interactional dominance and some common topics of discussion, it did not explore coaches' strategies for encouraging teacher growth. Collett's (2012) study examined coaches' interactional strategies in a university teacher education literacy practicum. It was found that as coaching progressed, while the strategies that led to teacher dependence on the coach (e.g. direct modeling) became less frequent, strategies that promoted interdependence (e.g. praise) became more frequent. Nonetheless, it neither explored teachers' perceptions nor the relationship between these strategies and teacher growth.

Investigating instructional coaching initiated and implemented by school districts, Coburn and Woulfin (2012) explored the discursive moves that district coaches used to help teachers accept and employ new state-endorsed literacy instructional practices. Interpreting coaching as a policy intervention, they examined how coaching impacted teacher uptake of new ideas. Their findings suggested that coaches employed markedly different strategies depending on teachers' attitudes toward the policy initiatives involved, emphasizing some aspects and downplaying others. Studying group instructional coaching interactions, Skinner *et al.* (2014) found that teacher acceptance of new pedagogical ideas (i.e. new literacies) was entangled with their professional identities.

While the research discussed above has focused on coaches' discursive strategies in helping teachers take up new practices, relatively little attention has been paid to how teachers' understandings of their students and teaching change over time and how coaches contribute to this process. Addressing this gap in research, we explore specific instances of interaction that proved to be turning points in the teacher's (Lisa's) learning to enact practices she initially considered impossible with her kindergartners, the majority of whom were learning English as an additional language. We also examine how the coach (Sabrina) assisted Lisa in developing and putting into practice a new vision for her classroom.

Method

School and participants

Lisa worked in Kennedy Elementary, an inner-city school in a large urban school district in the US Midwest. The school was located in a low socioeconomic neighborhood with a large number of immigrant families. Lisa, a White, middle-class female, had some working knowledge of Spanish. Her two kindergarten classes included many Spanish-speaking ELs. The school population was 75% Hispanic, 16% African American with small proportions of White, Asian and multiracial students; 95% of the students received free/reduced lunch. Limiting teacher autonomy, the district narrowed and scripted the curriculum in order to improve students' standardized test scores. Initial observations at the school revealed that the predominant mode of teaching was teacher-directed whole-class instruction with a preponderance of teacher talk and plentiful individual seat work. The school district gave approval for teachers at Kennedy Elementary, including Lisa, to participate in this PD project, allowing them to deviate from the mandated curriculum. The coach, Sabrina, also a White, middle-class female, had been an English–Spanish bilingual primary school teacher in California for nine years. After earning her doctorate in education, she then worked as an instructional coach for various PD projects in multiple US and international locations. Sabrina considered the role of an instructional coach to be that of helping teachers grow as professionals while respecting local school practices, teachers' experiences, their dispositions and their willingness to take risks. Lisa volunteered to participate in the one-year-long PD project, which consisted of a 30-hour summer workshop and seven cycles of instructional coaching across one academic year that introduced teachers to critical sociocultural teaching practices.

Study design, data sources and analytical procedures

Using a qualitative case study approach (Stake, 2013), multiple sources of data were collected, including video-recorded coaching sessions between Lisa and Sabrina over one academic year (seven pre-conferences, seven post-conferences), the coach's observational notes and ratings using the observation instrument called the Standards Performance Continuum Plus (SPC Plus), audio-recordings of Lisa's IC with her students and initial, exit and follow-up interviews with Lisa. SPC Plus is a validated observation rubric that describes a teachers' level of implementation of each of the six pedagogical principles (Doherty *et al.*, 2002; Teemant *et al.*, 2014).

For data analysis, we first reviewed all the data sources multiple times with Studiocode video-analysis, wrote analytical notes about how Lisa enacted different pedagogical principles and discussed our interpretations. Since we were interested in teacher growth, when analyzing video-recorded coaching sessions, we identified, extracted and transcribed 'episodes' in which, assisted by the coach, Lisa addressed the challenges she experienced in implementing critical sociocultural teaching practices. We defined episodes as consisting of 'the interaction that takes place in carrying out some recognizable task or sub-task' with episode boundaries being signaled by a change of task (Wells, 2000: 8–9). The repeated viewing of selected episodes led us to focus on two principles: IC and CS. Lisa initially found these standards to be challenging, but later came to regard them as key to achieving her pedagogical goals. In other words, these principles provide a window to witness Lisa's professional learning.

We wrote detailed analytical memos about each episode, describing the nature of the challenges the teacher identified, the way in which the coach's moves used particular 'speech functions' and the way in which Lisa took up or resisted the coach's moves. Throughout, we paid particularly close attention to how alternative possible actions were negotiated between coach and teacher. We then cross-referenced the analyses of the coaching conversations with each of the other types of data collected. Any evidence against the proposed interpretation of the discourse data was discussed among the authors until agreement was reached.

Assisted Performance: Vignettes

Lisa brought her 19 years of teaching experience to bear on the way she took up the critical sociocultural teaching practices introduced in the summer workshop and subsequent instructional coaching. Despite her strong self-identification as a 'whole-language' teacher, the pressure of high-stakes testing and curriculum mandates had increasingly caused her to abandon the kind of practices to which she had previously been committed. However, while attending the summer workshop, she discovered that the critical sociocultural teaching principles resonated well with her whole-language teaching philosophy and, by the time instructional coaching began, she had already started to enact Joint Productive Activity, Language and Literacy Development and Contextualization in her teaching. Despite this smooth start, she found the IC and CS challenging to incorporate into her current practice. Yet, it was by grappling with these two principles that she grew as a professional over the seven cycles of instructional coaching. Using vignettes, we narratively report Lisa's pathways to appropriating these two principles that posed different types of challenges to her.

Jumping into instructional conversation

Following the summer workshop, Lisa started the new academic year by experimenting with learning centers. She organized them around themes and a range of small group activities in order to address the diversity of her students' needs – a key component of implementing the IC. When asked by the coach what she hoped would result from ICs, Lisa replied 'I want them to form an opinion and justify it' (Cycle 2, Pre-conference). Lisa perceived ICs to be valuable both in terms of language development and critical thinking. Nevertheless, despite her expressed goal, she hesitated in attempting to enact it for two reasons. First, she was worried that while she held an IC with one group, the rest of the class might have difficulty staying on task at their independent centers. Lisa noted that 'I'd be interrupted a million times'. Second, Lisa was concerned her kindergartners, many of whom were ELs, were 'still learning the ins and outs of school' (Lisa's words) and might not be able to hold ICs in English with her. Noting Lisa's concerns, Sabrina asked Lisa to project when she might feel ready to conduct an IC. In response, Lisa proposed a six-week timeline. Following that, Sabrina helped Lisa to identify discrete steps for conducting ICs. Despite her own six-week projection, Lisa proceeded to 'jump into' ICs only six days after this conversation occurred.

Vignette 1: 'I decided to jump into it' (Cycle 2, Post-conference)

Having for the first time observed a lesson in which Lisa conducted an IC with a small group of students, Sabrina asks 'So, worst fears?' Leaning back, smiling, and shaking her head, Lisa responds, 'I pretty much said it was going to take, what, six weeks to do this, didn't I?' She laughs as Sabrina bangs on the table. 'Yes, you did! Six weeks was your goal... Six days. What was the change from the idea that it was going to take you six weeks that you could do it in six days?' Lisa pauses for a moment, and replies 'Probably just deciding to jump into it'. As Sabrina makes a note of this, Lisa continues. 'The longer I allowed them [students] to keep in the traditions that they wanted, or in the habits that they wanted, it was going to be worse to break. So, I decided to jump in with both feet and say 'You're gonna do it my way'. She laughs. Sabrina nods, and replies 'OK. So, breaking the habits'. Lisa continues. 'Yeah. So, before, they were all, you know, dependent on me. I wouldn't allow them to be dependent, but just make them independent little souls to begin with, so...' Sabrina nods. 'What about breaking your own habits? Anything you had to consciously break?' Lisa considers this. 'Um, allowing a little more chaos. But it wasn't that much'. Sabrina continues 'Do you feel like if you had been [moving from table to table], would there have been that big a difference in the amount of...' Lisa shakes her head, 'No'.

Lisa went on to note that the students in the non-IC groups were able to stay on task, and that small group discussion in learning centers allowed typically quiet students an opportunity to contribute. Vignette 1 shows the celebratory tenor of this exchange, as well as Lisa's rationale for 'just jump[ing] in and doing it'. Sabrina spent much of this conference affirming and celebrating Lisa's success while also encouraging her to identify ways to improve. Building on this success, Lisa was able to develop and refine her IC practices in the remaining cycles. Reflecting on her initial reservation, Lisa said:

> I didn't think we could get it going as much as we have it going now. I guess it's just MY control issues. [...] I knew that we could do the centers, I just didn't think they would be able to handle me being in a group, and not babysitting them...

Whereas Lisa had begun by doubting her students' ability to stay on task in a center-based classroom, her reflections following implementation suggest that her reservations may have had more to do with her need to regulate the behaviors of her students or engage in 'crowd control' in Lisa's words. Lisa noted that she was accustomed to teaching kindergartners in a whole class setting, engaging students as a group rather than as individuals.

Coming to terms with 'Critical Stance'

With Sabrina's support, Lisa proceeded to use her ICs to enact CS, which she initially did not think her students were able to handle because of their age and with the constraints of mandated basal readers.

Vignette 2: Introducing Critical Stance (Cycle 4, Post-conference)

Lisa and Sabrina sit facing each other at a conference table, each with their attention on the SPC Plus rubric between them. At this point, Lisa has successfully implemented five of the six principles in her classroom, all except CS. With her pen, Sabrina points to CS. 'Here's one I'm gonna poke you on', Sabrina says, 'because this is an interesting idea, Critical Stance'. As they both look at the rubric, Sabrina adds, 'It's just something to think about because it's a new idea'. Sabrina pauses a moment, then looks at Lisa, and reads the definition of CS out loud: 'How do we empower children, or students, to see how they can make change in their own realm?' Sabrina sits silently, letting these words sink in, and Lisa nods. Focusing again on the SPC Plus, Sabrina continues, 'And at that highest level you're creating an activity where they're having a conversation, but this is interesting', she quotes the rubric, 'engages learners in interrogating conventional wisdom and practices'. Sabrina looks up from the rubric and laughs briefly, and Lisa replies with a sardonic 'Sure'. Sabrina continues quoting, 'and reflecting on the ramifications of such practices and actively seeking to transform inequities within their scope of influence within the classroom and larger community'. She takes a breath, leans back, and again looks at Lisa. 'So, I'm gonna challenge you, I don't come back til January, but just to start thinking about how can we (pause) show kindergartners how to take a critical step of thinking further' about what they can contribute to equity at school 'in their scope of influence'. Lisa nods, and says decisively 'Bucket fillers, bucket dippers'.

This was the first time that Sabrina explicitly, but gently, pushed Lisa to consider incorporating the principle of CS into her instruction. Discussing future goals, in Vignette 2 (Cycle 4, post-conference), Sabrina introduced CS as a challenging concept to think about rather than as a practice that Lisa needed to implement immediately. Lisa instantly connected this with 'bucket fillers' and 'bucket dippers', an element of the school culture stressing consideration for others and collective responsibility (McCloud, 2015). In essence, these terms refer to those who take from others or make life more difficult (bucket dippers) and those who help others or contribute to the collective good (bucket fillers). Sabrina acknowledged this connection and encouraged Lisa to think further about the concept, possibly in conjunction with the IC. At this point, it appears that Lisa perceived CS to be compatible with materials currently used in the school. However, reflecting in a later conference, Lisa stated that she was initially skeptical of CS. This skepticism emerged in the Cycle 5 pre-observation conference.

Vignette 3: Understanding Critical Stance in Local Context (Cycle 5, Pre-conference)

Discussing the upcoming observation, as Lisa and Sabrina are again going over the SPC Plus rubric, Sabrina directs Lisa's attention to CS.

Sabrina leans back as Lisa reads the text that describes CS. Sabrina continues, 'It's not one we paid much attention to in terms of really focusing on…' She trails off as Lisa crosses her arms and studies the text. After several moments have passed silently, Lisa looks up and says, with amused skepticism in her voice, 'But how would you do that… in "Hide, Clyde!"?'[2] She lowers her head and, laughing, says 'Help me here!' Sabrina seems caught off guard, but recovers quickly. Thinking aloud, she states that Clyde lives in the rain forest that is getting destroyed and then asks Lisa, 'So why do you think it's important to save Clyde's habitat?' Lisa seems to understand Sabrina's point about connecting the book to the environmental themes that Lisa has been developing in her classes. Noting Lisa's comprehension, Sabrina continues, 'that's not somewhere you're gonna go right now. I don't want you to change to do that, but I want you to start thinking about Critical Stance'. Sabrina leans back and, with both hands, draws a circle in the air. 'In their scope of influence what can they control?' She lets her words stand, and after a moment of silence, Lisa asks, 'What can they control for…?' Sabrina replies, 'That's what we have to think about'.

As shown in Vignette 3, when Sabrina offered Lisa the official definition of CS, Lisa's reaction was mildly incredulous, indicating that she had to approach CS within the constraints of the mandated text *Hide, Clyde!* (Benfanti, 2002). However, initially taken aback, Sabrina responded by offering some suggestions linking the required text to environmentalism. She then gently encouraged Lisa to think more about CS. In response, Lisa immediately connected CS to an element of the school culture ('bucket fillers'). A major turning point came, however, when, in the Cycle 5 post-conference, without any prompting from Sabrina, Lisa identified a way in which she could have incorporated CS into an IC on the Lorax[3] by questioning the children as to the consequences on the animals of cutting trees. This link with environmentalism was affirmed by Sabrina. In their Cycle 6 pre-conference, Lisa informed Sabrina with some pride that she had incorporated CS into an IC on penguins in one of her previous classes. During the Cycle 5 observation, Lisa conducted the same penguin IC with a different group of kindergartners. Using a mandated basal reader on penguins, Lisa connected the topic to endangered animals, and prompted her kindergarteners to list actions people could take to prevent the deterioration of the environment in which penguins live. This culminated in the students creating posters to spread awareness of endangered penguins.

Vignette 4: Enacting Critical Stance (Cycle 6, Post-conference)

Having observed Lisa's IC about the consequences of oil spill on penguins, Sabrina says, 'You did Critical Stance in a big way this time'. Lisa smiles and winks. 'I did'. Smiling, Sabrina replies, 'Hard, difficult, over the top. I don't know how you dared do it'. Lisa laughs, 'They [her kin-dergartners] did it'. Sabrina asks, 'Was it hard?' and Lisa easily replies, 'No'. Sabrina continues, 'Okay, then what is difficult about the idea of Critical Stance in kindergarten?' This gives Lisa pause. 'I think it – I mean this story, obviously, was easy to come up with something'. Lisa holds up her hands, comparing and balancing. 'Now, "The Little Engine That Could", Critical Stance...' She trails off and laughs, letting her face communicate her doubt. Sabrina shifts the focus, saying, 'So it was an authentic connection'. As Lisa agrees, she continues, 'That's a big differ-ence between what you're saying. You needed an authentic connection. Did the kids buy into this, this connection? Totally over the top'. Lisa replies 'And it kind of helped that we had already discussed it with Lorax and had it in science. We just kind of took that whole step further. So, they could totally connect the text'. Sabrina says, 'Not a difficult idea'. As Lisa agrees, Sabrina continues, 'That's what is so exciting to me about this. Now you're thinking about it differently. These children have influ-ence...They have voice'. Lisa replies saying that 'it wasn't that hard at all'. Sabrina continues. 'I'm so glad because when we talked at the begin-ning you told me Critical Stance, no way lady. There's no way. There's no way'. Lisa has been laughing, but suddenly becomes serious, expressing her remaining concerns about the applicability of CS to other stories in the basal reader. She states, 'I mean, when I get the story "Little Engine That Could",...I mean, it depends on, obviously, what story we're on'.

In Vignette 4, they celebrated Lisa's success with CS. However, Lisa expressed some lingering doubts about the applicability of CS to a wider range of mandated curricular materials. Rather than address this skepticism directly, Sabrina responded by highlighting reasons why the previous IC was successful, emphasizing the authentic connection of the activity and the actions the students were able to think about taking. However, although Lisa had had success with CS, it seemed that she was still struggling with CS on a conceptual level. Sabrina continued to work with Lisa's expressed concerns by highlighting ways that Lisa's IC had been effective.

In the three cycles discussed thus far, each of the required basal read-ers lent themselves to environmentalist interpretations of CS (relating to the rainforest, animal habitat conservation and endangered species). In the seventh and final cycle, Lisa was required to teach a unit on trans-portation. While this represented a contrast to previous themes, Lisa was surprised to discover during her IC that her students were able to draw connections between transportation and previous topics that she herself had not seen:

Lisa: I had thought through some more questions, and we talked about, let's pretend there is no school bus. We talked about, there's no fire engine, there's no -

Sabrina: So, what did they say?
Lisa: We're gonna die like the penguins!

Using a CS approach along with other standards such as contextualization and IC, students were able to consider their own communities as 'habitats' and to consider the ramifications of dominant modes of transportation in their lives. Arguably, without the use of ICs and CS, these young students would not have had the opportunity to make this connection.

Later reflecting on the coaching process, Lisa noted how Sabrina's support had not only helped her develop contextualized understanding of the six pedagogical principles, but also pushed her to reconceptualize her kindergartners' capabilities and her own teaching practices. What she had thought was unimaginable with kindergartners and within her restricted curriculum was made possible.

Discussion

Turning points as examples of assisted performance

The narrative account of Lisa's learning trajectory illustrates turning points in a teacher's beliefs that serve as good examples of assisted performance with relevance beyond this individual case. Unlike the findings of previous research on instructional coaching (Collett, 2012; Heineke, 2013), Lisa was not offered direct modeling of instructional practices; instead, what was being modeled by the coach was how to conceptualize and enact IC and CS in relation to her existing practices. Lisa witnessed the coach, acting as a more competent other (Tharp & Galimore, 1988), articulate two principles, revisit them and create expectation for progress. In the conceptual space created in her ZPD by the coach, Lisa was able to express her concerns and grapple with the principles until she began to see the pedagogical situation from the viewpoint of new possibilities and connections. Once Lisa experimented with IC and CS, she was assisted by the coach in interpreting and refining her understanding. The opportunity to grapple with, enact and then reflect upon her teacher–student interactions resulted in changed beliefs.

Teacher growth

The narrative account suggests a number of interesting issues to consider with respect to teacher growth. Change in teaching practice might involve new ways of balancing control and autonomy in the classroom such that students are given more ownership of their own learning. In Lisa's case, success with the IC hinged upon a shift in her assessment of her emergent bilingual five-year-old students' abilities: to engage in a relatively long conversation with her in an IC group; and to function and learn independently in small group centers without her supervision. Through dialogue, Lisa was assisted by the coach in articulating her pedagogical vision (i.e. of helping her kindergartners become independent thinkers), in framing her goal for the IC and in creating a realistic timeline for enacting the necessary changes in her practice. Together, Lisa and the coach considered and evaluated possible ways of introducing the IC, identified challenges to be met and created concrete steps to overcome them. In the end, however, Lisa launched her first IC much sooner than she had expected and found, to her surprise, that her kindergartners were well able to engage in sustained discussions with the aid of linguistic scaffolding. Lisa learned she could trust her kindergartners to be independent learners, letting go of her own need to control. Without the dialogic space created through coaching, Lisa's experimentation with the IC might not have happened.

By contrast, the challenge that CS posed for Lisa was qualitatively different from that of the IC. Lisa felt that mandated basal readers were conceptually incompatible with the equity orientation of CS. However, she was gently guided by the coach to reconceptualize her stance toward basal readers; instead of following the curriculum as script *per se*, she could attempt to prioritize what she held to be meaningful learning for her students. In other words, following the coach's suggestion, Lisa found an alternative way of using the required basal readers by connecting them to her ongoing environmental themes, giving value to students' interests and identifying ethical problems to solve that were within her students' ability to address. Thus, assisted by the coach, Lisa came to see CS as conducive to the sort of meaningful learning she wished her students to engage in, and this helped her to conceptualize CS as compatible with her own pedagogical goals. Thus, by aligning her own goals with the goal of CS, Lisa was able to take greater control of her teaching. In sum, Lisa's interaction with the coach prepared her to launch a successful incorporation of CS, and her students' competent participation, in turn, helped her to recognize her kindergarteners' ability to be independent learners. Skinner *et al.* (2014) noted that teachers have to reconcile the differences they perceive to exist between new literacy practices introduced through instructional coaching and their professional identities as teachers. By contrast, Lisa's participation in coaching allowed her to enact her professional identity to a greater degree than she had previously been able to do in her district context.

For Lisa, embarking on agentive action took the form of (a) regaining control over and responsibility for her curricular and pedagogical decisions and (b) putting into practice her deeply held belief that young children can become independent critical thinkers, and this, in turn, required her to take on a new role as a teacher. This involved her in reconceptualizing herself as an agent of change who pushed back against the 'one-size-fits-all' approach to instruction epitomized by a prepackaged curriculum. Responding to the coach's encouragement, Lisa, in turn, came to expect her students to also take greater responsibility for their own learning.

The coach's interactional role

Throughout instructional coaching, the coach consistently modeled a collaborative form of knowledge building (also see Collet, 2012). Sabrina helped the teacher treat the pedagogical challenges she faced as a means of achieving greater alignment with her personal vision of teaching. The coach presented the IC and CS not only as effective pedagogical strategies but also as a means for Lisa to reclaim ownership of her own practices. In other words, the coach guided Lisa to use critical sociocultural teaching practices as a way of overcoming, while minimally complying with, the constraints of the district's test-driven demands.

The coach offered Lisa assistance in two specific ways. By encouraging Lisa to reconceptualize IC and CS, she provided conceptual assistance. By engaging Lisa in discussion of hypothetical courses of action for implementing the IC and CS, she provided strategic assistance. Reconceptualization was her preferred strategy on those occasions when Lisa had difficulty in fully understanding the pedagogical principles. Echoing the findings of Coburn and Woulfin (2012), Sabrina helped Lisa make sense of CS by mediating between the official text and Lisa's classroom reality. However, when conceptual aspects of the principles did not pose a problem, as in the case of the IC, the coach chose to engage in discussion of possible actions to address the logistics of implementation (e.g. how to organize non-IC centers so students could work together without the teacher's help). With CS, on the other hand, the coach posed questions, offered comments and suggestions and engaged in experimental enactment of possible courses of action, which the teacher rehearsed together with the coach. As a result, the coach helped Lisa develop greater understanding of how the IC and CS could enrich her students' learning.

Conclusion

Based on our analysis of the coach–teacher interactions, we suggest that an important starting point for successful coaching is for the coach to value the teacher's own beliefs and goals. Through consistent efforts to build a dialogic relationship with the teacher on this basis (Freire, 1970/2002), the coach is able to assist the teacher to see how a new approach to learning and teaching, in this case critical sociocultural teaching, can assist in enacting the teacher's own beliefs and goals, even in a restrictive institutional context. In this respect, the coach's practices illustrate the actual enactment of the recommendations for literacy coaches proposed by Skinner *et al.* (2014):

> [W]e posit that literacy coaches must step back from what has become an exclusive focus on the transfer of methods/best practice in literacy instruction to recognize, validate, and build upon the expertise, identities, and subjectivities that the literacy educators they are collaborating with possess. (Skinner *et al.*, 2014: 229)

In Lisa's case, the changes were related to the nature of the constraints she felt in her instructional setting, her young students' capabilities and even her role within the classroom. However, as the current findings show, teacher change – particularly in their beliefs – takes time, and must be willingly undertaken rather than externally imposed. In sum, despite this being a single case, Lisa's changing beliefs highlight the importance of constructive professional dialogue between a coach and a teacher. It also demonstrates the importance of teachers' engaging in constructive dialogue with their students, acting agentively and making decisions that shape their teaching practices and work life (e.g. Dovemark, 2010; Dover et al., 2016).

Notes

(1) The first author, Haneda, was introduced to sociocultural theory, including the concept of assisted/assisting performance in the ZPD, in Merrill Swain's graduate course at the *Ontario Institute for Studies in Education* (OISE). Further, Swain has assisted the performance of many scholars, including the three co-authors, through her scholarship. We therefore thought the focus on this concept in our chapter as appropriate.
(2) *Hide, Clyde!* is a children's book written by Benfanti about Clyde the chameleon with trouble blending into his jungle environment.
(3) *The Lorax* (1971) is a children's book written by Dr Seuss. *The Lorax* is an ecological warning that still rings true today amid the dangers of clear-cutting, pollution and disregard for the earth's environment.

References

Bean, R.M., Draper, J.A., Hall, V., Vandermolen, J. and Zigmond, N. (2010) Coaches and coaching in Reading First schools: A reality check. *The Elementary School Journal* 111 (1), 87–114.
Benfanti, R. (2002) *Hide, Clyde!* New York: Ipicturebooks.
Blase, J. and Blase, J. (1998) *Handbook of Instructional Leadership: How Really Good Principals Promote Teaching and Learning.* Thousand Oaks, CA: Corwin.
Coburn, C.E. and Woulfin, S.L. (2012) Reading coaches and the relationship between policy and practice. *Reading Research Quarterly* 47 (1), 5–30.
Collet, V.S. (2012) The gradual increase of responsibility model: Coaching for teacher change. *Literacy Research and Instruction* 51 (1), 27–47.
Doherty, R.W., Hilberg, R.S., Epaloose, G. and Tharp, R.G. (2002) Standards performance continuum: Development and validation of a measure of effective pedagogy. *Journal of Educational Research* 96 (2), 78–89.
Dovemark, M. (2010) Teachers' collective actions, alliances and resistance within neo-liberal ideas of education: The example of the individual programme. *European Educational Research Journal* 9, 232–244.
Dover, A., Henning, N. and Agarwal-Rangnath, R. (2016) Reclaiming agency: Justice-oriented social studies teachers respond to changing curricular standards. *Teaching & Teacher Education* 59, 457–467.
Freire, P. (1970/2002) *Pedagogy of the Oppressed.* London: Bloomsbury Publishing.
Heineke, S.F. (2013) Coaching discourse. *The Elementary School Journal* 113 (3), 409–433.
Lewis, C., Enciso, P. and Moje, E.B. (2006) *Identity, Agency, and Power: Reframing Sociocultural Research on Literacy.* New York: Routledge.

McCloud, C. (2015) *Have You Filled Your Bucket Today: A Guide to Daily Happiness for Kids*. Brighton, MI: Bucket Fillers Incorporated.

Milner, H.R. (2013) *Policy Reforms and De-Professionalization of Teaching*. Boulder, CO: National Education Policy Center. See http://nepc.colorado.edu/publication/policy-reforms-deprofessionalization (accessed 15 August 2018).

Neuman, S.B. and Wright, T.S. (2010) Promoting language and literacy development for early childhood educators: A mixed-methods study of coursework and coaching. *The Elementary School Journal* 111 (1), 63–86.

Skinner, E.N., Hagood, M.C. and Provost, M.C. (2014) Creating a new literacies coaching ethos. *Reading & Writing Quarterly* 30 (3), 215–232.

Stake, R. (2013) *Multiple Case Study Analysis*. New York: Guilford Press.

Stetsenko, A. (2014) Transformative activist stance for education. In T. Corcoran (ed.) *Psychology in Education: Critical Theory-Practice* (pp. 181–198). Rotterdam: Sense Publishers.

Swain, M. (2000) The output hypothesis and beyond: Mediating acquisition through collaborative dialogue. In J.P. Lantolf (ed.) *Sociocultural Theory and Second Language Learning* (pp. 97–114). Oxford: Oxford University Press.

Swain, M. and Lapkin, S. (2001) Focus on form through collaborative dialogue: Exploring task effects. In M. Bygate, P. Skehan and M. Swain (eds) *Researching Pedagogic Tasks: Second Language Learning, Teaching, and Testing* (pp. 99–118). London/New York: Routledge.

Teemant, A., Wink, J. and Tyra, S. (2011) Effects of coaching on teacher use of sociocultural instructional practices. *Teaching and Teacher Education* 27 (4), 683–693.

Teemant, A., Leland, C. and Berghoff, B. (2014) Development and validation of a measure of critical stance for instructional coaching. *Teaching and Teacher Education* 39, 136–147.

Tharp, R.G. and Gallimore, R. (1988) *Rousing Minds to Life: Teaching, Learning, and Schooling in Social Context*. New York: Cambridge University Press.

Tharp, R.G., Estrada, P., Dalton, S.S. and Yamauchi, L. (2000) *Teaching transformed: Achieving Excellence, Fairness, Inclusion, and Harmony*. Boulder, CO: Westview.

Vossoughi, S. and Gutiérrez, K.D. (2016) Critical pedagogy and sociocultural theory. In I. Esmonde and A.N. Booker (eds) *Power and Privilege in the Learning Sciences: Critical and Sociocultural Theories of Learning* (pp. 139–161). New York: Routledge.

Vygotsky, L. (1997) *Educational Psychology*. Boca Raton, FL: St Lucie.Walpole, S. and Blamey, K.L. (2008) Elementary literacy coaches: The reality of dual roles. *The Reading Teacher* 62 (3), 222–231.

Wells, G. (2000) Coding scheme for the analysis of classroom discourse. Unpublished manuscript. Toronto: Ontario Institute for Studies in Education of the University of Toronto.

Young, J.R., Bullough, Jr, R.V., Draper, R.J., Smith, L.K. and Erickson, L.B. (2005) Novice teacher growth and personal models of mentoring: Choosing compassion over inquiry. *Mentoring & Tutoring: Partnership in Learning* 13 (2), 169–188.

14 An EMCA Approach to Capturing the Specialized Work of L2 Teaching: A Research Proposal

Joan Kelly Hall

Introduction

Merrill Swain's research has had a far-reaching impact on the field of second language acquisition (SLA). The specification of communicative competence for second language (L2) teaching and testing (Canale & Swain, 1980), the development of the comprehensible output hypothesis (Swain, 1995, Swain & Lapkin, 1995) and the concept of languaging (Swain, 2006; Swain & Lapkin, 2011), and her more recent exposition on the integral role of emotions in L2 learning (Swain, 2013) have significantly expanded the field's understandings of L2 learning. Equally significant is the intellectual open-mindedness with which she has approached her work. Her scholarly trajectory is marked by dogged explorations fueled by endless curiosity about people's lived experiences in L2 teaching and learning. Swain has traversed epistemological territories, undeterred by disciplinary boundaries, to engage in extended dialogue with others about the theoretical, methodological and practical complexities and opportunities afforded by the teaching and learning of additional languages. Her intellectual engagement was especially evident in extended discussions we had as members of the Douglas Fir Group (2016), which culminated in a proposal for a transdisciplinary framework for SLA.

This chapter is an extension of these discussions. It takes as axiomatic that L2 teaching is deliberate, sophisticated professional work (Ball & Forzani, 2009, 2011; Cohen, 2011; Macbeth, 2011; Waring, 2016). Teaching in ways that advance the pedagogical activity while promoting individual learner participation, maintaining the shared attention of the larger cohort and displaying and engendering demonstrations of positive affect from the learners requires a range of complex specialized repertories composed of a wide array of multilingual, multimodal semi-otic resources for taking action.

Noting that much of what is known about the specialized nature of teaching is typically represented as knowledge and beliefs *about* teaching, scholars of teaching and teacher education have called for broader and deeper understandings of the practical nature of teaching (Ball & Forzani, 2009, 2011; Cohen, 2011; Macbeth, 2011). What is needed, they have argued, is a specialized framework that affords the identification of the features and components of teaching actions. The challenge to the development of such a specialized framework has been finding a theoretically grounded approach to the study of social action that is capable of identifying and describing the rich empirical details of the specialized actions of L2 teaching, the learner actions they engender and the larger pedagogical projects they accomplish, without reducing them to an 'atomized collection of discrete and unconnected tiny acts' (Ball & Forzani, 2009: 507).

As a dominant situated or practice-based approach to the study of social action, ethnomethodological conversation analysis (EMCA) is in a unique position to lay the groundwork for such a framework (Koschmann *et al.*, 2007; Macbeth, 2011). EMCA considers the nature and source of human sociality to be fundamentally cooperative, locally accomplished and grounded in real-world activity. Its theoretical strength lies in its grounding of mutual understanding in the sequential organization of interaction. Its methodological strengths are that it is data driven and analytically inductive, substantiating claims about how actions are built and interpreted in public observables. It also relies on a set of robust transcription conventions to capture the fine-grained details of the multiple, simultaneously and sequentially deployed multimodal resources used by parties to an interaction to achieve mutual understanding of the work they are doing together.

The purpose of this chapter is to lay out the basic organization of a framework grounded in EMCA that is capable of describing the specialized actions by which L2 teaching is accomplished as they unfold, in real time and real space (Garfinkel, 2002). The intent behind the framework is not to impose a view of how L2 teaching *should* be done, but rather to illuminate its complexities and in so doing, reveal instructive distinctions between idealized understandings of the work of L2 teaching and its 'interactional reality' (Freebody, 2013: 73). Discovering the particulars of what L2 teachers and learners are doing in their local classroom settings can inform and support prudential, i.e. sensible, decision-making by teachers, researchers and other stakeholders in their own contexts (Erickson, 2012).

In what follows, I first provide an overview of EMCA and then lay out five themes about the specialized nature of L2 teaching and four defining features of EMCA research. Next, I summarize current EMCA research efforts on L2 teaching, discuss some challenges for continued EMCA research efforts on L2 teaching contexts and offer a brief conclusion.

EMCA: A Situated Approach to the Study of Social Interaction

EMCA is founded on two interrelated sociological approaches to the study of social life: ethnomethodology (EM) and conversation analysis (CA). EM considers the nature and source of social order to be fundamentally empirical and locally accomplished (Garfinkel 1964, 1967; Heritage, 1984). It was founded by Harold Garfinkel as a radical alternative to sociological theories that posit the existence of an objective social order and appeal to theoretical constructs to explain the lived experiences of members of society. Such theories attribute the production of stability in everyday life, Garfinkel (1964: 244) argued, to compliance by members of society to 'pre-established and legitimate alternatives of action that the common culture provides'. Members have no influence on these alternatives of action; they can only internalize them and act in response to them. According to Garfinkel (1964), such formal analyses of social life treat individuals as 'cultural dopes', i.e. passive bearers of theorized constructs; in ignoring the concreteness of social facts, they lose the phenomena they are meant to study.

EM is a radically different approach to the study of social life. In EM, there is no separation between a theorized social world and individuals' experiences of it. Rather, the facts of social life are practical constructions, produced in and through mutually recognizable common-sense reasoning practices, i.e. methods used by members of society to achieve actual social phenomena in their local contexts (Garfinkel, 1967, 2002; Heritage, 1984; Maynard & Clayman, 2003). These methods are the public, reflexively accountable and observable ways in which members of society jointly construct their social worlds. For the conduct of their daily affairs, persons take for granted that what is done and said at any local moment is understood on the basis of these shared methods. These methods do not stand for something else, that is, they are not texts that represent or signify something else. They are exhibits of social order, and thus 'constitutive of their own reality' (Garfinkel, 2002: 97).

In their work together, persons hear and are heard by others to be 'engaged in the objective production and objective display of common-sense knowledge of everyday activities as observable and reportable phenomena' (Garfinkel & Sacks, 1970). These observable and reportable phenomena, i.e. members' methods through which courses of action are produced and recognized, are the topics of EM study.

Emerging from EM's interests in the empirical study of the methods by which members of society achieve social order, but asserting a fundamental role for interaction as 'the primordial site of human sociality' (Schegloff, 2006: 70), CA narrowed its focus to the interactional bases of social order. Founded by Sacks in association with Schegloff and Jefferson around the same time as EM was being developed, the approach is based on the premise that social order is an interactional achievement, informed by stable, identifiable, interactional organizations to which participants normatively orient (Heritage, 1984; Sacks, 1984). These social structures comprise a common-sense knowledge, i.e. an interactional competence, of all ordinary members of society and are exhibited in the methods they use in their interactions with others to achieve social order (Maynard, 2012).

Empirical research from the first generation of scholars revealed three methods to be fundamental to the achievement of social order in interaction: turn taking, sequence organization and repair. The organization of turn taking concerns the construction and coordination of turns among participants in an interaction. It comprises two components: turn constructional units, which are the basic units by which turns are constructed, and can include potentially any verbal and non-verbal means for making meaning, e.g. prosodic cues, words, clauses, gestures, eye gazes and so on; and turn allocational units, which are the methods by which next speakers are selected (Sacks *et al.*, 1974).

The second method, sequence organization, is the 'vehicle for getting some activity accomplished' (Schegloff, 2007: 2), and is concerned with the normative, reflexive relationship between turns. Each turn is formed to be coherent with the immediately prior action and at the same time, implicative of the next turn and of larger stretches or sequences of actions. As explained by Schegloff (1968: 1083), 'given the first [turn], the second is expectable; upon its occurrence it can be seen to be a second item to the first; upon its nonoccurrence it can be seen to be officially absent – all this provided by the occurrence of the first item'.

A key concept in the ascription of meaning to actions in their sequential organization is preference. Many types of actions involve at least two relevant options that differ in terms of how they forward the interaction. An action that complies with the structural expectation of the prior turn is the preferred action. For example, greetings anticipate return greetings; questions project answers. Preferred actions are typically offered straightaway, without delay or any kind of qualification. Dispreferred actions do not comply with the structural expectations of prior actions and are designed with delays, mitigating particles, e.g. *well*, *uh*, accounts and other features that mark deviation from the expected action. Disagreements, rejections and disconfirmations are typically performed as dispreferred actions (Pomerantz & Heritage, 2012).

The third interactional method, repair, is the 'self-righting' mechanism (Schegloff *et al.*, 1977: 381) by which troubles in maintaining intersubjectivity are dealt with such that the action, the action sequence and the larger interactional project can move to possible completion (Levinson, 2012). When trouble arises, repair practices temporarily stop the course of action so that the trouble can be dealt with. Repair practices do not address '*all* divergences or difficulties of understanding' (Schegloff, 1992: 1341, italics added). Instead, they deal with 'only the narrower domain of understanding what someone has just said' (Schegloff, 2000: 207), that is, with difficulties presented by 'the production and uptake of the talk itself' (Schegloff, 1992: 1341).

Early CA studies primarily used audio recordings of interactions for their analyses, and thus, focused on participants' verbal practices, i.e. prosodic cues and grammatical items, and temporal and sequential practices such as overlapping turns and pauses within and between turns, which are used to build and ascribe meaning to actions and action sequences. Impelled by technological advancements in video-recording resources over the last two decades, CA has expanded its analytic scope to include the use of other semiotic resources to build actions including gesture, gaze, head movements, facial expressions, body posture, body movements and artifacts (Goodwin, 2000, 2013; Mondada, 2014; Nevile, 2015; Streeck *et al.*, 2011). This consideration of other modes in addition to verbal conduct has changed CA's understanding of the organization of social interaction. As Mondada (2016: 341) notes, while earlier studies of talk-in-interaction viewed action formation as strictly linear, current studies that 'integrate and intertwine multiple simultaneous sequentialities and temporalities' illustrate the wide range of possible modalities in building multilayered forms of actions and action sequences.

Institutional interaction

The central domain of EMCA studies is everyday, mundane conversation, i.e. 'forms of interaction that are not confined to specialized settings or to the execution of particular tasks' (Heritage, 2005: 104). In mundane conversation, very little of what is done is determined in advance. Rather, the context is dynamically built and managed turn by turn, with the sequence of prior actions heavily shaping the meaning of current actions and with the allocation and length of turns locally managed by all the parties to the interaction (Sacks *et al.*, 1974). Institutional interaction is more restrained in comparison. While there are no clearly marked, fixed boundaries between the two types, three elements distinguish institutional interaction (Drew & Heritage, 1992; Heritage, 2005).

First, institutional interaction involves institutional goals that make relevant institution-specific identities and roles. Interactions in courtrooms, for example, are organized around legal proceedings, which make relevant such institutional identities as judges, lawyers, jurors, plaintiffs and defendants. Similarly, in medical clinics, interactions typically center on the identification of a person's medical issues and the specification of medical care. These goals make relevant the institutional identities of patients and health practitioners such as physicians and nurses.

Second, special constraints are placed on what are allowable interactional structures and actions in working to achieve the institutional goals (Levinson, 2012). News interviews, for example, are a major means of broadcasting information on current events. They are organized by a specialized question-answer turn-taking system in which interviewers are normatively restricted to asking questions and interviewees to responding to the questions (Clayman, 2012). Likewise, in pedagogical contexts, instructing actions may normatively include questioning, directing and providing feedback, but not vow taking. It is not that such actions cannot take place in pedagogical settings, but rather, they may not be considered normal actions for achieving their institutional goals.

Finally, institutional interaction involves special inferential frameworks that are specific to the context. In medical settings, for example, physician questions directed to patients are expected to deal with patients' medical issues and not with their financial health. Likewise, in pedagogical interaction, teacher questions are expected to elicit student responses that display their knowledge of that which is being instructed. Departing from the work that is typically associated with the goals of the institutional context can warrant negative or questionable inferences about the work being accomplished and even about the participants themselves.

Themes on the Situated Nature of L2 Teaching and Implications for Research

Arising from an EMCA understanding of social action are five themes on L2 teaching. Together, they lay a foundation for a research agenda on the study of the specialized work of L2 teaching.

(1)   L2 teaching is a form of institutional interaction.

As a form of institutional interaction, L2 teaching entails complex sets of practices for forming and interpreting pedagogical actions, their larger pedagogical projects and the pedagogical goals informing these projects. Individuals come to their L2 teaching contexts with a set of expectations about the practices that are likely to be used to form and interpret actions in the accomplishment of particular projects, e.g. mathematical problem-solving or reflective writing tasks, and how these projects achieve particular pedagogical goals. They also come with a set of expectations about the types of materials, e.g. textbooks, writing devices and physical aspects of the setting, e.g. lighting fixtures and arrangements of desks and chairs, in addition to language and other semiotic resources, which may contribute to the organization of the institutional work they are doing together. Finally, they come with some knowledge about what each member of the context is responsible for or can be held accountable for knowing and doing (Levinson, 2012).

(2)   The institutional context of L2 teaching makes relevant the institutional identities of L2 teacher and L2 learner.

Individuals come together in L2 classroom contexts with specific institutional roles as teachers and learners and in these roles, work toward specific pedagogical goals. To do this work cooperatively, and to enable further development of their pedagogical activities, the participants must be competent members, that is, they must know and understand these roles and the activities they are pursuing together. It is not that individuals can *only* act in their institutional identities of teachers and learners in these contexts; it is through their goal-oriented interactions together that the parties co-construct the instructional context and make relevant their roles within it.

(3)   L2 teaching is inextricably linked to L2 learning.

From an EMCA approach, L2 learning is not an unobservable matter, residing in the heads of learners. Rather, it is an 'accountable, public, and locally occasioned process' (Koschmann, 2012: 1040), enacted in the embodied methods whereby teachers and students, together, carry out courses of action with each other as they attend to the larger pedagogical projects within which their actions are embedded (Goodwin, 2000; Goodwin & Goodwin, 2004; Koschmann, 2012; Levinson, 2012). In their jointly constructed actions, relevant aspects of the subject matter as objects of learning and methods for detecting these objects and displaying understandings are made publicly observable. The work of L2 teaching and learning, then, is done 'not propositionally OR "behaviorally" but praxiologically, as practical tasks and orientations' (Macbeth, 2000: 59, emphasis in original).

To locate L2 learning entails uncovering the methods, i.e. the specific actions and practices comprising the courses of action and pedagogical projects jointly accomplished by the members of the L2 teaching contexts. Locating learning, however, is not easy. As Stahl (2006) notes,

> Learning is subtle. It rarely expresses itself in syntactically perfect complete propositions, like one would think based on textbook presentations of knowledge... Learning is situated; someone might be able to use a new resource in the context where it was learned, but not yet elsewhere. (Stahl, 2006: 368)

(4)   L2 teaching participant frameworks are multiple and embodied.

L2 teaching contexts are composed of multiple, embodied participation frameworks arranged to accomplish varied pedagogical goals. Participant frameworks are constituted through the mutual attention and alignment of multiple parties as they carry out courses of action in concert with each other (Goodwin, 2007). They can include lectures, whole group and small group discussions, group or team projects, pair tasks and individual work. Participant frameworks are embodied in that the actions of the participants are accomplished not just through talk, but through mutual orientation to the 'temporally unfolding juxtaposition of multiple semiotic fields' (Goodwin, 2000: 1517), including gestures, eye gazes, body positionings and spatial organizations.

The organization of the varied participant frameworks comprising L2 teaching contexts does not rest solely with the teacher. The students are equally important to their accomplishment. As recipients of teacher actions, they use gestures, eye gazes, facial expressions and body positionings to display to the teacher and to other students whether and how they are analyzing and participating in the unfolding actions. Via the ongoing public production and displays of mutual orientation in their embodied participation frameworks, teachers and students demonstrate a cooperative stance toward the work they are doing together. A cooperative stance is a 'visible display that one is organizing one's body toward others and a relevant environment in just the ways necessary to sustain and help construct the activities in progress' (Goodwin, 2007: 70). Certainly, possibilities for non-cooperation in L2 teaching contexts, as in all human interaction, exist; such possibilities demonstrate that the cooperative accomplishment of embodied participation frameworks are actively constructed and maintained through the ongoing work of the teacher and students (Enfield, 2012; Goodwin, 2007).

(5)   L2 teaching actions are in the service of pedagogical projects.

L2 teaching actions are organized by larger projects. Projects are 'course[s] of action that at least one participant is pursuing, which may at first be opaque to others then retrospectively discernible' (Levinson, 2012: 122). As noted earlier, in L2 teaching contexts, pedagogical goals are usually pre-set and serve as organizers of the pedagogical projects and their actions and practices constituting the contexts. The meanings of actions then depend not only on their local placement in a sequence or course of action, but also on the larger project being accomplished. For example, the directive 'open your books to page 34' not only projects a compliant response from the recipients, but it also serves as a pre-announcement of the next pedagogical activity to take place, likely something to do with what is on the page to which learners are directed. Anticipating what pedagogical project a turn foreshadows is part of the knowledge that teachers and students use to construct and interpret their actions together (Goodwin, 2013; Levinson, 2012).

Implications for research on L2 teaching

The program of research implicated by an EMCA perspective on L2 teaching has the following four characteristics.[1]

(1)   It is a descriptive analytic program.

The L2 teaching worlds we study are competent worlds of social action. As noted above, members of these contexts are competent participants, having developed from childhood a fundamental interactional competence for achieving social order in interaction with others (Maynard, 2012). Researchers of L2 contexts encounter these worlds already in place, with participants 'already competent to their affairs, including the competence to teach and learn them' (Macbeth, 2011: 76). The purpose for research is to capture the natural features of the classroom life as they are produced 'in their situated and lived detail' (Francis & Hester, 2004: 187). In other words, to do research of these worlds is to adequately account for 'how participants actually *do* the teaching plan or *do* the instructional model as ongoing interactional achievement' (Koschmann *et al.*, 2007, emphasis in the original).

(2)   It is indifferent.

One of Garfinkel's (1967) major policies for doing research is what Koschmann *et al.* (2007) refer to as ethnomethodological indifference. Garfinkel (1967) explains,

> An indefinitely large domain of appropriate settings can be located if one uses a search policy that *any occasion whatsoever* be examined for the feature that 'choice' among alternatives of sense, of facticity, of objectivity, of cause, of explanation, of communality *of practical actions* is a project of members' action. (Garfinkel, 1967: 32, emphasis in the original)

To do indifferent research on L2 teaching contexts does not mean that anything goes or that care does not need to be exercised by the researcher. Rather, it means that since an EMCA perspective on social action assumes that interaction always entails the orderly construction and interpretation of meaning, researchers of L2 teaching contexts can analyze *any* L2 teaching interaction and find interesting processes of action formation and interpretation. As Koschmann *et al.* (2007: 4) note, 'any circumstance, situation or activity that participants treat as one in which instruction and learning is occurring can be investigated for how instruction and learning are being produced by and among participants'. This stance of indifference suggests not only that the examination of any activity of interaction will demonstrate some occurrence of import, but also that 'such a demonstration can be based on a single case' (Koschmann *et al.*, 2007). It further suggests that EMCA L2 studies of teaching need not reference exogenous theories or arguments to bolster findings. Garfinkel (1967) explains,

> Ethnomethodological studies…do not formulate a remedy for practical actions, as if it was being found about practical actions that they were better or worse than they are usually cracked up to be. Nor are they in search of humanistic arguments, nor do they engage in or encourage permissive discussions of theory. (Garfinkel, 1967: viii)

(3)   It does not yield causative variables.

EMCA research on L2 teaching is different from formal analysis in that it is not meant to produce or theorize about abstracted sets of causal variables. Nor is it undertaken to decide whether some occasion of teaching is successfully implemented based on some exogenous criteria. Rather, EMCA research focuses on how the life of the classroom, as lived by its members, is accomplished (Koschmann *et al.*, 2007). EMCA studies produce natural histories of situated pedagogical actions and activities, supporting their findings with actual cases *in situ*, and their reproducibility with next actual cases *in situ*. What is treated as relevant in any occasion is up to the members of that occasion to work through in their interaction; it is the researcher's task 'to discover what these relevancies might be' (Koschmann *et al.*, 2007: 8).

(4)   It requires special consideration in producing video-recorded data.

What distinguishes an EMCA research program is its 'careful and precise attention to temporally and sequentially organized details of actions that account for how co-participants orient to each other's multimodal conduct, and assemble it in meaningful ways, moment by moment' (Mondada, 2016: 240). To produce ecologically valid descriptions of the fine-grained coordination of these details of action in L2 teaching contexts requires special consideration in producing video-recorded data.

Kimura *et al.* (2018) emphasize two institutional characteristics of L2 teaching contexts that afford special considerations in the production of video recordings: the multiplicity of spatial arrangements and the interplay of interactional routines and pedagogical projects. Regarding the first consideration, they note that L2 teaching contexts typically comprise multiple pedagogical activities within one time period or lesson, which, as noted earlier, engender different participation frameworks and different physical arrangements of interactional space. In terms of the second, they note that L2 teaching actions are organized by larger institutional projects. This means that not only is any one action contingent on the prior turn, but it is also oriented to a larger pedagogical project, which at the same time amplifies and constrains the meaning of any one action (Levinson, 2012). To describe the assemblage of an activity as the participants who are responsible for its production understand it, then, may require institutionally specific contextual information in addition to recordings that extend beyond any single stretch of interaction.

In sum, an EMCA approach to the study of social action yields five themes on L2 teaching and four defining characteristics of research. Together, they lay a foundation for a research agenda for the study of the specialized work of L2 teaching. Although the EMCA approach has a long history as a dominant approach to the study of social action in the field of sociology, it has only recently begun to inform studies of L2 teaching. In the next section, I offer an illustrative review of this small, but growing body of work.

Review of EMCA Studies of L2 Teaching Contexts

The organization of the complex work of teaching in contexts other than L2 has been a focus of EMCA studies for well over 40 years (e.g. Baker, 1992; Heap, 1992; Hester & Francis, 2000; Lerner, 1995; Macbeth, 1991, 1994, 2000; McHoul, 1978; Mehan, 1979; Payne & Hustler, 1980). In comparison, initial interest in EMCA studies of L2 teaching contexts began fewer than 15 years ago, with a significant jump in studies occurring only within the last 10 years. A major impetus for this interest can be traced back to the 2004 special issue of *The Modern Language Journal* on an approach labeled CA for SLA. Addressing what the research tradition of CA offered to the field of SLA, the studies examined the situated nature of L2 learning and L2 learners' competent use of the L2.[2] These interests in documenting L2 learning and L2 learners' interactional competencies in classrooms have continued to grow since the publication of that issue (see e.g. Cekaite, 2009; Hall *et al.*, 2011; Hellermann, 2008; Markee & Seo, 2009; Pallotti & Wagner, 2011; Sert & Jacknick, 2015).

Alongside this strand of research drawing on CA methods to address SLA concerns and more to the concern of this chapter has been the growing interest in uncovering the complexities of instructional sequences and the design of turn allocation systems in the accomplishment of teaching and learning. These interests have grown out of and thus are more directly tied to early EMCA work on teaching contexts, and in particular to the work of Mehan (1979), Macbeth (1991, 2000) and McHoul (1978). Early studies on the organization of instructional sequences of turns found a ubiquitous three-action sequence of direct instruction, referred to first by Mehan (1979) as *Initiation-Response-Evaluation* (IRE), where I refers to teacher initiation, R to student response and E to teacher evaluation of the response. As noted by Macbeth (2011: 446), the power and usefulness of this canonical three-action sequence 'lies in how it writes filaments of understanding into public, witnessable organizations of interactional regularity and coherence'.

Lee (2007) offers perhaps the most detailed examination of L2 teacher management of learner turns in the three-action instructional sequence, showing the practical and procedural details of a range of actions that the third turn accomplishes in responding to and acting on student responses and at the same time moving the instructional project forward. Additional work on this instructional sequence in L2 teaching contexts includes Sert's (2013) study of teacher management of student claims of insufficient knowledge in the second turn; Waring's (2008) study of explicit positive assessments; Park's (2014) study of teacher repetitions of student responses in the third turn; and Waring's (2009) study of learner post-expansion turns.

Related studies have built on early work on the specialized turn allocation system of teaching contexts (e.g. Lerner, 1995; McHoul, 1978; Mehan, 1979), which revealed that, unlike in informal interaction where any participant has the right to self-select as next speaker, the responsibility for coordinating turns lies with the teacher. The teacher determines whether students must wait to be called on, whether and how they can bid for the opportunity to speak, when they can speak at will and whether the turn is to be taken by a single student, two or more students or as a collective turn by the cohort. The small body of research on turn allocation routines in L2 contexts includes studies of teacher practices for nominating and managing student turns (Kääntä, 2012; Waring, 2013), and of student behaviors for bidding for and securing turns (Mortensen, 2009; Sahlström, 2002).

Finally, it is worth noting that while much of this research has focused heavily on vocal behaviors, i.e. prosodic cues and word choice, in the design of actions and sequences of actions, the embodied turn (Neville, 2015) in research on social interaction is changing research emphases in studies of L2 teaching contexts. There is now increasing focus on the multimodal constitution of L2 teaching actions through the concurrent and sequential use of such resources as gestures, facial expressions, eye gaze, posture and body positioning and movement and the manipulation of material objects in addition to verbal resources (e.g. Eskildsen & Wagner, 2013; Kääntä, 2012; Matsumoto & Dobs, 2016; Sert, 2013).

Challenges for Future Research on L2 Teaching Contexts

In this chapter, I have outlined a research program that can offer much-needed insight into the sophisticated and specialized work of teaching. As a central theoretical approach to the sociological study of social action, EMCA offers much to those concerned with documenting and understanding the specialized complexities of teaching and of L2 teaching in particular. The increasing number of studies on various L2 teaching contexts that are being published notwithstanding, there are at least three challenges this budding field of research must deal with if it is to become an established program with the power to offer pedagogical insights that can inform decision-making by stakeholders in their particular contexts of teaching.

The first challenge has to do with gaining access to a wider range of L2 teaching contexts. Perhaps because of the ease of access to adult-level English as a second language (ESL) classes in the US and elsewhere, a fairly substantial portion of the published studies features this context. Research using video-recorded data in settings involving minors, i.e. individuals under the age of 18, requires special consideration to ensure participants' confidentiality is respected and their welfare and safety are protected. In the US public school systems, for example, district and school regulations in addition to more stringent institutional review board (IRB) requirements for collecting videos featuring children and young adults make grades K-12 difficult sites to maneuver.[3] Moreover, the diverse spatial arrangements of desks and chairs typically found in the classrooms of these sites, which can include rows, small groupings or pairs, horseshoe shapes and even large circles, can complicate the collection of video data.[4] These constraints in turn may constrain the reach of this research program.

A second challenge has to do with the requirements of EMCA research methods. Those unfamiliar with EMCA methods cannot appreciate how time-consuming the processes of producing and transcribing video-recordings of naturally occurring interaction is. Nor can they appreciate fully how steadfast the analyst must be in capturing all of the interactional details in the transcripts and in scrutinizing the video materials and transcripts to allow 'a precise interpretation of the trajectories, temporalities and qualities of these multiple resources' (Mondada, 2016: 361). An EMCA research program requires, then, at the very least, analysts who are fully committed to making sense of real L2 teaching contexts.

The third challenge has to do with the changing fabric of communities brought about in large part by large-scale migration of individuals and families taking place in regions around the world and which has resulted in L2 teaching contexts that are increasingly more racially, ethnically, culturally and linguistically diverse (Douglas Fir Group, 2016). In his treatise on EM's program, Garfinkel (2002: 113) specified that to document the methods members *are* using to jointly produce their worksite-specific practices rather than those they *should be* using requires 'work-site-specific, discipline-specific' analysts, i.e. individuals who are qualified to recognize and account for the work that is being done. He refers to this requirement as the principle of unique adequacy.

Researching contemporary L2 teaching contexts, then, calls for analysts who know and understand the multilingual, multicultural, multi-ethnic worlds they are describing. Forming research collaborations is one way to meet this challenge; overcoming institutional and other constraints for forming such collaborations may be more difficult.

Conclusion

In this chapter, I have sketched a promising research approach to the empirical study of the specialized, complex work of L2 teaching. Despite its challenges, the EMCA framework affords studies that document and describe the specialized repertoires of actions and action plans comprising L2 teaching done at a level of articulation that allows teachers, researchers and other stakeholders to see the work that teachers accomplish in their classrooms in new and potentially transformative ways.

To be sure, such studies of L2 teaching are not meant to stand for something else, that is, they do not represent abstract phenomena of social order. Nor are they meant to inform prescriptive guidelines or to be reframed as generic implications for how to do L2 teaching. As Macbeth (2011: 449) compellingly states, such studies 'neither begin with complaints nor offer solutions for the "problems of education". They promise nothing for the efficiencies of the institution. They do not pose as arbiters – or designers – of things like "best practices"'.

Instead, as practical, publicly observable exhibits of the interactional achievements comprising L2 teaching contexts, EMCA descriptive studies are interchangeably tutorials, and are meant to be studied 'in their unmediated details' (Garfinkel 1996: 8). The remedial expertise their findings offer is 'described with questions "What did we do? What did we learn? More to the point, what did we learn, but only in and as lived doings, that we can teach? And how can we teach it?"' (Garfinkel, 1996: 9). As both descriptions and instructions, that is, as 'praxeologizing descriptive accounts' (Garfinkel, 1996: 19), EMCA studies of L2 aim for more than the development of a reflective capacity for understanding the specialized nature of L2 teaching. More significantly, they aim to re-specify the work of L2 teaching by making possible new perspectives for formulating pedagogical possibilities. For as Heap (1990: 43) notes, 'if some activity is important in our lives, then knowing how it is organized may make a difference to how we act'.

Notes

(1) These are adapted from Garfinkel's (1967) policies for doing ethnomethodology and from Koschmann *et al.*'s (2007) re-specification of the policies.
(2) The mainstream cognitive research approach to the study of learning and learners was the main issue brought up by Firth and Wagner (1997) in their seminal critique of SLA. The 2004 special issue was a follow-up to the issues raised by Firth and Wagner.

(3) Assuming that one can access these sites, once video-recordings are produced, technological innovations can help in editing them so that participants' identities are kept
confidential.
(4) I thank an anonymous reviewer for pointing this out.

References

Baker, C. (1992) Description and analysis in classroom talk and interaction. *Journal of Classroom Interaction* 27, 9–14.

Ball, D. and Forzani, F. (2009) The work of teaching and the challenge for teacher education. *Journal of Teacher Education* 60, 497–511.

Ball, D. and Forzani, F. (2011) Building a common core for learning to teach, and connecting professional learning to practice. *American Educator* 35,17–21, 38–39.

Canale, M. and Swain, M. (1980) Theoretical bases of communicative approaches to second language teaching and testing. *Applied Linguistics* 1, 1–47.

Cekaite, A. (2009) Soliciting teacher attention in an L2 classroom: Affect displays, classroom artefacts, and embodied action. *Applied Linguistics* 30, 26–48.

Clayman, S. (2012) Conversation analysis in the news interview. In T. Stivers and J. Sidnell (eds) The *Handbook of Conversation Analysis* (pp. 630–656). Malden, MA: Wiley-Blackwell.

Cohen, D. (2011) *Teaching and Its Predicaments.* Cambridge: Harvard University Press.

Douglas Fir Group (D. Atkinson, H. Byrnes, M. Doran, P. Duff, J. Kelly Hall, K. Johnson, J. Lantolf, D. Larsen-Freeman, B. Norton, J. Schumann, M. Swain and E. Tarone) (2016) A transdisciplinary framework for SLA in a multilingual world. *The Modern Language Journal* 100, 19–47.

Drew, P. and Heritage, J. (1992) Analyzing talk at work: An introduction. In P. Drew and J. Heritage (eds) *Talk at Work: Interaction in Institutional Settings* (pp. 3–65). Cambridge: Cambridge University Press.

Enfield, N. (2012) Sources of asymmetry in human interaction: Enchrony, status, knowledge and agency. In T. Stivers, L. Mondada and J. Steensig (eds) *The Morality of Knowledge in Conversation* (pp. 285–312). New York: Cambridge University Press.

Erickson, F. (2012) Comments on causality in qualitative inquiry. *Qualitative Inquiry* 18, 686–688.

Eskildsen, S.W. and Wagner, J. (2013) Recurring and shared gestures in the L2 classroom: Resources for teaching and learning. *European Journal of Applied Linguistics* 1, 139–161.

Firth, A. and Wagner, J. (1997) On discourse, communication and (some) fundamental concepts in second language acquisition research. *The Modern Language Journal* 81, 285–300.

Francis, D. and Hester, S. (2004) *An Invitation to Ethnomethodology.* London: Sage Publications.

Freebody, P. (2013) School knowledge in talk and writing: Taking 'when learners know' seriously. *Linguistics and Education* 24, 64–74.

Garfinkel, H. (1964) Studies in the routine grounds of everyday activities. *Social Problems* 11, 225–250.

Garfinkel, H. (1967) *Studies in Ethnomethodology.* Englewood Cliffs, NJ: Prentice-Hall.

Garfinkel, H. (1996) Ethnomethodology's program. *Social Psychology Quarterly* 59, 5–21.

Garfinkel, H. (2002) *Ethnomethodology's Program: Working out Durkheim's Aphorism.* Lanham, MD: Rowman & Littlefield.

Garfinkel, H. and Sacks, H. (1970) On formal structures of practical actions. In J.D. McKinney and E.A. Tiryakian (eds) *Theoretical Sociology* (pp. 337–366). New York: Appleton-Century Crofts.

Goodwin, C. (2000) Action and embodiment within situated human interaction. *Journal of Pragmatics* 32, 1489–1522.

Goodwin, C. (2007) Participation, stance, and affect in the organization of activities. *Discourse & Society* 18 (1), 53–73.

Goodwin, C. (2013) The co-operative, transformative organization of human action and knowledge. *Journal of Pragmatics* 46, 8–23.

Goodwin, C. and Goodwin, M.H. (2004) Participation. In A. Duranti (ed.) *A Companion to Linguistic Anthropology* (pp. 222–244). Oxford: Blackwell.

Hall, J.K., Hellermann, J. and Pekarek-Doehler, S. (eds) (2011) *L2 Interactional Competence and Development*. Bristol: Multilingual Matters.

Heap, J.L. (1990) Applied ethnomethodology: Looking for the local rationality of reading activities. *Human Studies* 13, 39–72.

Heap, J. (1992) Seeing snubs: An introduction to sequential analyses of classroom interaction. *Journal of Classroom Interaction* 27, 23–28.

Hellermann, J. (2008) *Social Actions for Classroom Language Learning*. Clevedon: Multilingual Matters.

Heritage, J. (1984) *Garfinkel and Ethnomethodology*. Cambridge: Polity Press.

Heritage, J. (2005) Conversation analysis and institutional talk. In R. Sanders and K. Fitch (eds) *Handbook of Language and Social Interaction* (pp. 103–146). Mahwah, NJ: Erlbaum.

Hester, S. and Francis, D. (2000) Ethnomethodology and local educational order. In S. Hester and D. Francis (eds) *Local Educational Order: Ethnomethodological Studies of Knowledge in Action* (pp. 1–17). Amsterdam: John Benjamins.

Kääntä, L. (2012) Teachers' embodied allocations in instructional interaction. *Classroom Discourse* 3, 166–186.

Kimura, D., Malabarba, T. and Hall, J.K. (in press) Data collection considerations for classroom interaction research: A conversation analytic perspective. *Classroom Discourse*.

Koschmann, T. (2012) Conversation analysis and learning in interaction. In C. Chapelle (ed.) *The Encyclopedia of Applied Linguistics* (pp. 1038–1043). Oxford: Wiley-Blackwell.

Koschmann, T., Stahl, G. and Zemel, A. (2007) The video analyst's manifesto (or the implications of Garfinkel's policies for studying practice within design-based research. In R. Goldman, D. Barron, S. Derry and R. Pea (eds) *Video Research in the Learning Sciences* (pp. 133–143). Mahwah, NJ: Lawrence Erlbaum.

Lee, Y.-A. (2007) Third turn position in teacher talk: Contingency and the work of teaching. *Journal of Pragmatics* 39, 1204–1230.

Lerner, G. (1995) Turn design and the organization of participation in instructional activities. *Discourse Processes* 19, 111–113.

Levinson, S.C. (2012) Action formation and ascription. In T. Stivers and J. Sidnell (eds) *The Handbook of Conversation Analysis* (pp. 103–130). Malden, MA: Wiley-Blackwell.

Macbeth, D. (1991) Teacher authority as practical action. *Linguistics and Education* 3, 281–313.

Macbeth, D. (1994) Classroom encounters with the unspeakable: 'Do you see, Danelle?' *Discourse Processes* 17, 311–335.

Macbeth, D. (2000) Classrooms as installations: Direct instruction in the early grades. In S. Hester and D. Francis (eds) *Local Education Order: Ethnomethodological Studies of Knowledge in Action* (pp. 21–72). Philadelphia, PA: John Benjamins.

Macbeth, D. (2011) Understanding understanding as an instructional matter. *Journal of Pragmatics* 43, 438–451.

Markee, N. and Seo, M-S. (2009) Learning talk analysis. *International Review of Applied Linguistics in Language Teaching* 47, 37–64.

Matsumoto, Y. and Dobs, A.M. (2016) Pedagogical gestures as interactional resources for teaching and learning tense and aspect in the ESL grammar classroom. *Language Learning* 67, 7–42.

Maynard, D. (2012) Everyone and no one to turn to: Intellectual roots and contexts for conversation analysis. In J. Sidnell and T. Stivers (eds) *The Handbook of Conversation Analysis* (pp. 11–31). Oxford: Wiley-Blackwell.

Maynard, D. and Clayman, S. (2003) Ethnomethodology and conversation analysis. In L. Reynolds and N. Herman-Kinney (eds) *Handbook of Symbolic Interactionism* (pp. 173–202). Walnut Creek, CA: Altamira Press.

McHoul, A. (1978) The organization of turns at formal talk in the classroom. *Language in Society* 7, 183–213.

Mehan, J. (1979) *Learning Lessons: Social Organization in the Classroom.* Cambridge, MA: Harvard University Press.

Mondada, L. (2014) The local constitution of multimodal resources for social interaction. *Journal of Pragmatics* 65, 137–156.

Mondada, L. (2016) Challenges of multimodality: Language and the body in social interaction. *Journal of Sociolinguistics* 20, 336–366.

Mortensen, K. (2009) Establishing recipiency in pre-beginning position in the second language classroom. *Discourse Processes* 46, 491–515.

Nevile, M. (2015) The embodied turn in research on language and social interaction. *Research on Language and Social Interaction* 48, 121–151.

Pallotti, G. and Wagner, J. (eds) (2011) *L2 Learning as a Social Practice: Conversation-analytic perspectives* (pp. 135–162). Honolulu, HI: University of Hawai'i, National Foreign Language Resource Center.

Park, Y. (2014) The roles of third-turn repeats in two L2 classroom interactional contexts. *Applied Linguistics* 35, 145–167.

Payne, G. and Hustler, D. (1980) Teaching the class: The practical management of a cohort. *British Journal of Sociology of Education* 1, 49–66.

Pomerantz, A. and Heritage, J. (2012) Preference. In J. Sidnell and T. Stivers (eds) *The Handbook of Conversation Analysis* (pp. 210–228). Oxford: Wiley-Blackwell.

Sacks, H. (1984) On doing 'being ordinary.' In J. Maxwell Atkinson and J. Heritage (eds) *Structures of Social Action: Studies in Conversation Analysis* (pp. 413–429). Cambridge: Cambridge University Press.

Sacks, H., Schegloff, E. and Jefferson, G. (1974) A simplest systematics for the organization of turn-taking for conversation. *Language* 50, 696–673.

Sahlström, F. (2002) The interactional organization of hand raising in classroom interaction. *Journal of Classroom Interaction* 37, 47–57.

Schegloff, E. (1968) Sequencing in conversational openings. *American Anthropologist* 70, 1075–1095.

Schegloff, E. (1992) Repair after next turn: The last structurally provided defense of intersubjectivity in conversation. *American Journal of Sociology* 97, 1295–1345.

Schegloff, E. (2000) When others initiate repair. *Applied Linguistics* 21, 205–243.

Schegloff, E. (2006) Interaction: The infrastructure for social institutions, the natural ecological niche for language, and the arena in which culture is enacted. In N.J. Enfield and S. Levinson (eds) *The Roots of Human Sociality: Culture, Cognition and Interaction* (pp. 70–96). London: Berg.

Schegloff, E. (2007) *Sequence Organization in Interaction.* Cambridge: Cambridge University Press.

Schegloff, E., Jefferson, G. and Sacks, H. (1977) The preference for self-correction in the organization of repair in conversation. *Language* 53, 361–382.

Sert, O. (2013) 'Epistemic status check' as an interactional phenomenon in instructed learning settings. *Journal of Pragmatics* 45, 13–28.

Sert, O. and Jacknick, C. (2015) Student smiles and the negotiation of epistemics in L2 classrooms. *Journal of Pragmatics 77*, 97–112.

Stahl, G. (2006) *Group Cognition: Computer Support for Building Collaborative Knowledge.* Cambridge, MA: MIT Press.

Streeck, J., Goodwin, G. and LeBaron, C. (2011) Embodied interaction language and body in the material world. In J. Streeck, C. Goodwin and C. LeBaron (eds) *Embodied Interaction: Language and Body in the Material World* (pp. 1–28). Cambridge: Cambridge University Press.

Swain, M. (1995) Three functions of output in second language learning. In G. Cook and B. Seidelhofer (eds) *Principle and Practice in Applied Linguistics: Studies in Honor of H.G. Widdowson* (pp. 125–144). Oxford: Oxford University Press.

Swain, M. (2006) Languaging, agency and collaboration in advanced language proficiency. In H. Byrnes (ed.) *Advanced Language Learning: The Contribution of Halliday and Vygotsky* (pp. 95–108). London: Continuum.

Swain, M. (2013) The inseparability of cognition and emotion in second language learning. *Language Teaching 46*, 195–207.

Swain, M. and Lapkin, S. (1995) Problems in output and the cognitive processes they generate: A step towards second language learning. *Applied Linguistics 16*, 371–391.

Swain, M. and Lapkin, S. (2011) Languaging as agent and constituent of cognitive change in an older adult: An example. *Canadian Journal of Applied Linguistics 14*, 104–117.

Waring, H.Z. (2008) Using explicit positive assessment in the language classroom. *The Modern Language Journal 92*, 577–594.

Waring, H.Z. (2009) Moving out of IRF: A single case analysis. *Language Learning 59*, 796–824.

Waring, H.Z. (2013) Managing Stacy: A case study of turn-taking in the language classroom. *System 41*, 841–851.

Waring, H.Z. (2016) *Theorizing Pedagogical Interaction: Insights from Conversation Analysis.* New York: Routledge.

Conclusion

Hossein Nassaji and Mari Haneda

The aim of this edited volume is to pay tribute to Professor Merrill Swain, honoring her scholarly contributions to the field of applied linguistics – particularly in the area of immersion education and second language acquisition (SLA). More specifically, it explores how her scholarship has helped advance our understanding of the processes involved in second language (L2) learning and teaching and how others have built on her scholarship to conduct their own research. The volume addresses a number of key constructs proposed and developed by Swain and her colleagues, including the output hypothesis, the importance of meta-talk, languaging and collaborative dialogue. In this concluding section, we provide a brief overview of key threads of discussion in this volume, as they relate to Swain's legacy.

One of the main areas of research to which Swain has made significant contributions is her substantive body of research on French immersion. In brief, Swain's findings established that immersion students successfully learned content materials to the level of comparison groups (i.e. those who learn content in their first language [L1]), 'progress in their home language kept pace (and sometimes overtook) that of their regular English program peers'; and 'their levels of French proficiency far exceeded what was possible in "traditional" French second language programs' (Lapkin, 2013: 5480). Swain's research and its implications in this area have been discussed in a number of chapters throughout the book. In their chapter titled 'Context Matters: Translanguaging and Language Immersion Education in the US and Canada', Fortune and Tedick, for example, highlighted Swain's contribution to the principles underlying the medium of instruction in immersion programs and her support for separation of languages in such contexts. The authors recognized the value of translanguaging, the seamless use of two or more languages in communication by bilinguals, in educating language minority students. However, they questioned the uncritical, universal application of the idea of translanguaging to other L2 teaching and learning contexts, such as immersion education, where students' exposure to the target language is typically limited to language immersion classrooms. Thus, the authors argued that the instructional context should be taken into account when choosing the medium of instruction and language use in the classroom. Duff (Chapter 12) discussed the controversies around multiple uses of languages in the classroom and reviewed the research that addressed these debates and the various positions proposed as solutions. Björklund (Chapter 3) highlighted Swain's pioneering research on language immersion and its impact on such programs in different countries, including the Swedish immersion program in Finland and the research in that area.

One of the groundbreaking theoretical constructs that Swain has developed, based on her cumulative program of research, concerns the role and significance of L2 output. Swain has contended that while exposure to 'comprehensible input' (Krashen, 1982) helps L2 students develop semantically based comprehension strategies, it is not sufficient to enable them to process language syntactically. The research findings reported in a number of chapters of this book provide strong support for this idea. Swain (1985: 248) has also argued that for students to produce the target language accurately, they need to be pushed 'toward the delivery of a message that is not only conveyed, but that is conveyed precisely, coherently, and appropriately'. Pointing out the limitations of the language input in a typical French immersion classroom, she asserted that content-based language teaching alone is not good language teaching; it needs to be complemented to maximize L2 learning. Building on this early work, Swain (1995) proposed three functions for output: a noticing function, a hypothesis-testing function and a metalinguistic function. The noticing function refers to the idea that when L2 learners produce output, they will become aware of what they do not know or cannot say. Output provides learners with occasions for testing hypotheses about language by providing opportunities for trying out different ways of saying the same thing. The third function, its metalinguistic function, can be summarized as follows (Swain, 1997: 119): 'as learners reflect on their own target language use, their output serves a metalinguistic function, enabling them to control and internalize linguistic knowledge'.

To date, many studies have provided evidence for the need to incorporate output opportunities in language teaching. In Chapter 1, Lyster discussed ways in which Swain inspired inquiry into this area of research and how this pushed the field of immersion education to pay attention both to the development of grammatical accuracy and to meaningful communication. This, in turn, broadened our understanding of what it means to effectively integrate language and content in L2 teaching.

Closely related to the notion of output is that of languaging. The term 'languaging' 'derives from Vygotsky's work that demonstrated the critical role language plays in mediating cognitive process' (Swain & Watanabe, 2013: 3218). Swain (2005) pointed out:

Speaking (and writing) are conceived of as cognitive tools – tools that mediate internalization; and that externalize internal psychological activity, resocializing, and recognizing it for the individual; tools that construct and deconstruct knowledge; and tools that regulate and are regulated by human agency. (Swain, 2005: 480)

Her theoretical claim was that languaging, which functions as a cognitive tool, creates important opportunities for L2 learning. To reiterate the important role played by languaging in L2 learning, it is best to use Swain's (2013: 5–6) own words, which were also in Lapkin's chapter:

In my view, the concept of languaging opens up how we might see the role of language in cognition: as an agent in the creation of higher mental processes and as a mediator of them. If it were not for language, how would we focus attention, consider the past, plan, and imagine the future? A person is also languaging when reasoning, problem-solving, and so forth.

The role of languaging as a tool to mediate cognition is a recurring theme in several chapters, including Kim (Chapter 5) and Van Compernolle and Kinginger (Chapter 6). Van Compernolle and Kinginger applied the notion of languaging to concept-based pragmatic instruction for French as an additional language, focusing on the complex French address forms *tu* versus *vous*. Further, Kim provided support for the role that languaging played in enhancing learners' motivation to learn English as a foreign language (EFL). In her chapter, Lapkin (Chapter 9) focused on the contribution of languaging to older learners' well-being and described how it provided opportunities for them to improve their cognition. As cited in Lapkin's chapter, Swain pointed out:

My hypothesis is that if an older adult is not given opportunities to language, then the power to create meaning, to plan, to attend, to organize, and to problem solve will dissipate. Thus, one possible reason for mild cognitive loss among older adults may lie in the lack of opportunities they have to language. If opportunities are limited, then cognitive loss rather than cognitive maintenance or development might occur. If this is the case, then providing opportunities to language may be one route to cognitive maintenance and development, and positive affective change.

In keeping with her growing interest in sociocultural theory, Swain (1995) also advocated what she called 'collaborative dialogue', which refers to dialogue in which language is used to negotiate meaning and solve linguistic problems. In her 1995 publication, Swain introduced the Vygotskian idea that learning occurs during social activity, specifically during dialogue in which students solve problems they encounter in their language learning (Lapkin, 2013: 5481). Such collaborative dialogue between learners, involving problem-solving and knowledge building, can be seen as learning in progress (Swain, 2000). Collaborative dialogue also provides opportunities for feedback from peers, which can then contribute to language accuracy. Several chapters in the book have examined dialogue between L2 learners as they interact with each other or the teacher to co-construct knowledge. For example, Watanabe (Chapter 4) explored how collaborative dialogue assisted the writing development of university EFL students. Her study highlighted how it was not just working together that mattered but how students interacted. Nassaji (Chapter 7) discussed collaborative output tasks and their application to L2 teaching and showed how such opportunities enhance learning in L2 classrooms.

Another key area in Swain's scholarly work is that of assessment. Her contribution in this area began with the seminal paper co-authored with Michael Canale in 1980 (Canale & Swain, 1980): 'Theoretical Bases of Communication Approaches to Second Language Teaching and Testing'. In that article, three components of language proficiency (grammatical, sociolinguistic, strategic) were identified and theorized and subsequently extended by Canale (1983) by the addition of discourse competence. In 1983, Swain articulated four principles of communicative test development.

Several chapters of this book have also highlighted Swain's contributions to a number of other related contexts. Tarone (Chapter 11), for example, demonstrated how Swain's multiple perspectives on language research help us develop a better and more fine-tuned understanding of the complexity of bilingualism and bilingual education. García (Chapter 8) highlighted Swain's contribution to the appreciation of the relationship among emotion, cognition and learning. Drawing on the sociocultural theoretical concept of assisted performance, Haneda, Sherman and Teemant (Chapter 13) showed how through particular kinds of languaging practices, an experienced instructional coach promoted teacher learning. And in her chapter, Hall (Chapter 14) brought together a number of key socially grounded concepts embodied in the framework of ethnomethodological conversation analysis to shed light on language teaching as a sophisticated professional enterprise.

In sum, all the chapters in this Festschrift have discussed many issues related to language as action, an idea to which Swain's scholarship contributed over the years. The volume has been prepared to provide a forum for discussing and reflecting on the impact of Swain's work in various areas of research in SLA and L2 education. The contributors have discussed key theoretical notions derived from Swain's work and have explored their implications in various instructional contexts, including K-12 immersion education, university-level foreign language classrooms and other educational settings. We hope that the book serves to honor

Swain's contributions, to promote further discussion and to inspire new investigations in the areas presented and beyond.

References

Canale, M. (1983) From communicative competence to communicative language pedagogy. *Language and Communication* 1, 1–47.

Canale, M. and Swain, M. (1980) Theoretical bases of communicative approaches to language teaching and testing. *Applied Linguistics* 1, 1–47.

Krashen, S. (1982) *Principles and Practice in Second Language Acquisition.* New York: Pergamon Press.

Lapkin, S. (2013) Swain, Merrill. In C.A. Chapelle (ed.) *The Encyclopedia of Applied Linguistics* (pp. 5479–5483). Hoboken, NJ: Wiley.

Swain, M. (1985) Communicative competence: Some rules of comprehensible input and comprehensible output in its development. In S. Gass and C. Madden (eds) *Input in Second Language Acquisition* (pp. 235–253). Rowley, MA: Newbury House.

Swain, M. (1995) Three functions of output in second language learning. In H.G. Widdowson, G. Cook and B. Seidlhofer (eds) *Principle and Practice in Applied Linguistics: Studies in Honour of H.G. Widdowson* (pp. 125–144). Oxford: Oxford University Press.

Swain, M. (1997) Collaborative dialogue: Its contribution to second language learning. *Revista Canaria de Estudios Ingleses* 34, 115–132.

Swain, M. (2000) The output hypothesis and beyond: Mediating acquisition through collaborative dialogue. In J.P. Lantolf (ed.) *Sociocultural Theory and Second Language Learning* (pp. 97–114). Oxford/New York: Oxford University Press.

Swain, M. (2005) The output hypothesis: Theory and research. In E. Hinkel (ed.) *Handbook on Research in Second Language Teaching and Learning* (pp. 471–483). Mahwah, NJ: Lawrence Erlbaum Associates.

Swain, M. (2013) Cognitive and affective enhancement among older adults: The role of languaging. *The Australian Review of Applied Linguistics* 36, 4–19.

Swain, M. and Watanabe, Y. (2013) Languaging: Collaborative dialogue as a source of second language learning. In C. Chapelle (ed.) *The Encyclopedia of Applied Linguistics* (pp. 3218–3225). Hoboken, NJ: Wiley Blackwell.

Afterword

G. Richard Tucker

After completing my PhD under the supervision of Wally Lambert in Spring 1967, I was hired by the Ford Foundation as a Project Specialist in Language Education and posted to their office in Manila, Philippines. In January 1969, I returned to McGill to join the faculty with a joint appointment in Psychology and Linguistics.

At the time, Merrill was a doctoral student at the University of California Northridge, but she was residing in Quebec at Laval University where she was working on her doctoral dissertation that examined the acquisition of bilingualism as a first language. During the Spring 1969 semester, much to my delight, Merrill and her fellow Quebec-resident student, Jack Richards drove to Montreal weekly to sit in on a seminar that I was offering around the topic of Research Methods in Psycholinguistics. That began a 48-year, and continuing, friendship that continues to this day (in fact, Merrill came to Carnegie Mellon University in Spring 2017 as a Visiting Scholar and I had the pleasure of attending her presentation and sharing dinner with her at my house).

What are my lasting impressions of Merrill as a scholar and as a human being? As a scholar, Merrill epitomizes the person who: (1) knows how to pose an interesting question, (2) knows how to collect diverse types of relevant information; (3) knows how to examine the information that she has collected from diverse perspectives; and (4) knows how to tell a relevant 'story' using this information. Merrill epitomizes the type of scholar that we hope that our graduate students will become…and she has shared these insights with numerous students over the years.

This has led Merrill along a 'road less traveled' from examining diverse aspects of immersion education in the primary years of schooling to working with 'senior citizens' and examining their language experiences.

As a human being, Merrill epitomizes the person who: (1) is concerned about the well-being of her students and her colleagues; (2) ensures that her students and her colleagues maintain the highest ethical standards in all that they do; and (3) ensures that her students and her colleagues have opportunities to experience relaxation and enjoyment.

I consider myself blessed to have had the opportunity to know and to interact continually with Merrill and her colleagues at OISE (the University of Toronto) over the years – the experiences have enriched my life and have afforded all of us the opportunity to contribute to the advancement of our profession.

Thank you Merrill!

Index